Windows® XP Professional Little Black Book Quick Reference

Windows XP Shortcut Keys

Although Windows XP is better used with a mouse, you cannot deny that keyboard shortcuts are a handy way of quickly navigating through the XP interface. The following tables will highlight many of the different shortcuts within Windows XP.

Table 1 lists the shortcuts that are found in nearly every Windows application.

Table 1   Universal keyboard shortcuts.

Shortcut	Action
Alt+Enter	Display properties
Alt+Esc	Switch between items in the order opened
Alt+F4	Close the active item; quit the active program
Alt+spacebar	Open the shortcut menu for the active window
Alt+Tab	Switch between open windows
Alt+underlined letter in menu bars	Display the menu
Ctrl+A	Select all
Ctrl+C	Copy
Ctrl+down arrow	Move the insertion point to the beginning of the next paragraph
Ctrl+drag item	Copy an item
Ctrl+Esc	Display the Start menu
Ctrl+F4	Close the active document in multidocument applications
Ctrl+left arrow	Move the insertion point to the beginning of the previous word
Ctrl+right arrow	Move the insertion point to the beginning of the next word
Ctrl+Shift+any arrow key	Highlight a block of text
Ctrl+Shift+drag item	Create a shortcut to an item
Ctrl+up arrow	Move the insertion point to the beginning of the previous paragraph
Ctrl+V	Paste
Ctrl+X	Cut
Ctrl+Z	Undo
Delete	Delete
Esc	Cancel the current task
F1	Display Help
F10	Activate the menu bar
F10, left arrow	Open the next menu to the left or close the submenu
F10, right arrow	Open the next menu to the right or open the submenu
F2	Rename an item
F3	Search for files or folders
F5	Refresh the active window
F6	Switch between screen elements in the window or desktop
Shift+any arrow key	Select multiple items
Shift+Delete	Delete and bypass the Recycle Bin
Shift+F10	Display the shortcut menu for an item
Shift+insert CD into CD-ROM drive	Halt AutoRun
Underlined letter in an open menu	Run menu command

If you have a newer keyboard, you likely have a WinKey (⊞). You probably know about using the WinKey to open the Start menu, but the WinKey has some other important uses, as shown in Table 2.

Table 2   WinKey keyboard shortcuts.

Shortcut	Action
⊞	Display the Start menu
⊞+Break	Display the System Properties dialog box
⊞+D	Show the desktop
⊞+E	Open My Computer
⊞+F	Search for files or folders
⊞+F1	Display Windows Help
⊞+ L	Lock the computer
⊞+M	Minimize all windows
⊞+R	Open the Run dialog box
⊞+U	Open Utility Manager
Ctrl+ ⊞+F	Search for computers
Shift+ ⊞+M	Restore minimized windows

Every Windows application has the ubiquitous dialog box. In Windows XP, these interface devices come in all sizes and forms. Table 3 describes the shortcut keys that will let you navigate through any dialog box.

Table 3   Dialog box keyboard shortcuts.

Shortcut	Action
Arrow keys	Select radio buttons
Backspace	Open the folder one level up in Save As or Open dialog boxes
Ctrl+Shift+Tab	Move the cursor backward through tab pages
Ctrl+Tab	Move the cursor forward through tab pages
Enter	Run the command on an active item
F4	Display list items
Shift+Tab	Move the cursor backward through fields
Spacebar	Select or clear the checkbox
Tab	Move the cursor forward through fields

Not only do dialog boxes have their own set of keyboard shortcuts, but the Windows Explorer also has its own special set of keyboard shortcuts, as shown in Table 4.

Table 4   Windows Explorer keyboard shortcuts.

Shortcut	Action
Backspace	View the folder one level up
End	Display the bottom of the active window
F4	Display the Address bar list
Home	Display the top of the active window
Left arrow	Collapse the current selection if expanded; select the parent folder
Num Lock+- (numeric keypad)	Collapse the folder
Num Lock+ + (numeric keypad)	Display folder contents
Num Lock+* (numeric keypad)	Display all subfolders
Right arrow	Expand the current selection if collapsed; select the first subfolder

4. When the time is near the total capacity for the blank CD, click the Copy Music button. A conversion and copying process will begin. When this process is complete, the CD will be ejected from the drive.

Running Windows Update

1. Click Start|All Programs|Windows Update. Internet Explorer will open to the Windows Update Web page.
2. Click Scan For Updates. The list of updates will be downloaded and compared to the configuration of your machine. If updates are found, they will be listed in the category list within the Windows Update pane on the left side of the screen.
3. Click a Category link to view the list of updates in that category.
4. If you decide to select an update to download and install, click the Add button next to the update to select it.
5. After you select all the updates you want, click the Install Now button. The Install page will appear, and the updates will be downloaded and installed to your computer.
6. Click the close icon to close the Internet Explorer window.

Running Automatic Updates

When notified of updates:

1. Click the Automatic Updates icon or the balloon notification message. The Automatic Updates window will open to the Updates For Your Computer page.
2. Click a Read Me First link for one of the upgrade packages. The information window for the update will open.
3. Click the Close link to close the update information window.
4. Click the checkbox for any link you don't want to download to clear it.
5. Click the Start Download button. The Automatic Updates window will close, and the application will begin to acquire the selected packages from the Windows Update site.

When the downloads are complete:

1. Click the Automatic Updates icon or the balloon notification message. The Automatic Updates window will open to the Ready To Install page.
2. Click Install. A new Ready To Install page will appear, listing the updates that were downloaded.
3. Click Install. The Installation In Progress page will appear, and the updates will be installed. When the installation is finished, the Installation Complete page will appear.
4. Click OK to close the Automatic Updates window.

Defragmenting a Hard Drive

1. Click Start|All Programs|Accessories|System Tools|Disk Defragmenter to open the Disk Defragmenter window.
2. Click a hard drive to select it.
3. Click the Analyze button to begin analyzing the contents of the drive. When this process is complete, the Disk Defragmenter dialog box will appear, notifying you of the results.
4. Click the View Report button. The Disk Defragmenter dialog box will close, and the Analysis Report dialog box will open.
5. Examine the report. If you agree with its findings, click Defragment. The Analysis Report dialog box will close, and the defragmentation process will begin.
6. When the process is complete, the Disk Defragmenter dialog box will open.
7. Click Close to accept the notification. The Disk Defragmenter dialog box will close.

Compressing Data

1. Click Start|My Computer to open the My Computer window.
2. Navigate to the file or folder you want to encrypt.
3. Right-click the file or folder. The context menu will appear.
4. Click Properties to open the object's Properties dialog box.
5. Click Advanced to open the Advanced Attributes dialog box.
6. Click the Compress Contents To Save Disk Space checkbox to select it.
7. Click OK to close the Advanced Attributes dialog box.
8. Click Apply to open the Confirm Attribute Changes dialog box.
9. Click the Apply Changes To This Folder, Subfolders, And Files radio button to select it.
10. Click OK. The Confirm Attribute Changes dialog box will close, and the Applying Attributes dialog box will open to mark the progress of the compression.
11. Click OK to close the object's Properties dialog box.

9. Click Next to move to the Completing The Add Printer Wizard page.
10. Click Finish. The Add Printer Wizard will close, the test page should be printed on your new printer, and a notification dialog box for the test page will appear.
11. If the page printed correctly, click OK to close the notification dialog box.

Sharing a Folder on the Network

1. In Windows Explorer, navigate to the folder you want to share.
2. Click the Share This Folder link. The folder's Properties dialog box will open.
3. Click the Share This Folder On The Network checkbox to select it.
4. To allow users to edit files in this folder, confirm that the Allow Network Users To Change My Files option is checked.
5. Click Apply to apply the settings.
6. Click OK to close the folder's Properties dialog box.

Setting Up a Dial-Up Networking Account

1. Click Start|Control Panel to open the Control Panel.
2. Click the Network And Internet Connections link to open the Network And Internet Connections page.
3. Click the Set Up Or Change Your Internet Connection link to open the Internet Properties dialog box.
4. Click Setup to open the New Connection Wizard.
5. Click Next to move to the New Connection Type page.
6. Click the Connect To The Internet radio button to select it.
7. Click Next to move to the Getting Ready page.
8. Click the Set Up My Connection Manually radio button to select it.
9. Click Next to move to the Internet Connection page.
10. Click the Connect Using A Dial-Up Modem radio button to select it.
11. Click Next to move to the Connection Name page.
12. Enter the proper name of the ISP connection in the ISP Name field.
13. Click Next to move to the Phone Number To Dial page.
14. Enter the phone number your modem needs to contact the ISP's modem in the Phone Number field.
15. Click Next to move to the Internet Account Information page.
16. Enter the username provided by the ISP in the User Name field.
17. Enter the password provided by the ISP in the Password field.
18. Enter the password again in the Confirm Password field.
19. Confirm the selected options for connection.
20. Click Next to move to the Completing New Connection Wizard page.

21. Click the Add A Shortcut To This Connection To The Desktop checkbox to select it.
22. Click Finish. The New Connection Wizard and Internet Properties dialog boxes will close, and a shortcut for the connection will appear on the desktop.
23. Click the close icon in the Network And Internet Connections page to close the Control Panel.

Sharing an Internet Account

1. Click Start|Control Panel to open the Control Panel.
2. Click the Network And Internet Connections link to open the Network And Internet Connections page.
3. Click the Network Connections link to open the Network Connections page.
4. Click the Set Up A Home Or Small Office Network link to open the Network Setup Wizard.
5. Click Next to move to the Before You Continue page.
6. Review the instructions and click Next. The Select A Connection Method page will appear.
7. Click the option that is appropriate to your setup.
8. Click Next to move to the Select Your Internet Connection page.
9. Select the connection tied to the network card that is connected to the cable modem or represents the primary dial-up Internet connection.
10. Click Next to move to the Give This Computer A Description And Name page.
11. Enter a descriptive phrase for the computer in the Computer Description field.
12. Enter a network name for the computer in the Computer Name field.
13. Click Next to move to the Name Your Network page.
14. Enter a name for your network in the Workgroup Name field.
15. Click Next to move to the Ready To Apply Network Settings page.
16. Review the settings and click Next. You will need to wait as the network settings are applied, and then the You're Almost Done screen will appear.
17. Click the Create A Network Setup Disk radio button to select it.
18. Click Next to move to the Insert The Disk You Want To Use page.
19. Insert a blank, formatted floppy disk into the disk drive.
20. Click Next. The network setup file will be copied to the floppy disk, and the Completing The Network Setup Wizard page will appear.
21. Click Finish to close the Network Setup Wizard.

Burning Music CDs

1. Insert a blank CDR into the CD Writer drive.
2. Click the Record To CD Or Device link to open the Record To CD Or Device page.
3. Click the checkboxes for the music files you want to record. A total time will appear as you add files.

If you need or want to use the Accessibility functions within Windows XP, you can quickly access them through a special set of keyboard shortcuts, listed in Table 5.

Table 5   Accessibility keyboard shortcuts.

Shortcut	Action
Left Alt +Left Shift+Num Lock	Toggle MouseKeys
Left Alt+Left Shift+PrtScr	Toggle High Contrast
Num Lock (5 seconds)	Toggle ToggleKeys
Right Shift (8 seconds)	Toggle FilterKeys
Shift (5 times)	Toggle StickyKeys

Windows XP Tasks

Throughout this book, you'll find many examples illustrating how to accomplish important tasks within Windows XP. Following are some of the most commonly used tasks and the quick steps showing how to perform them.

Copying Files and Folders

1. In Windows Explorer, click the file or folder you want to copy to select it.
2. In the File And Folder Tasks window, click the Copy This File link to open the Copy Items dialog box.
3. Using the expansion icons, navigate to the folder in which you want to place the copied file.
4. Click the destination folder to select it.
5. Click Copy to copy the file to the destination folder.

Moving Files and Folders

1. In Windows Explorer, click the file or folder you want to move to select it.
2. In the File And Folder Tasks window, click the Move This File link to open the Move Items dialog box.
3. Using the expansion icons, navigate to the folder in which you want to place the file.
4. Click the destination folder to select it.
5. Click Move to move the file to the destination folder.

Deleting Files and Folders

1. In Windows Explorer, click the file or folder you want to delete to select it.
2. In the File And Folder Tasks window, click the Delete This File link to open the Confirm File Delete dialog box.
3. Click Yes to send the file to the Recycle Bin and close the dialog box.

Creating New Folders

1. In Windows Explorer, open the folder in which you want to place a new folder.
2. Click the Make A New folder link. A New Folder icon will appear, with the name highlighted.
3. Type a new name for the folder.
4. Click anywhere else within Windows Explorer or press Enter. The new name will be applied and the folder ready to use.

Customizing Folders

1. In Windows Explorer, right-click the folder you want to customize. The context menu will appear.
2. Click Properties to open the Properties dialog box.
3. Click the Customize tab to open the Customize page.
4. Click the drop-down list for the Use This Folder Type As A Template field. A list of folder type templates will appear.
5. Click the appropriate folder type to select it.
6. Click the Change Icon button to open the Change Icon For Folder dialog box.
7. Click a desired icon to select it.
8. Click OK to close the Change Icon For Folder dialog box.
9. Click OK. The Properties dialog box will close, and the changes will be made to the folder.

Pinning an Application to the Start Menu

1. In a folder, on the desktop, or in the Start menu, right-click the application icon you want to pin. The context menu will open.
2. Click the Pin To Start menu option. The application icon will appear in the pinned applications section.

Adding the Quick Launch Toolbar to the Taskbar

1. Right-click an empty portion of the taskbar. The context menu will appear.
2. Select Toolbars to open the Toolbars submenu.
3. Click the Quick Launch option to make the Quick Launch toolbar appear on the taskbar.

Setting Up a New Local Printer

1. Connect the printer to the PC using the appropriate port and turn on the printer. If the printer is connected through a USB or Firewire port, the printer will automatically be detected and installed immediately.
2. If the printer is not detected, click Start|Printers And Faxes to open the Printers And Faxes window.
3. Click the Add A Printer link to open the Add Printer Wizard's Welcome screen.
4. Click Next to move to the Local Or Network Printer page.
5. Click the Local Printer Attached To This Computer option to select it.
6. Confirm that the Automatically Detect And Install My Plug And Play Printer option is checked.
7. Click Next. The New Printer Detection page will appear as Windows searches for the connected printer.

   If the detected printer is not recognized by Windows XP, the Add New Hardware Wizard will appear. Use this tool to install your printer's software.

   If the detected printer is recognized by Windows XP, the New Printer Detection page will display a message asking you to print a test page.
8. Click the Yes option to select it.

Windows® XP Professional
Professional
Little Black Book

Brian Proffitt

President and CEO
Roland Elgey

Publisher
Al Valvano

Acquisitions Editor
Jawahara Saidullah

Product Marketing Manager
Tracy Rooney

Project Editor
Karen Swartz

Technical Reviewer
Felicia Buckingham
Diana Bartley

Production Coordinator
Wendy Littley

Cover Designer
Carla Schuder

Windows® XP Professional Little Black Book

Limits of Liability and Disclaimer of Warranty

The author and publisher of this book have used their best efforts in preparing the book and the programs contained in it. These efforts include the development, research, and testing of the theories and programs to determine their effectiveness. The author and publisher make no warranty of any kind, expressed or implied, with regard to these programs or the documentation contained in this book.

The author and publisher shall not be liable in the event of incidental or consequential damages in connection with, or arising out of, the furnishing, performance, or use of the programs, associated instructions, and/or claims of productivity gains.

Trademarks

Trademarked names appear throughout this book. Rather than list the names and entities that own the trademarks or insert a trademark symbol with each mention of the trademarked name, the publisher states that it is using the names for editorial purposes only and to the benefit of the trademark owner, with no intention of infringing upon that trademark.

The Coriolis Group, LLC
14455 North Hayden Road
Suite 220
Scottsdale, Arizona 85260

(480) 483-0192
FAX (480) 483-0193
www.coriolis.com

Library of Congress Cataloging-in-Publication Data

Proffitt, Brian
   Windows XP Professional little black book/by Brian Proffitt
      p. cm.
   Includes index.
   ISBN 1-58880-253-1
   1. Microsoft Windows XP.   2. Operating systems (Computers)   I. Title.
QA76.76.O63 P7628   2001
005.4'4769--dc21   2001047680

Printed in the United States of America
10 9 8 7 6 5 4 3 2 1

CORIOLIS

The Coriolis Group, LLC • 14455 North Hayden Road, Suite 220 • Scottsdale, Arizona 85260

A Note from Coriolis

Coriolis Technology Press was founded to create a very elite group of books: the ones you keep closest to your machine. In the real world, you have to choose the books you rely on every day *very* carefully, and we understand that.

To win a place for our books on that coveted shelf beside your PC, we guarantee several important qualities in every book we publish. These qualities are:

- *Technical accuracy*—It's no good if it doesn't work. Every Coriolis Technology Press book is reviewed by technical experts in the topic field, and is sent through several editing and proofreading passes in order to create the piece of work you now hold in your hands.

- *Innovative editorial design*—We've put years of research and refinement into the ways we present information in our books. Our books' editorial approach is uniquely designed to reflect the way people learn new technologies and search for solutions to technology problems.

- *Practical focus*—We put only pertinent information into our books and avoid any fluff. Every fact included between these two covers must serve the mission of the book as a whole.

- *Accessibility*—The information in a book is worthless unless you can find it quickly when you need it. We put a lot of effort into our indexes, and heavily cross-reference our chapters, to make it easy for you to move right to the information you need.

Here at The Coriolis Group we have been publishing and packaging books, technical journals, and training materials since 1989. We have put a lot of thought into our books; please write to us at **ctp@coriolis.com** and let us know what you think. We hope that you're happy with the book in your hands, and that in the future, when you reach for software development and networking information, you'll turn to one of our books first.

Coriolis Technology Press
The Coriolis Group
14455 N. Hayden Road, Suite 220
Scottsdale, Arizona
85260

Email: ctp@coriolis.com
Phone: (480) 483-0192
Toll free: (800) 410-0192

For all the heroes of 9/11/01.
Your courage and bravery have shown us all the true spirit of
Humankind.
❧

About the Author

Brian Proffitt is a professional author and computer consultant whose work on Windows and Linux technology has caused the New York Times to bestow the title "übergeek" upon him. Brian was not sure whether to be proud or deeply disturbed by this anointment.

A follower of all things technical, Brian is the author of 15 computer books and hundreds of Windows, Linux, and Internet Technology articles for INT Media Services (formerly Internet.com). Currently, he is a contributing editor to LinuxPlanet.com and Linux Today.

In his spare time, Brian is a private pilot, a serious fan of the Food Network, and makes one mean Chicken Kiev.

Acknowledgments

This book may rank as the most insane project I have ever tried to do. But, somehow, I managed to pull it off on schedule. Though not without some serious help from a lot of good people.

First off, Jawahara Saidullah, my acquisitions editor at Coriolis. It was she who called me up literally on the eve of despair as I lay awash in the aftermath to the dot.com implosion. She went to bat for me for this book and told everyone else that she worked with that if anyone could produce this book on a five-week schedule, it was me. Her confidence was a real motivator.

The efforts of the other editors are also much appreciated. project editor Karen Swartz (who thinks I am an android), copyeditor Chuck Hutchinson, and tech reviewers Felicia Buckingham and Diana Bartley did a tremendous job putting this book together and have been most forgiving of my dangling participles. Many thanks also to production coordinator Wendy Littley, cover designer Carla Schuder, and product marketing manager Tracy Rooney.

Lynette Quinn, my acquisitions editor at (ahem!) another publishing company, deserves many thanks for letting me take some time away from a project I was doing for her to tackle this book. Lynette has moved on to better things, but her efforts here do not go unnoticed.

Joli Ballew gets a big thanks from me for her assistance with Chapter 17, which threatened to drive me insane, because my laptop was far too old for XP's tastes. Joli is the author of the upcoming *Windows XP Professional—The Ultimate User's Guide*, due out this Christmas from Coriolis.

Robert Bogue, another fellow author and a good friend as well, has my thanks for all of his help during the beginning stages of putting this book together. His knowledge of Windows 2000 is invaluable and his sense of humor is as well.

Acknowledgments

Finally, my deepest love and gratitude goes to my family: my wife, my two daughters, and even my mother, who emailed me every day to make sure I was getting my chapters in on time. Without their love, their patience, and their help, this book would not be in your hands today.

Contents at a Glance

Table of Contents

Introduction

You hold in your hands the *Windows XP Professional Little Black Book*. It is a reference guide and how-to manual to the latest operating system to come out of the Microsoft Corporation: Windows XP Professional.

Windows XP Professional, along with its companion system Windows XP Home Edition, represents a large leap forward in interface design and background technology for Windows 95 and Windows 98 users. Granted, this has all been said before, but this time it's really true.

Windows XP is the first Microsoft operating system offered to consumers that is based on the Windows NT kernel. Until this release, all the consumer-targeted operating systems from Microsoft were based on the Windows 95 kernel. Businesses were the primary customers for the other branch of Windows, Windows NT.

Ever since the first release of Windows NT, executives at Redmond have wanted to combine the two forms of Windows into one operating system. Windows 2000 was supposed to be the first product of this merger, but huge delays forced the merger to be delayed, until now.

Without knowing it, many consumers have missed the passing of an era. Windows Millennium Edition was the last version of Windows 9x, the operating system that revolutionized personal computing. From this point on, there will be only one core version of Windows, the one based on Windows NT.

Because of this merger, users of Windows 9x operating systems are going to be in for quite a few surprises. The change from Windows 9x to Windows XP is significant, and this book will serve as a guide not only to Windows XP but also to the Windows NT way of operating.

Users of Windows 2000 will find themselves on more familiar ground with Windows XP, but they, too, can benefit from this book because several interesting changes and improvements have been made beyond the features of Windows 2000. With this book, NT and 2000 users will be able to more efficiently navigate the areas of XP that are not *quite* the same as they are used to.

First and foremost, the *Windows XP Professional Little Black Book* is your best guide to finding out all about the new features in Windows XP and how to capitalize on them to make your work and play sessions more efficient. Along the way, you will learn more details about the technology behind Windows XP Professional and why things are the way they are.

On October 25, 2001, Microsoft officially released other products besides Windows XP Professional. Windows XP Home Edition and Microsoft Plus for XP were also made available, as well as a new version of the Windows Messenger client. Progress, it seems, does not stop to catch its breath—or wait for a book. You will find this book to be comprehensive nonetheless, and hopefully an excellent guide to the new technologies before us.

Is This Book for You?

The *Windows XP Professional Little Black Book* was written with the intermediate or advanced user in mind. The following are just some of the Windows XP Professional topics covered in this book:

- Preparing for installation
- Managing hardware and software
- Mastering the multi-user and networking tools
- Administering and troubleshooting

Both home and business users will find out how to perform important tasks in Windows XP—tasks they should learn to increase their prowess with their computers.

How to Use This Book

In Chapters 1 through 9, you will be guided through the all-important steps of getting Windows XP installed on your home or office system. You will also review the new features of the Luna interface and ways to configure your software and hardware with XP.

Chapters 10 through 14 will address the need for all users everywhere to connect their computers to something. Whether it's a network, the Internet, or the printer down the hall, all but a few PCs are truly standalone devices anymore. The chapters in this part of the book will provide the solutions to getting your computer hooked up right the first time.

When you get Windows XP running and connected, you just have to check out some of the tools. That will be the overriding topic of Chapters 15 through 17. Here, you will learn about maximizing your multimedia experience, using the latest Windows remote tools, and using Windows XP on that oddest of breeds, the laptop.

Finally, Chapters 18 through 21 will guide you through the solutions needed to improve and repair your basic XP installation. From automatic updates to network user management, Windows XP Professional has the tools you need to help you get your work done fast.

The Little Black Book Philosophy

Written by experienced professionals, Coriolis *Little Black Books* are terse, easily "thumb-able" question answerers and problem solvers. The *Little Black Book*'s unique two-part chapter format—brief technical overviews followed by practical immediate solutions—is structured to help you use your knowledge, solve problems, and quickly master complex technical issues to become an expert. By breaking down complex topics into easily manageable components, this format helps you quickly find what you're looking for. A lot is happening in the world of Windows XP, and with this book, you won't miss a thing.

I welcome your feedback on this book. You can either email The Coriolis Group at **ctp@coriolis.com** or email me directly at **bkproffitt@home.com**. Errata, updates, and more are available at **www.coriolis.com**.

Chapter 1

Prepare for Windows XP Professional

In Brief

You have just purchased one of the latest and greatest offerings from Microsoft: Windows XP. Amid all the glitz and glamour of the software's premiere is one overwhelming need: You just want the thing to work well on your computer.

Sometimes, in the haste to deliver something in a pretty package, Microsoft Windows products have fallen a bit short in the performance department. Things look good, but they crash, giving us all more than a few looks at the infamous "Blue Screen of Death."

Windows XP is making good on a promise Microsoft made quite some time ago: the merger of the two separate Windows platforms that have been the basis of the company's client and server platform offerings. Microsoft will still have client and server offerings, of course, but now they will all be based on the same technology.

But how did this division of technology come about in the first place? And why did getting it back together take so long?

Why Windows XP Is Different from Its Predecessors

In the beginning, there was Windows 1.0. And, it was pretty bad. Application windows would not overlap, and hardly anyone had written applications for this fledgling platform.

After that came Windows 2.0, which allowed for overlapping windows and enabled the protected mode that let applications take up more memory than the DOS 640KB limit.

Windows 2.1 came seven months later and was named Windows 286. Windows 286 was the first version of Windows I had ever seen, and it was awful. The interface was tabbed windows, and the whole thing was a pure resource hog for my poor, beleaguered IBM PS/2-30.

I never saw Windows 386, which also came out soon after Windows 2.0. This OS was supposed to be good at multitasking on the new Intel 80386 machines that were just coming out at the end of 1987.

In 1990, Windows finally became a real GUI for the DOS operating system with the release of Windows 3.0. Windows 3.0 was the first Windows interface that looked and felt like the Windows many of us were first exposed to. The File Manager interface that is still the basic premise for Windows operating systems today was first introduced in this release.

Two years later, in 1992, Windows 3.1 was introduced. Not much changed in the interface, but many stability issues that plagued Windows 3.0 were fixed.

The Windows 3.x series of releases were 16-bit operating systems, which were all well and good for the 286 and 386 processors that were on the market at the time. But, more powerful 486 chips were on the way, and Microsoft wanted to take full advantage of their power. So, in that same year, Microsoft announced the development of a 32-bit operating system called Windows NT. This new NT architecture would eventually replace the existing Windows platforms, though that promise would not be fulfilled for another nine years.

NT's new architecture offered developers a stable and secure platform on which to create new applications. But, when it came out in 1993, Windows NT 3.1's reception was mixed. The developers loved it, but end users were saddled with an operating system that ran only on the more powerful PCs, and even then not terribly well. It would take until the release of Windows NT 3.51 for the market to readily accept this product.

NT was also the first Windows product that was a true independent operating system—not something running on top of an invisible DOS. But, Microsoft was not done with DOS yet, wanting to capitalize on the host of 16-bit and DOS-based applications that were still out on the market and introduce an operating system that did not have high resource requirements like Windows NT. Instead of supplanting the current 16-bit Windows 3.x architecture with Windows NT, the developers at Microsoft introduced something in between: a 32-bit operating system that still ran on top of DOS.

This OS would become Windows 95. And, although Windows 95 and Windows NT (from version 4.0 on) would look the same, functionally they were very different. NT's emphasis on a totally secure platform meant that crashing applications would not bring down the whole platform. Network and user management was much better on NT than 95, too. In short, 95 would be for the home users and NT would take care of the business machines.

Unfortunately, it didn't quite work out that way. Windows NT itself split into two offerings: Server and Workstation. But, despite the better security of NT, businesses were reluctant to move over to the new platform because it was expensive and required too many hardware resources to run. Besides, everyone reasoned, Windows 95 (and later, Windows 98) runs well enough and has a lot lower expense threshold.

Windows NT 5.0, which would be named Windows 2000, was initially going to effect the merger of the two separate Windows development tracks. But, Windows 2000's completely blown production schedule plus some real problems getting Windows 2000 to be a proper games platform (a prerequisite for home users) soon put a stop to that notion. Windows 2000 closed the gap with Windows 98 compatibility, but they were still as separate as could be.

Today, we have Windows XP, the operating system that will deliver on the promise of One Combined Windows. For home users and business users who have stayed with the Windows 9x line, this will represent a huge increase in stability. When (not if) an application crashes, the entire operating system will not come down with it. System uptime will increase dramatically. And, the cost of moving to this new platform will not be significantly larger than past Window 9x upgrades, both in terms of licensing and hardware support.

These are the major benefits of the new XP platform, the ones that will mean the most to users. Sure, XP has a snazzy new interface and some really nifty tools, but Microsoft is delivering to users something they really need: a platform for everyone that won't cause as many problems as it solves.

Choose the Right Version of Windows XP for You

Two flavors of the new Windows XP have been released: Windows XP Home Edition and Windows XP Professional. Looking at those labels, you would think it would be easy to figure out which platform to use. If the PC is at home, use Home Edition. If it's at work, use Professional. For many cases, this will certainly be true. But, not always.

If you are looking at system requirements to be the deciding factor between these two flavors of XP, you'll get no help here. The published requirements for each flavor are practically identical, according to this list adapted from the Microsoft Web site:

- PC with 300MHz or higher processor clock speed recommended; 233MHz minimum required; Intel Pentium/Celeron family, AMD K6/Athlon/Duron family, or compatible processor recommended

- 128MB of RAM or higher recommended (64MB minimum supported; may limit performance and some features)

- 1.5GB of available hard disk space

- Super VGA (800×600) or higher resolution video adapter and monitor

- CD-ROM or DVD drive (with DVD decoder card or DVD decoder software)

- Keyboard and MS-compatible pointing device

In fact, the only difference between the two sets of system requirements is that XP Professional can support dual-processor systems, and the Home Edition can't. If you are among the few users who have a dual-processor system, your choice is clear. For the rest of us, the real determinant of which version of Windows XP to use will not be where the computer is located or how it is configured, but rather who needs access to it.

Windows XP Home Edition is a good platform to use for any system that is standalone or connected to a small network. It has all the things even power users are going to need for their systems: networking and firewall support, laptop support, and an improved interface, just to name a few.

For a single user, or even a family at home, Windows XP Home Edition should be enough. It should also serve well for small businesses that have a small number of users on a small network. Keep in mind the word *small*. And, also keep in mind the term *slow-growth*. For families, new computer users are typically not going to show up without notice. The same may hold true in some small businesses, where success is not measured by the number of employees.

But, if the rate of new users being added to the system is high or if your users travel outside the office (or home) and still need access to the network, choosing Windows XP Professional is the better decision for you.

Windows XP Professional comes with all the solutions offered by the Home Edition plus quite a few more that are geared toward the needs of growing and mobile businesses. The Remote Desktop, Access Control, and an encrypted file system are some of the connectivity features Windows XP Professional has to offer.

NOTE: *For a complete comparison of features in Windows XP Home Edition and Professional, visit* ***www.microsoft.com/windowsxp/guide/comparison.asp****.*

After a comparison of the feature differences between the two XP versions and an examination of your needs, you should be able to decide which is best for you.

Immediate Solutions

Preparing Your System for Windows XP

How well do you really know your PC? *Really* know it? Are you just passing acquaintances, or do you know it down to its very soul (or at least the jumper settings on your sound card)? To find out just how well Windows XP will run on your PC, you need to know the workings of your machine fairly well.

You will need to do several things to prepare your system for using Windows XP. Don't let the fact that your system is relatively new lull you into a false sense of security, either. Newer systems are more likely to be compatible with Windows XP, but this is not a guarantee.

The problem is this: Windows XP, like its Windows NT predecessors, deals with hardware in a different manner than the Windows 9x platforms. It has specific hardware drivers and something many Windows 9x users have never even heard of: a hardware compatibility list (HCL).

Because an HCL is available, planning an installation of Windows XP becomes all the more important.

In general, you should take these steps before installing Windows XP:

• Take a hardware inventory of your entire system.
• Check your hardware inventory against the Windows XP HCL.
• Make any changes that are needed to your system.
• Back up all your data.

If you follow these steps, you should have a safe and easy migration.

NOTE: *Windows XP includes a new system compatibility tool that will automate much of the process outlined in these Immediate Solutions. If you want to forego much of the system inventory steps and trust the new compatibility tool to handle the check, it is available on the Windows XP Professional CD-ROM.*

Conducting a System Inventory

As you begin examining your computer, notice that a lot of the information you need to know is right there in front of you. Your monitor, for instance, is sitting on your table or desk with its brand name and model displayed on the front or back. The same is probably true for your printer and any other external devices you might have. You'll want to take note of both the brand name and model as they appear on the device.

Performing an Inventory with Device Manager

In addition to identifying external devices, you'll need to determine what's actually inside your computer. One place to start is by displaying a list of devices as identified by your existing operating system. Windows 95, 98, and 2000 use a built-in applet called the Device Manager to list known devices. In Windows NT, perhaps the best place to view installed devices is the Windows NT Diagnostics applet, located in the Administrative Tools menu.

To identify the devices attached to your computer, follow these steps:

1. In Windows 95 and 98, open the Device Manager by clicking the Start button on the Windows taskbar and then choosing Settings|Control Panel.

2. When the Control Panel window appears, double-click the System icon to open the System Properties dialog box, shown in Figure 1.1.

3. Click the Device Manager tab to list the inner workings of your computer, as shown in Figure 1.2.

Now, you need to do some old-fashioned detective footwork. Your computer may (or may not) actually use a device for each of the device types listed in the Device Manager. For example, to determine whether you have a CD-ROM drive installed in your computer and to find its brand, first expand the CD-ROM list by clicking its expansion control—the little plus sign (see Figure 1.3).

As you can see in Figure 1.3, this computer has one CD-ROM drive, with a rather cryptic label. To find out more about a device, select it and then click the Properties button. (Alternatively, double-click the selected device.) For example, click the listed CD-ROM device and then click Properties. The Properties dialog box for the CD-ROM drive appears (see Figure 1.4).

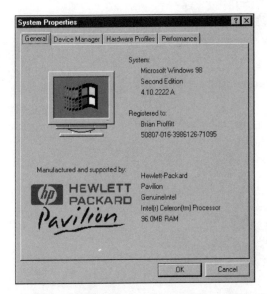

Figure 1.1   The System Properties dialog box is the home of the Device Manager.

Figure 1.2   The Device Manager will show you nearly every hardware device used by your computer (at least as identified by your current operating system).

Figure 1.4 shows a classic example of a device that has been made to conform to Windows' standards—so much so that Windows does not care who manufactured it. As far as Windows is concerned, this device is just a CD-ROM drive that follows Western Digital's AT Attachment Packet Interface (ATAPI) standard. Even so, recording the

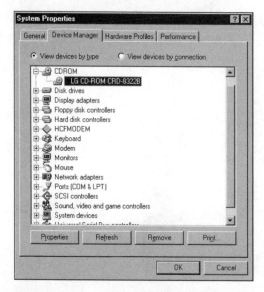

Figure 1.3   Open a list of devices by clicking the expansion box.

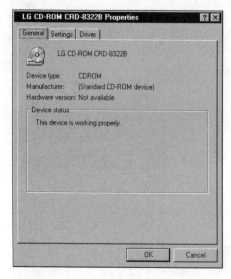

Figure 1.4   The Properties dialog box. Not too much information here, but
every little bit helps.

information is still a good idea so that you can check it against the
Windows XP HCL.

You may want to keep a journal to track and record all the PC's hardware along with any other issues that may arise while installing Windows XP. Jotting down all this information with a pencil and paper,

however, can be an onerous job. Follow these steps to simplify the task and print all your PC's hardware information in one fell swoop:

1. In the System Properties dialog box, click the Print button. The Print dialog box will appear, as shown in Figure 1.5.

2. Select All Devices And System Summary and then click OK. All the information available to the Device Manager will be printed.

You will find this information to be very technical—most of which you will not need. If you want to successfully install Windows XP, the most important information you need is for those devices that make your computer operable, as listed in Table 1.1.

In addition to the critical hardware, other hardware types that may be part of your computer system should also be recorded in your journal. These hardware types are listed in Table 1.2.

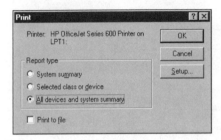

Figure 1.5   Getting your device information on paper.

Table 1.1   Primary hardware information needed for Windows XP installation.

Hardware	Information Needed
CPU	Manufacturer, model, speed
Motherboard	Manufacturer, model
Buses	Manufacturer, model
Memory (RAM)	Size
Video card	Manufacturer, model, video RAM size
Monitor	Manufacturer, model, horizontal and vertical synchronization rates
Hard drive	Manufacturer, model, size, type (Small Computer System Interface (SCSI) versus Integrated Drive Electronics (IDE))
Network card	Manufacturer, model
CD-ROM drive	Manufacturer, model, size
Floppy drive	Manufacturer, model, size
Modem	Manufacturer, model, transmission speed

(continued)

11

Table 1.1   Primary hardware information needed for Windows XP installation *(continued)*.

Hardware	Information Needed
Printer	Manufacturer, model
Mouse	Manufacturer, model, type (PS/2 versus serial)
Keyboard	Manufacturer, model, number of keys, language
SCSI card and devices	Manufacturer, model, type of device controlled
IDE adapters	Manufacturer, model, type of device controlled

Table 1.2   Secondary hardware information needed for Windows XP installation.

Hardware	Information Needed
Zip/Jaz drive	Manufacturer, model, size
Tape drive	Manufacturer, model, size
Sound card	Manufacturer, model
Scanner	Manufacturer, model
Infrared device	Manufacturer, model, type of device controlled
Joystick	Manufacturer, model
Serial device	Manufacturer, model, type of device controlled
Parallel device	Manufacturer, model, type of device controlled
Personal Computer Memory Card International Association (PCMCIA) device	Manufacturer, model, card type

Most of the information you require is included in the Device Manager output you printed, but not all. For example, you can locate information on the amount of RAM installed on your computer by clicking the Performance tab in the System Properties dialog box. Another option might be to right-click your hard drive letter as listed in My Computer or Windows Explorer, checking the Properties option to see how large your drive space is. A little detective work will go a long way toward making your Windows XP installation easier.

Performing an Inventory of Your Network

Checking for network information now will save you time as you actually perform your Windows XP installation. Although all the information should be carried over to the new Windows XP platform, it's a good idea to make sure you have a copy of all your settings first.

To check your dial-up settings, follow these steps:

1. Click the Start button on the Windows taskbar. Then, choose Programs|Accessories|Communications|Dial-Up Networking to open the Dial-Up Networking window, shown in Figure 1.6.

2. Right-click your connection's icon to open the shortcut menu; then, select Properties from the menu to open the dialog box for your dial-up connection (see Figure 1.7).

3. Click the Server Types tab. Note the Type Of Dial-Up Server setting in your journal, as well as any other settings on this page of the dialog box.

Figure 1.6   Exploring your computer's connections.

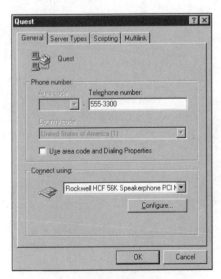

Figure 1.7   The properties of a dial-up networking connection.

4. When you're ready, click the TCP/IP Settings button. The TCP/IP Settings dialog box will appear (see Figure 1.8).

   The information contained in this dialog box is essential to any connection to the Internet. These settings dictate how your computer talks to other computers on the network after you dial in. Every connection is different, so you should record these settings exactly.

5. When you're finished, click the Cancel button to close the TCP/IP Settings dialog box.

6. Click Cancel once more to leave the connection dialog box.

TIP: *Don't forget to record your username and password for the connection! You can usually find them in the Network settings in your Windows Control Panel.*

If you have any other connections in the Dial-Up Networking window that you want to be sure to retain in Windows XP, repeat the procedures in this section for each of them to determine their settings.

Related solutions:	Found on page:
Configuring Power Options	350
Customizing the XP Desktop	56

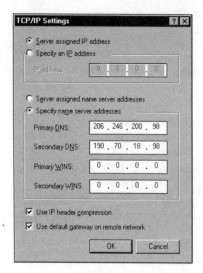

Figure 1.8   TCP/IP settings are the heart of most Internet connection settings.

Investigating Potential Trouble Spots

Now that you have a list of hardware for your system, you need to check it against the Windows XP HCL to be sure no pieces of equipment connected to your PC might have a problem with Windows XP, or vice versa.

The best place to get the HCL for Windows XP is from the horse's mouth itself: the Microsoft Web site at **www.microsoft.com/hcl/ default.asp**. There, you will find a good list of data regarding the hardware that is known to work with Windows XP. You can search for each hardware item on your inventory and see whether it appears as a match for Windows XP.

A device may have three levels of compatibility for Windows XP: no compatibility, basic compatibility, and fully Windows compliant. You will want at least basic compatibility for your device to work properly.

But, what if your device is not listed among the compatibles? Should you just chuck it into a trash can? The answer really depends on what the device is. For instance, if the device is an external modem, it's a pretty safe bet that Windows XP will be able to use it because nearly all modems have default standard settings that most operating systems can use. Plus, an external modem may not be a critical device on your system, so it would be safe to install Windows XP.

For something more important, such as the motherboard, you need to exercise a lot more caution. If the motherboard is not listed, and it fails to run upon installing Windows XP, you will have spent a whole lot of time for nothing.

In instances such as these, you need to contact the device's manufacturer to see whether its device has been tested on Windows XP yet. If not, contact Microsoft's technical support to see whether there are any known issues with the device working on Windows XP. You may get lucky and find out the HCL simply hasn't been updated yet.

If the device is important, and you do not feel comfortable risking an upgrade to Windows XP, you will need to replace the device with something new.

Fixing Hardware Trouble Spots

If your inventory has concluded that you need to replace some trouble-some devices on your system, now—before the Windows XP installation—is the time to do so.

One of the most common incompatibilities will be the system's basic input/output system (BIOS). The BIOS is what enables your computer to boot up when you turn on the power. It contains, in a special ROM chip, all the information needed to start the disk drives, screen, and various buses on the system without accessing the operating system.

A BIOS incompatibility is a serious thing, but luckily one of the easiest to fix. In fact, fixing it is so easy that it is recommended you do so as a matter of course before performing any upgrade. It will give your system a nice little tune-up and get your machine up to current industry standards.

To locate the type of BIOS your system has, you can restart your system and press whatever key your BIOS needs to enter the BIOS Setup screen. It is usually the Esc or F2 key (or even the Delete key), but it may be different on your own machine. Look for the "setup" message during the system startup routine.

After you identify the type of BIOS you have, exit the BIOS Setup and continue back to Windows. You can run a search on the Internet to find the company Web site for your BIOS manufacturer, but a good place to start is Wim's BIOS Page at **www.wimsbios.com**. Here, you will find a very complete listing of BIOS manufacturers and their contact information.

Here is a typical set of steps you could use to upgrade your system BIOS:

1. Different BIOSs have different upgrade routines, but they usually follow a similar pattern.
2. Download the available upgrade for your BIOS to your computer.
3. Create a bootable floppy by formatting a floppy disk with the Copy System Files setting.
4. If the BIOS file is compressed (and it usually is), uncompress the file. Typically, you do so by double-clicking the file icon.
5. Copy all the uncompressed files to the bootable floppy.

6. Leaving the bootable floppy in the drive, restart your system. The system will boot from the floppy and start the upgrade process.

7. Follow the upgrade instructions on your screen.

TIP: Some newer motherboards protect the BIOS ROM from accidental overwriting or malicious damage with a physical jumper switch. If you have problems upgrading the BIOS, you may need to open the PC case and change the jumper setting. Consult your PC owner's manual or manufacturer's Web site.

Although performing BIOS upgrades is easy, some risk is involved. Read-only memory (ROM) is sensitive to power fluctuations during an upgrade, so be sure you perform the upgrade with full access to power and during a time when the power is not likely to go out (such as during a major storm). Also, don't try to rush things. Rewriting the ROM can take a while—and may even look like it's stuck.

WARNING! Don't interrupt the upgrade process at any time!

Another potential hardware problem may be your PC's onboard memory, or RAM. Recall that Windows XP recommends 128MB of RAM on your machine. That's quite a bit, and many machines don't have that much. If you were hoping to squeak by with the minimum requirement of 64MB, you are going to be in for some really bad times.

There is an adage among those who are familiar with Windows products: Whatever Microsoft says you need, double it. And, that is certainly the case here. Early beta results strongly indicate that the minimum amount of RAM for an XP system should be 128MB, and the recommended should be 256MB. So, even if you think you have enough memory, you are strongly encouraged to add more.

And, quite frankly, adding more memory is not such a bad thing. Memory is ridiculously cheap and easy to install, so you have no reason not to add the memory. You'll thank yourself later.

Before purchasing new RAM, you will need to identify what type of RAM slots you have on your machine. You can choose from two kinds: Dual Inline Memory Modules (DIMMs), which have 168 contacts, or Synchronous Inline Memory Modules (SIMMs), which have 72 contacts. The best way to tell is to open the PC case and see what kind your PC has. Look for two closely spaced parallel slots that may or may not have narrow little cards within them.

After you determine the type of RAM you need and purchase the additional memory, you will need to put the new RAM into your computer. Before opening the PC case, be sure to disconnect every cable connected to your PC and move the machine to a reasonably static-free area. (The kitchen is usually a good place.)

TIP: *Before you touch anything inside the case, touch your finger to a metal object to discharge any static remaining on your body.*

When you remove the RAM memory modules from their plastic shipping material, never clasp the module in the middle. Hold the module by the short ends, with your fingers only on the plastic edges.

Different motherboards put their RAM slots in different places, but usually the RAM slots are in an easily accessible spot. Now that you have a module in your hands, you can look for a similar unit inside your PC if you're still not sure. Check the slots to see whether they have any manual locks (they are found at the ends of the slots). If you find any plastic tabs in these locations, gently push them down and away from the slots to release the locks.

If a DIMM RAM module is already in the slot and you are swapping, you can now gently but firmly pull the module out of its slot. If it is a SIMM module, you will need to push the memory component back at an angle before pulling it out of the slot.

Now, you can place the new module in the slot. Notice the little notch in the module on the edge with the contacts. This notch will ensure that you get the module in the slot the right way because the module will fit only one way.

For SIMM modules, hold the RAM module so it's at an angle to the motherboard and lined up correctly with the slot (aimed down from the module in front). Push it slowly into the slot while angling it up until it's perpendicular to the motherboard and its edge is parallel to the existing modules. When it's in the right position, the module should snap into place.

With DIMM modules, the procedure is the same, but you don't angle the module in—you just push it straight into the slot.

Backing Up Your Data

After you ascertain your hardware compatibility with Windows XP, you will need to get your computer ready for the installation. One of the first things you should do is back up the data on your PC.

It is always a good idea to back up your valuable data, thus guarding against system catastrophe. At the very least, you'll want your data protected from power surges, virus attacks, computer theft, or anything else that can affect your ability to access the data on your machine.

Upgrading to Windows XP certainly should not be classified as a catastrophic event. But, you are going to be adding a new operating system or perhaps possibly even changing the file system on your hard drive. These events have the potential to erase data completely.

It is very likely that you have used a backup program at least once and have found them easy to use. Many backup programs are available, including an excellent one found with Norton System Utilities. The principles for backup utilities are pretty much the same: Locate and identify the files you wish to archive, specify the location of the new archive file, and then create the file. Restoration is simply the reverse of this action.

Microsoft Windows has its own utility for backup that can be used to archive your data. The next few paragraphs describe how to work with the Windows Backup utility.

1. From the Windows 98 taskbar, click the Start button.

2. Choose Programs|Accessories|System Tools|Backup. The Microsoft Backup application will start with the Welcome To Microsoft Backup dialog box open (see Figure 1.9).

NOTE: *The Backup application in Windows 95 is similar to that in Windows 98, except for the lack of a wizard to step you through operations.*

---

3. You can now choose to create a new backup file, open an existing backup job, or restore archived data. Select Create A New Backup Job and then click OK. The Backup Wizard will appear, as shown in Figure 1.10.

4. Here, you can either choose to back up your entire set of computer files or to back up only selected files. If you have the storage space and the time, go ahead and archive your entire PC. If not, select the Backup Selected Files, Folders, And

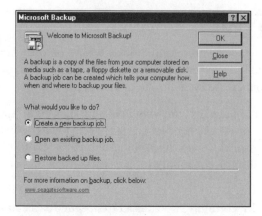

Figure 1.9   Microsoft's Backup utility.

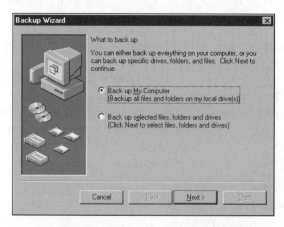

Figure 1.10   The first step in the Backup process.

Drives option and then click Next. The second dialog box of the Backup Wizard will open.

5. On the left side of the dialog box, select the checkboxes for the drives and folders you want to back up. As necessary, use the expansion icons in the directory listing to view subfolders. Note that selecting a folder automatically selects all the files within the folder. Alternatively, select or clear the checkboxes for the specific files you want to include or exclude from the file list on the right side of the dialog box. Figure 1.11 shows an example of selected files in the My Documents folder.

6. After you select all the files you want to include in your backup job, click Next to continue to the next dialog box of the Backup Wizard. You are asked whether you want to back up all the selected files or just the ones that have changed since a prior backup.

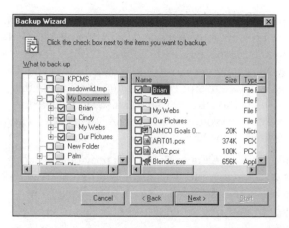

Figure 1.11   You can select all or part of a folder's contents.

7. Because this is likely your first backup, select the All Selected Files option and click Next to continue.

8. In the fourth dialog box (see Figure 1.12), you are asked where you want to store the backup file. Choose your preferred location and type a file name for your backup file.

9. When you are finished, click Next to continue.

TIP: Make sure you save this information on a drive other than your hard drive. Zip, Jaz, or tape drives are good places.

10. The fifth dialog box gives you two choices on how to back up your data. The first specifies that you want your data to be double-checked to make sure it was successfully archived.

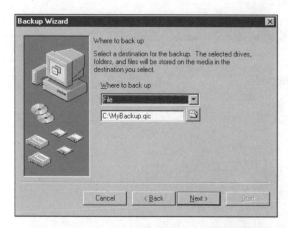

Figure 1.12   Where do you want to store your backup file?

Double-checking your data as it's being archived will slow down the process, but I recommend that you do so. After all, what's the point of backing up erroneous data? The second option asks whether you want to compress the backup data. Unless you have virtually unlimited space to store your backup, you'll want this option checked, even though doing so will also slow down the backup process. Choose your preferences and then click Next to continue to the final dialog box of the Backup Wizard.

11. In the last dialog box (see Figure 1.13), you provide a descriptive name for your backup file. This name is different from the file name you previously selected. Use a name to help you remember the contents of the backup archive file.

12. After you confirm the choices you have made, simply click the Start button to begin the backup process. The Backup Progress window will appear to display the process' progress.

13. When the process is complete, the backup file will be verified (if you chose to do this), and you will be notified that the operation is complete.

14. Click OK to acknowledge the notification.

15. Click OK again to close the Backup Progress window.

16. Make sure the file is stored away from your hard drive (that is, in a Jaz or Zip drive, a CD, or a tape drive).

NOTE: *You should be aware that Windows 98 backup files can only be restored within Windows 98—not Windows XP. If you choose to perform a clean installation, you will eliminate any chance of reverting your system back to Windows 98 and making use of these backup files. Keep this in mind when you decide how to install Windows XP.*

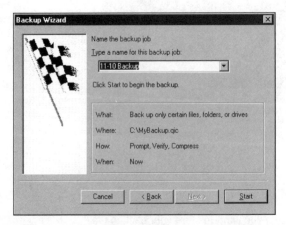

Figure 1.13   Confirm your backup choices in this dialog box.

Chapter 2

Install Windows XP Professional

In Brief

You have certain expectations when you get ready to install a new operating system—the secret little thrill you get that quickens your pulse. As you wonder what's over the next hilltop, so you also wonder what nifty little tricks the new OS will bring.

Perhaps this description is a bit more poetic than it needs to be, and you just want to get on with the installation. After all, you have a lot of work in your near future, and you don't have time to fool around with installing a new version of Windows. Microsoft has vastly simplified the stages of its installation routine with Windows XP Professional. Gone are the confusing phrases and geekology—they're now replaced by straightforward, everyday English. Or Japanese. Or Bulgarian.

Migration Paths

You can put Windows XP onto your system in more than one way. The first, and perhaps easiest, is to go out and buy a computer that has XP pre-installed. If you are in this situation, you may as well just give this chapter a miss and move on to Chapter 3.

If you are like a vast majority of users, however, you already are running some version of Windows on your PC and are looking to upgrade. *Upgrading* is the process by which you carry over all the settings and applications in your existing version of Windows to Windows XP. From a programming point of view, upgrading is one of the hardest operations a computer application can take because the transposition of so many variables can easily introduce an error.

Conversely, upgrading is by far the simplest form of installation from the user's perspective. After all, you start the Setup program, and all your files and programs eventually find their way to a new home.

The other form of installation is called a *clean install*. In a clean install, you have Windows XP completely ignore any previous installations and install itself as if you were getting a new machine out of the factory. Performing a clean install is not often done because there is very little call for it. For the Setup application, this is the easiest operation to perform. And, as you may have already guessed, it's the most difficult for the user to deal with.

Clean installs are not recommended for most users for a big reason: Performing such an installation will completely change the Windows Registry. The Registry is a collection of files that serves as an electronic roadmap of every single application file on your computer.

Such a roadmap is necessary because when an application is installed on a Windows system, it is not made up of just one file. Because of the complex nature of programming for Windows, many Windows programmers take a shortcut with their code. Instead of placing every single action of their program into a single file, they set up many actions to be shared with other programs.

For instance, Word, Internet Explorer, and virtually every other Windows program uses menus. So, instead of putting the code for menu creation into all these programs, you can just make a shared library of the menu code that every application can refer to. These library files make up a lot of the graphical instructions for Windows applications, and it's a good thing, too. Otherwise, every Windows application would be incredibly huge.

These shared code files are often referred to as dynamic link libraries, or DLLs. You may recall seeing a reference to them once or twice in Windows 95 and 98—usually behind a maddening error message that said, "Can't find or missing." The Registry tracks these DLLs and any other special helper files for every installed program on your Windows machine.

If you were to implement a clean install on your Windows machine, all your existing files and applications would pretty much be in the same place. Nothing would really be lost. But, the Registry would be completely different and would no longer be able to help your application find any of the files it needs to run. Not only that, but Windows XP may have new locations for some of these shared files, so any self-configuration settings your application has may be useless as well.

With all this at stake, you may be wondering why Microsoft even gives people this option. Basically Microsoft recognizes that some users will be coming to Windows from other operating systems, such as Linux or Solaris. Those people clearly will not have any Windows settings to carry over. This set of users will need something that will build a Windows XP operating system from the ground up.

The clean install option also exists as a last-resort fallback for those rare occasions when a regular upgrade has gone completely awry. Some users (myself among them) have configured and hacked their way through an existing Windows system to such an extent that Windows XP can find little to make use of. The resulting installation, therefore, is riddled with all sorts of pitfalls and errors—to the point that a clean install may be your best option.

Set Up an Upgrade

If you are like the majority of Windows users who simply want to move to the next level of Windows with XP, you will need to bear the burden of performing an upgrade. This statement is more than a little tongue-in-cheek because upgrading is perhaps the easiest thing for a user to do.

Before you begin the upgrade, you need to make sure you have backed up your machine as completely as possible. This is one point that bears repeating because it really is important. At the very least, save the most important files (finances, work files, pictures of the kids) somewhere else.

One thing you *won't* need before you begin is a blank, floppy disk like you needed before all the other Windows installations you may have done in the past. That's because Windows XP, like NT and 2000 before it, does not employ a floppy disk to use as an emergency boot device. It's not that it can't, but the use of an emergency boot floppy is a bit of a security risk—something that the NT family of Windows has taken great pains to avoid.

Finally, you will need some time. Although much of the Windows XP installation is automated, it does need some user input at the beginning and end of the process. Depending on the size and speed of your computer, you are looking at a little over an hour of time on average. I usually try to block out an hour and a half, to anticipate those little slowdowns that invariably creep into a Windows installation. Besides, with the extra time on your hands, you will be far more relaxed about your installation on the off chance something odd does happen.

Mass Deployment of Windows XP

If you are an IT manager, the thought of sitting around for even an hour for each and every machine you want to upgrade to Windows XP is enough to trigger a dull headache behind your eyes. On the other hand, the thought of letting your users perform the upgrade themselves is likely enough to give you a migraine. The best way around this little conundrum is to perform a large-scale deployment for Windows XP. But, with so many options available, which way should you choose?

One of the most popular techniques for getting Windows XP out to the masses is to perform an unattended installation. The principle behind this procedure is pretty simple. Using Microsoft's Setup Manager, you create a script that will automatically answer all the questions the Windows XP Setup will ask the user. Then, all you need to do is take the Windows XP CD-ROM and a floppy disk that has the scripted answers on it to the various computers and run the installation. For an upgrade, you can even use this technique across a network connection.

TIP: *You can find the Setup Manager application in the Support\Tools\deploy.cab file on the Windows XP Professional CD-ROM.*

Another method for rapid deployment is to use Sysprep for creating a master image of a baseline PC's hard disk with Windows XP installed. This image can then be copied to other computers, thus cloning the original computer.

Sysprep is not for everyone or for every situation. Sysprep will perform only a clean install of Windows XP, which means that if you are going to clone systems that have data on them already, you will need to find a way to migrate user files and settings off the computers to be cloned and then migrate them back when the cloning procedure is finished.

TIP: *You can find the Sysprep application in the Support\Tools\deploy.cab file on the Windows XP Professional CD-ROM.*

Another way to perform a clean installation of Windows XP is to use the Remote Installation Service (RIS). RIS also uses an answer file generated by the Setup Manager to direct the setup of Windows XP simultaneously on multiple clients in your network. It does so by remote booting eligible clients with their network cards and connecting the clients to the network to download a full system image onto the client's hard drive.

There are some caveats to using RIS. First, you can use it only with Windows 2000 Server's Active Directory Service (ADS) and only with clients that are configured for ADS. And, it cannot be used for upgrading—clean installs only.

For mass remote upgrades, the best tool to use is the Systems Management Server (SMS), a Microsoft product designed to remotely manage client desktops throughout an organization. SMS will allow simultaneous upgrades of client machines to Windows XP, provided Windows XP Professional is somewhere in use on your network.

Immediate Solutions

Upgrading to Windows XP Professional

All the preparations are done. You've got the time, you've got the drive. It's time to install Windows XP Professional. You can start with these steps:

1. Insert the Windows XP Professional CD-ROM into your CD-ROM drive. The Welcome screen will appear (see Figure 2.1).

2. Click the Install Windows XP button. The Windows XP installation screen will open, with the Windows Setup dialog box (see Figure 2.2).

3. In the Installation Type field, select the type of installation path you want to take, Upgrade or Clean Install.

NOTE: *Though there is little difference between the two installation paths, this section will focus on the Upgrade path.*

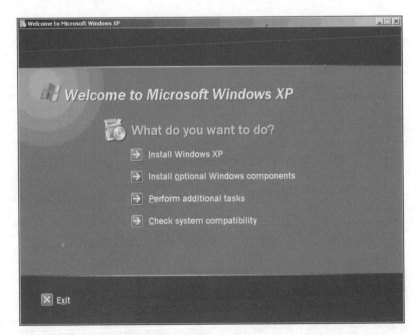

Figure 2.1   Welcome to Windows XP.

Figure 2.2   Choose what kind of installation you want to implement.

4. Click the Next button. The License Agreement dialog box will appear.

5. Click the I Accept This Agreement radio button.

6. Click the Next button. The Your Product Key dialog box will appear (see Figure 2.3).

7. Type the 25-digit code key into the key fields.

8. Click the Next button. The Get Updated Setup Files dialog box will open (see Figure 2.4).

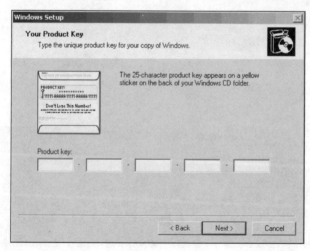

Figure 2.3   Proving you own the software you are about to install, Part 1.

Figure 2.4   Make sure you have the most current Setup files.

Every once in a while, various updates will come out for the Setup routines. Even if you just bought the software, your Setup files could be outdated due to a bug fix or improvement that Microsoft recently implemented. To make sure you have the very latest version of the Setup application, you should choose to download new Setup files as follows:

1. Click the Yes, Download The Updated Setup Files radio button.
2. Click Next. The Updated Setup Files dialog box will close, and Setup will automatically search for updated files.

If any new Setup files are located, they will be downloaded and installed on your computer. Afterward, the Setup application will immediately move on to the Preparing Installation phase. In this phase, Setup will check your system to make sure you have room on your hard drive and no system compatibility issues remain. It also will record the current settings of your existing Windows system.

If any problems are found with your current system, a series of dialog boxes will appear explaining them, such as the System Compatibility dialog box shown in Figure 2.5.

You must decide whether any of these issues are important enough to stop the installation. If the issues are noncritical, like the possible incompatible printer shown in Figure 2.5, then you can likely go ahead with the Setup.

After you deal with any issues that may appear, Setup will move into what is (for you) the boring part of the process: installing Windows XP.

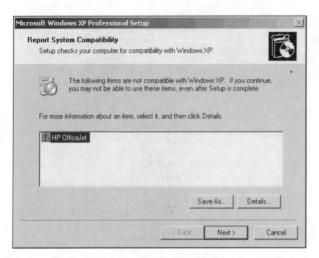

Figure 2.5   Any remaining issues you may have in Setup will appear just before the actual file copying begins.

First, the system will reboot and bring up a text mode Windows environment that will step you through the remainder of the installation process.

In the first part, the Installing Windows phase, the files needed to run Windows XP are uncompressed from the CD-ROM and placed in the appropriate place on your hard drive. This portion of Setup usually takes the longest, and you really can't do anything while you're waiting for it to complete. Go grab a cup of coffee or bother your cubicle-mates for a half hour or so.

When the copying process is complete, the system will reboot once more—this time actually running Windows XP.

Related solutions:	*Found on page:*
Backing Up Your Data	19
Migrating Users with the Files And Settings Transfer Wizard	221

Activating Windows XP Professional

You still need to complete a few steps before the process is complete, however. First, you will need to activate and possibly register Windows XP before you can use it.

In its efforts to combat technology piracy, something that all proprietary software developers loathe, Microsoft has begun to use a new
policy to protect its software from one of the least malicious, and yet
most prolific, forms of piracy: casual copying.

Casual copying is something that many of us have done, without really intending to harm anyone. Most often, it is done by users who
have more than one machine in their home or small office and have
decided to share one copy of a Windows product between all the PCs.
But, according to the End User's License Agreement (EULA), even
this most benevolent form of sharing is simply not allowed. Microsoft's
stance is very stringent: one license per machine. Period.

Granted, license enforcement is certainly needed because a great
deal of real piracy is going on. It is possible to download and install registered copies of almost any popular software today—all without paying
a single penny. But, is Microsoft going too far in this enforcement policy?

Regardless of how you feel about the new activation policy, it is—for
now—here for us to contend with. In a nutshell, here's how it works.
When you entered the 25-digit Product Key during the Setup process,
you basically inserted one key in a three-key "lock" designed to make
your copy of Windows XP yours and yours alone.

The second key in the process is the 20-digit Product Identification,
which is based in part on the Product Key. The Product ID is different
from the Product Key, but it is similar in function. Each copy of Windows XP has its own ID, which is inviolate.

TIP: *To see you computer's Product ID, click the View System Information link in the My
Computer window.*

The third key that makes up the lock is the hardware signature of
your PC. Certain system components are scanned and identified. This
information is then run through a special one-time-only algorithm to
create a Hardware Identifier that is unique to your system. This helps
to ensure the privacy of what's on your PC because no one would ever
be able to deduce your components based on this one-time-only code.

After all the keys are created, the lock is formed. The lock is called
the Installation ID, and only this information will need to be sent to
Microsoft to activate Windows XP.

Activation is mandatory, but it is anonymous. All Microsoft is tracking is
which instance of Windows XP is installed on what machine. In this way,

2. Install Windows XP Professional

if someone else tried to install the same copy of Windows XP on his or her system, the Product Key and Product ID parts of the lock would be the same as yours, and only the Hardware Identifier section would be completely different. If someone attempts to activate this installation, Microsoft's records would immediately know that this copy had already been installed somewhere else and would reject the activation.

If you are concerned that Big Brother is now going to come swooping down to get you for trying to run one copy of Windows XP on more than one machine, don't panic. Remember, the activation process is completely anonymous, so no one will come to get you. The worst thing that will happen is that the second installation will not be activated. After 30 days in this state, Windows XP will become completely nonfunctional—except for the Product Activation feature.

Product Activation can occur at two points, depending on how you installed Windows XP. If you performed an upgrade, you will have the opportunity to activate Windows XP just before starting Windows XP for the first time. If you performed a clean install, you will be asked to activate soon after you begin running the Windows XP desktop because activation can use an Internet connection and the developers of XP know you need some time to set up such a connection. In either case, the procedure is exactly the same. In the Let's Activate Windows screen (as shown in Figure 2.6), you are given the choice to activate Windows now or wait and be reminded later. Unless you have a pressing need not to do so, you may as well activate it as soon as you can.

You have two choices for activating Windows XP: over the Internet or over the phone. If you have an Internet connection already created (or perhaps carried over from your previous version of Windows), choose this option. It is much faster and completely automated.

The telephone option is just as good, though it takes a bit longer. Should you go this route, you will be given a phone number to call Microsoft, and the Installation ID will be displayed. When you have the representative on the phone, you can read the Installation ID to him or her. The representative will then give you a string of characters to type back into the activation screen. This set of characters will activate your copy of Windows XP.

After you activate Windows XP, you will be given the opportunity to register your copy. If this step seems redundant, it's really not. Activation is to enforce the EULA. Registration is the process in which Microsoft finds out more about you, the customer. Because of this, Registration is completely optional, as indicated in the Registration screen shown in Figure 2.7.

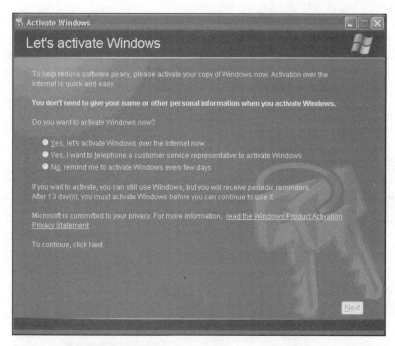

Figure 2.6   Activation is painless and quick.

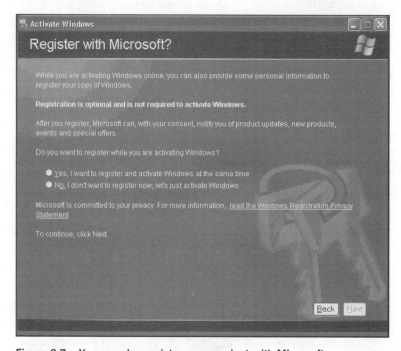

Figure 2.7   You can also register your product with Microsoft.

Should you register with Microsoft? There are many schools of thought about this question. With privacy a growing concern, sending your personal information to anyone may be a bit daunting. Even if you completely agree with Microsoft's privacy policy, your information is still sitting in a database somewhere for someone to look at. On the other hand, registration can offer some nice benefits, such as early notification of new Microsoft products and updates. The choice is really up to you.

Using Setup Manager

Setup Manager is a versatile tool designed to help create automated setups for Windows XP. Whether you are using the Unattended Installation, Sysprep cloning, or RIS methods, you will find Setup Manager to be a valuable tool.

Setup Manager is one of several deployment tools that are included with Windows XP Professional but not installed. To use Setup Manager, you first need to move it onto your PC as follows:

1. Insert the Windows XP Professional CD-ROM into your CD-ROM drive. The Welcome screen will appear.
2. Click Exit to close the Welcome screen.
3. Click Start|My Computer to open the My Computer window.
4. In the My Computer window, right-click the icon for the CD-ROM drive containing the Windows XP Professional CD-ROM. The drive's context menu will appear.
5. Click Open in the context menu. The contents of the CD-ROM will be displayed.

TIP: *If you try to double-click the CD-ROM drive icon, you will likely just get the Welcome screen again because Autoplay is activated by default in Windows XP.*

---

6. Double-click the Support folder to display its contents.
7. Double-click the Tools folder to display its contents (see Figure 2.8).
8. Double-click the deploy.cab file to display the contents of this compressed file.
9. Double-click the setupmgr.exe file. The Select A Destination dialog box will appear (see Figure 2.9).

Figure 2.8   Looking for the deployment tools.

Figure 2.9   Choose a spot to extract the Setup Manager application.

10. Click the folder to which you want to extract Setup Manager.

11. Click Extract so that setupmgr.exe will be extracted to the destination folder.

Now that you have Setup Manager on your PC, you can run it. Navigate to the executable file you just extracted using the My Computer window and double-click it to start Setup Manager and its wizard function. To continue, follow these steps:

1. The first screen of the Windows Setup Manager Wizard is a brief introduction screen. Click Next to continue to the next screen (see Figure 2.10).

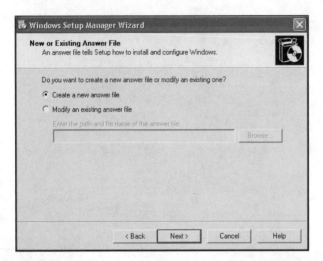

Figure 2.10   Start something new or work on something old?

2. Click the Create A New Answer File radio button if this is your first time running Setup Manager.

3. Click the Next button. The Product To Install dialog box will appear (see Figure 2.11).

4. Click the Windows Unattended Installation radio button.

5. Click the Next button. The Platform dialog box will appear.

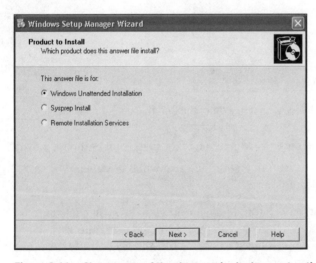

Figure 2.11   Choose one of the three main deployment options.

6. Click the platform option you want to install. In this case, click Windows XP Professional.

7. Click the Next button. The User Interaction Level dialog box will appear (see Figure 2.12).

   A brief explanation of the options in the User Interaction Level dialog box is in order. This dialog box essentially lets you decide how much or how little burden you want to put on the end user and, consequently, yourself. Table 2.1 provides some

Figure 2.12   How much do you want your users to work?

Table 2.1   Unattended installation options.

Option	Explanation	Administrator	User
Provide Defaults	Setup Manager fills in all the answers with default settings, but the user can override them at any time.	High	Medium
Fully Automated	You provide every answer for the installation; the user has no chance to change them.	High	Low
Hide Pages	Only pages you have not answered will be displayed to the user to answer.	Medium	Medium
Read Only	All Setup pages will be displayed, but those you have answered cannot be changed.	Medium	Medium
GUI Attended	The GUI portion of Setup must be attended; everything else is automated.	Medium	High

detail on just what these options mean for you and your users in terms of low, medium, or high involvement.

8. For this example, click the Provide Defaults option.

9. Click the Next button. The Distribution Folder dialog box will appear.

10. Choose whether you want to make all the installation files available on the network or just make an answer file for use with a CD-ROM installation.

11. Click the Next button to close the Wizard dialog box.

Now that the wizard has completed its task, you can step through all the available Setup page screens and provide the answers you wish.

Within the Setup Manager, either you can use the Next and Back buttons to step through the different Setup pages in order, or you can click the particular headings you want to fill in.

After you answer the questions you want, you need to click the Finish button on the final Additional Commands page. Doing so will open the Windows Setup Manager dialog box that tells you where the answer file for the unattended setup can be found. Click OK if this location is satisfactory. You will now see the Setup Manager Complete screen. You can close the application by clicking on the Close icon.

Installing Windows XP Professional Unattended

When the unattended answer files are completed, all you need to do is actually go out and use them and the rest of the Windows files to install Windows XP.

This example will show how to install Windows XP unattended with a CD-ROM. You will find this to be a pleasantly easy process. The most difficult aspect of this process, actually, is altering the unattended batch file so it knows where to find the (a) answer file and (b) Windows XP CD-ROM.

First, you should open the batch file so you can edit it to match the parameters on the machine(s) upon which you are going to install Windows XP. In the My Computer window, right-click the unattended.bat file the Setup Manager stored for you and click Edit in the context menu.

WARNING! Don't double-click the batch file or select Open from the context menu. This will start the batch file and quite possibly begin a Windows XP installation on your computer!

The contents of the unattended.bat file produced by the Setup Manager are shown here:

```
@rem SetupMgrTag
@echo off

rem
rem This is a SAMPLE batch script generated by the Setup Manager
rem Wizard.
rem If this script is moved from the location where it was
rem generated, it may have to be modified.
rem

set AnswerFile=.\unattend.txt
set SetupFiles=E:\i386

E:\i386\winnt32 /s:%SetupFiles% /unattend:%AnswerFile%
```

As you can see in the remarks section, moving this file may result in your having to edit it so it can work.

For example, on my machine, the sample script that was generated has the location of the Windows XP Setup files on drive E (which is the first CD-ROM drive on my system). On another user's system, the CD-ROM drive may be drive D or perhaps drive G. It is important, therefore, to make sure the location of the **SetupFiles** variable is pointing to the correct file path.

It is also critical that the command to run Setup (the last line of the batch file) is calling up the winnt32 application (which is Setup) from the right place.

If you are setting up for multiple users, be sure to point the batch file at the right answer file. If you had an answer file for user Jane and one for user Bill, you could easily make copies of unattended.txt and edit each copy with specific user information. Further, you could name one file janeunattend.txt and the other billunattend.txt. If you are managing your multiuser setup in this fashion, all you need to do is change the value of the **AnswerFile** variable to match the correct answer file for that user.

Editing the unattend.txt file is simplicity itself, as you can see in this small sample:

TIP: *This sample does not have a Product Key setting, but it's a good idea to have one set for each copy of Windows XP you will install.*

```
;SetupMgrTag
[Data]
   AutoPartition=1
   MsDosInitiated="0"
   UnattendedInstall="Yes"

[Unattended]
   UnattendMode=ProvideDefault
   OemPreinstall=No

[GuiUnattended]
   EncryptedAdminPassword=NO
   TimeZone=40

[UserData]
   FullName="Brian Proffitt"
   OrgName="Quantum Learning Group"

[Display]
   BitsPerPel=32
   Xresolution=800
   YResolution=600

[Identification]
   JoinWorkgroup=WORKGROUP

[Networking]
   InstallDefaultComponents=Yes
```

The variables here are straightforward, especially for user-centric information. You can change user and workgroup information with ease and then save the file under a new name as suggested earlier.

After you make all your changes, you need to save the unattended.bat file and the correct unattend.txt file onto a floppy disk. If you are in a multiuser scenario, be sure you have the correct batch file matched with the correct answer file.

TIP: *To make things easier, you can rename various copies of the batch file to include usernames.*

Now, all you have to do is take the floppy disk and the CD-ROM to the user's computer and do the following:

1. Insert the CD-ROM into the appropriate drive and click Exit on the Windows XP Welcome screen when it appears.

2. Click Start|Run to open the Run window.

3. Type the full command for running the batch file (for example, "A:\billunattended.bat").

4. Click OK. The batch file will run, and the unattended installation will begin.

2. Install Windows XP Professional

Chapter 3

Explore the Windows XP Desktop

In Brief

Contrary to popular belief, Microsoft did not invent the computer "desktop" with Windows. This distinction belongs to the folks at the Xerox Palo Alto Research Center (PARC) who, in their efforts to enter the personal computer market in the early 1980s, developed a wonderful graphical user interface (GUI) for their Xerox 8010 Star computer. This computer, which had a word processor and file/directory management system, would be the forerunner of everything Windows would later become.

There was only one little hitch: The Xerox 8010 Star cost $17,000 U.S. This was a tad pricey when compared to the $3,000 IBM PCs of the day, and the product never really took off.

The legacy of this first GUI with its windows, menus, and mouse lived on, with Apple Computer using it to create the interface for the Apple Lisa and later the Macintosh. Microsoft would soon pick up on this type of interface for its own new Windows product and, through a very strong marketing campaign, managed to convince most of the world that this whole thing was its idea. I'm not saying that Microsoft did not come up with any innovations on this basic interface. The introduction of the taskbar and Start menu in Windows 95 was not exactly new, but no one had figured out how to make it work so well before.

The interface within Windows XP is not a complete departure from the Windows design, though users of Windows 98 and Windows 2000 will be a bit surprised at some of the changes. Users of Windows ME will have less of a transition, but they will still discover significant changes from that interface as well.

Where Did All the Icons Go?

The first thing you will notice (particularly if you just finished a clean install for Windows XP) is that all the normal icons you would associate with Windows—My Computer, My Documents, and My Network Places—are gone from the desktop. In fact, if you perform a clean install, you are not going to see any icons on your desktop, save one: the Recycle Bin (see Figure 3.1).

Recycle Bin

start   9:23 PM

Figure 3.1   The (very stark) Windows XP desktop.

If you are wondering where all the icons went, they are still around. Only now, they are tucked neatly away in the Start menu, leaving the desktop nice and clean for your use. The rationale behind this change seems to be to make the desktop truly your own, and not Microsoft's. If this is indeed the case, this was a good move by the developers at Redmond because desktop space can be at a big premium in these days of working with multiple files at the same time.

Another interesting change to the desktop is the fact that you can have more than one of them. Actually, one desktop is available for each user assigned to the Windows XP machine. This capability really isn't anything new—Windows 98 has had multiple user capability for quite some time. What is new in Windows XP is the way the different user spaces are delineated.

In the past, the line between different users' desktops was rather fuzzy. Different desktops could be used, but managing them often involved a little guesswork. With Windows XP, desktop (and thereby user) management is crystal clear.

New XP Eye Candy

Perhaps the most significant change on the desktop is the new Start menu, which is now a large bright-green button that cannot help but catch your eye.

More than just the color of the Start menu has changed, however. If you look at the new Windows XP Start menu, you will be surprised by the radical changes within this central Windows component (see Figure 3.2).

Some of these features may be familiar, and some not. Using the new menu is like walking into your house and finding all the furniture has been moved around. It's still your house, it's still your furniture, but everything just looks *odd*.

On the very top of the Start menu is the username. In the past, it was located near the bottom of the Start menu, within the Log Off *Username* option. Now, the username is right in your face and (as you can see) has a nifty little picture next to it. You can choose from several included icons for your personal icon or import a graphic of your own.

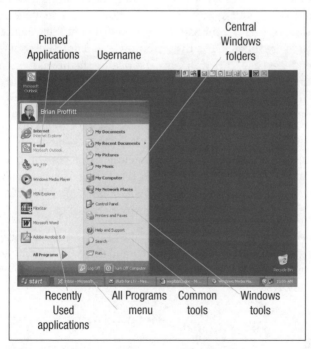

Figure 3.2   The components of the Start menu.

Immediately below the username section, on the left side, is the pinned applications section. You can put your most frequently used applications here. Windows XP has already put two likely applications here for you: the default browser and email applications. You can change or add any application you want to this section, too.

Below the pinned applications is the recently used applications section. In this section, the icons for the last six applications you started will appear. The assumption is that users tend to use the same applications over and over, and they can speed up their work if they can go back to them quickly. This is a fairly good assumption to make because the recently used applications section is definitely very useful. You can even increase or decrease the number of applications that you want to see, if you feel the need to shorten or lengthen the list.

NOTE: *Only applications that have been started with the Start menu will appear in the recently used applications section. Applications started manually with a **Run** command will not appear here.*

Under the recently used applications section is a menu link to the All Programs menu. This is an element that any experienced Windows user will find familiar. When you hold the mouse pointer on this menu link, the All Programs menu will appear, looking like an old friend from Windows gone by (see Figure 3.3).

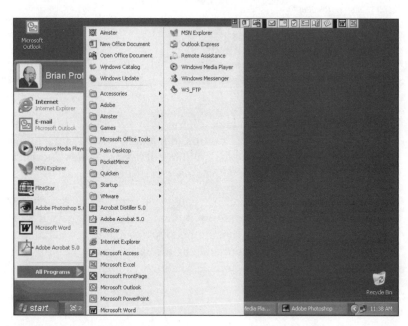

Figure 3.3   An old Windows standby: the All Programs menu.

3. Explore the Windows XP Desktop

At the top of the right column of the Start menu is the central Windows folders section. This is the place where all those missing desktop icons got off to, along with a few more. You can find five folder links in this section, to My Computer, My Network Places, My Documents, My Music, and My Pictures. You'll also find a menu link to My Recent Documents, which will display a brief menu highlighting the last 15 files you opened in Windows XP.

Below the central Windows folder section is the Windows tools section. Here, you can find commonly used Windows utilities, such as the ubiquitous Control Panel and the Printers and Faxes control settings.

Under these Windows tools are more common tools: Help and Support, Search (which replaces the Find function in previous versions of Windows), and Run. This section essentially mirrors its counterpart links in the older Windows releases.

Finally, you'll see the PC control buttons located along the bottom of the Start menu. Two buttons are located in this section: Log Off and Turn Off Computer. Each seems self-explanatory, but some nifty little tricks are found in these controls, which you will see later in this chapter.

NOTE: *For more information on shutting down your system, see the "Leaving Your Computer" section later in this chapter.*

As far as the rest of the Windows desktop, you will find that much has not changed from previous versions. Each window still has Minimize, Maximize/Restore, and Close buttons, though the Close button is bright red for emphasis.

The taskbar is also the same tool, though with one important difference. In the past, opening multiple documents in the same application would create an equivalent number of taskbar icons. These icons tended to eat up a lot of taskbar space very quickly.

In the Windows XP taskbar, you can group similar application icons. Grouped icons are indicated by a number denoting the number of documents found within that application group and a small menu arrow. When you click a grouped icon, a small menu containing all the available documents will appear, as shown in Figure 3.4.

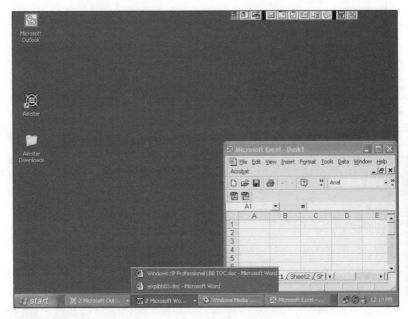

Figure 3.4   Grouped documents save a lot of taskbar space.

Immediate Solutions

Managing Shortcuts and Folders

One of Windows' most enduring features is the ability to organize your files and applications any way you want them. If you like to use the Start menu to reach all your files and documents, you are certainly welcome to do so.

For frequently used files and applications, you may want to put a shortcut to them right on the desktop or perhaps in a more prominent position on the Start menu. Your options here are wide open.

A shortcut is nothing new to Windows users. If you come from a Macintosh background, this shortcut is what you would call an alias. Shortcuts are little icons that do nothing but serve as a link to the file or application to which they are pointing. They are not the files and applications themselves, so moving or deleting them will do no harm to the original item.

A shortcut is typically denoted by a little black-and-white corner arrow within the shortcut icon. If you see this marker, you know you are looking at a shortcut. If you do not see it, it's likely you have the real McCoy, and you should use a little caution so you don't lose something you may need later.

Making a shortcut is a simple process with the Create Shortcut wizard. Just remember, you can point a shortcut to a document or an application. To create a shortcut on the desktop, follow these steps:

1. Right-click the Windows XP desktop or within any open folder. The context menu will appear.

2. Click New|Shortcut. A new shortcut icon and the Create Shortcut Wizard will appear (see Figure 3.5).

3. If you know the direct file path to the item you want to shortcut, type it into the Location field. Otherwise, click the Browse button. The Browse For Folder dialog box will appear, as shown in Figure 3.6.

4. Using the expansion icons, navigate through the folders until you locate the file for which you wish to create the shortcut.

5. Click the file name to select the file.

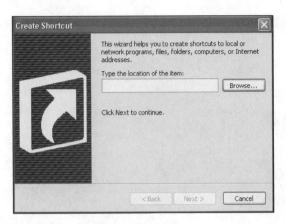

Figure 3.5   Creating a new shortcut.

Figure 3.6   Browsing to find the item to shortcut.

6. Click OK. The Browse For Folder dialog box will close, and the full file path of the file will appear in the Type The Location Of The Item field.

7. Click the Next button.

8. Type a new name (if desired) for the shortcut.

9. Click the Finish button. The Create Shortcut Wizard will close, and the new shortcut will appear on the desktop.

The preceding steps are the formal way of creating a shortcut. Here's a faster way if you have the file open in Windows Explorer:

1. In Windows Explorer, right-click the file you want to shortcut. The context menu for the file will appear.

2. Click Create Shortcut. A shortcut for the original item will appear in the same folder (see Figure 3.7).

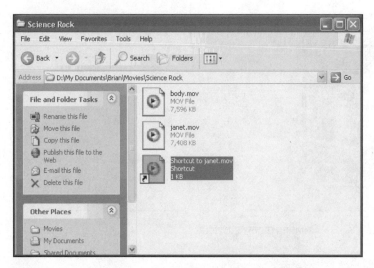

Figure 3.7   A shortcut to creating shortcuts.

You can now drag and drop or cut and paste the shortcut to any location you want.

Creating folders on the desktop is similar if you follow these steps:

1. Right-click the Windows XP desktop or within any open folder. The context menu will appear.

2. Select New|Folder. A New Folder icon will appear.

3. Type a new name for the folder.

4. Click anywhere on the desktop or the open folder window. The new folder name will be applied.

If you are like me, you likely have icons scattered all over your desktop. Having all these icons can be kind of messy, but if it works for you, so be it.

If you don't like how your icons look on the desktop, you can have Windows auto-arrange them by following these steps:

1. Right-click the Windows XP desktop. The context menu will appear.

2. Select Arrange Icons By to open the submenu (see Figure 3.8).

3. Select the option you want to arrange with. The icons will immediately be arranged in that manner.

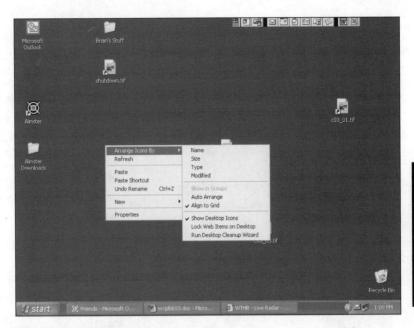

Figure 3.8   You can select to arrange the desktop icons by name, size, type, or date modified.

NOTE: *Any auto-arrangement will place the Recycle Bin icon at the upper-left corner of the screen. Not a major issue, but weird.*

If you have many icons on your desktop and want to get rid of some of them, you could select each icon and press the Delete key. Or, you could use the Desktop Cleanup Wizard as follows:

1. Right-click the Windows XP desktop. The context menu will appear.

2. Select Arrange Icons By|Run Desktop Cleanup Wizard to open the Desktop Cleanup Wizard (see Figure 3.9).

3. Click Next to leave the Welcome screen. The Shortcuts screen will appear, as shown in Figure 3.10.

4. Click the checkboxes of the shortcuts to select or deselect them as desired.

5. Click the Next button. The confirmation screen will appear.

6. If the list of shortcuts is correct, click the Finish button. The Desktop Cleanup Wizard will close, and the shortcuts will be removed from the desktop.

Figure 3.9   Now, you can automatically clean up your desktop.

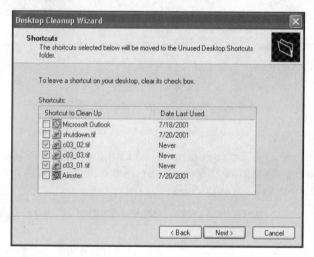

Figure 3.10   Choose the shortcuts to remove.

Customizing the XP Desktop

The look and feel of the Windows XP desktop are quite different from previous Windows incarnations. Users have jokingly referred to it as the "Playskool" effect, a reference to all the big controls and bright primary colors.

If you don't like the way the Windows XP environment looks, you are more than welcome to change it to suit your aesthetic desires. The quickest way to alter the look of the desktop is to add a new background. In earlier versions of Windows, you may have been told that backgrounds (which were also called wallpapers) were not recommended because they would take up memory that could be used elsewhere. If you are using a machine that is low on RAM, this recommendation is still true. But, today's new computers are so richly laden with RAM that using them should not be a big deal.

To add a background, follow these steps:

1. Right-click the Windows XP desktop. The context menu will appear.
2. Click Properties to open the Display Properties dialog box.
3. Click the Desktop tab to open the Desktop page (see Figure 3.11).
4. Scroll down the list of available backgrounds.
5. Select the background you want to use. A preview of the background will appear in the virtual desktop at the top of the dialog box.
6. Click Apply to apply the new background to your desktop (see Figure 3.12).

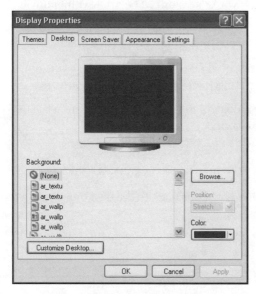

Figure 3.11   Picking a background is easier than picking out curtains.

Figure 3.12   This looks like a nice place.

If you want to forget the use of a background graphic, you can use color as follows to enhance your desktop look:

1. Right-click the Windows XP desktop. The context menu will appear.

2. Click Properties to open the Display Properties dialog box.

3. Click the Desktop tab to open the Desktop page.

4. Select the None option at the top of the Backgrounds list.

5. Click the drop-down control in the Color field to open the Color palette.

6. Click a color from the palette.

7. Click Apply to apply the new color to your desktop.

You can also add the Windows icons back to the desktop, if you want, by following these steps:

1. Right-click the Windows XP desktop. The context menu will appear.

2. Click Properties to open the Display Properties dialog box.

3. Click the Desktop tab to open the Desktop page.

4. Click the Customize Desktop button to open the Desktop Items dialog box (see Figure 3.13).

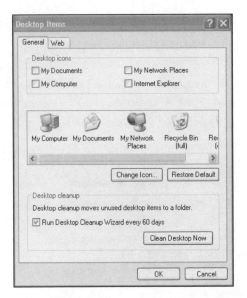

Figure 3.13 Choose the icons that will appear on your desktop.

5. Click the Desktop Icons checkboxes that you want to have on your desktop.

6. Click OK to close the Desktop Items dialog box.

7. Click Apply to add the new icons to your desktop.

8. When you're finished with the Display Properties dialog box, click OK.

Related solution:	Found on page:
Customizing the Start Menu	98

Customizing with Visual Themes

Another popular way to give your XP machine a custom look-and-feel is to use themes. Themes change far more than just the look of the desktop. Window borders, cursors, and even sounds are changed between themes.

Themes used to be add-on components of Windows, as part of the Microsoft Plus product. Now, they are a direct part of Windows XP.

To add a theme, follow these steps:

1. Right-click the Windows XP desktop. The context menu will appear.

2. Click Properties. The Display Properties dialog box will appear with the Themes tab open (see Figure 3.14).

3. Click the drop-down list control for the Theme field to open the themes list.

4. Scroll down the list and click an option to select it.

5. Click Apply to apply the new theme to your desktop.

6. If you like the theme, click OK to close the Display Properties dialog box.

Figure 3.14   What will your theme be?

Setting Up a Screen Saver

You surely have heard the story about screen savers—how they were originally designed to prevent screen "burn-in" on the older displays. Today, such a thing is not needed because displays are built in a better way.

Screen savers are now an expression of personal taste more than a functional tool, though they do have some uses—beyond mere aesthetics. For one, they can act as effective security barriers for the contents of your screen. Even without password protection, a running screen saver is less likely to attract the attention of a snoop than an open Word document with the title "Next Year's Salary Projections." And with password protection, it's a time-consuming barrier for those who go beyond being snoops and are outright information thieves.

You can set up a screen saver like this:

1. Right-click the Windows XP desktop. The context menu will appear.

2. Click Properties to open the Display Properties dialog box.

3. Click the Screen Saver tab to open the Screen Saver page (see Figure 3.15).

4. Click the drop-down list control for the Screen Saver field to open the screen saver list.

5. Scroll down the list and click an option to select it.

6. Click the Settings button. If available, the screen saver's Setup dialog box will appear.

7. Modify the settings and click OK to close the Setup dialog box.

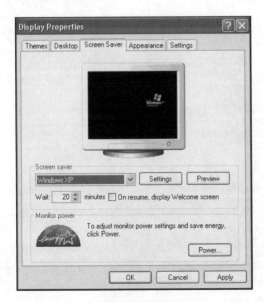

Figure 3.15   Setting up a screen saver.

8. Click the Preview button. The screen saver will fill the screen until you move the mouse to deactivate it.

9. Click Apply to apply the new screen saver.

10. Click OK to close the Display Properties dialog box.

Changing the Resolution of Your Screen

If you have a big monitor, you can adjust the screen resolution of your Windows desktop to take better advantage of all that real estate. You can also change the number of colors Windows will display on a monitor.

To change the resolution, follow these steps:

1. Right-click the Windows XP desktop. The context menu will appear.

2. Click the Properties menu to open the Display Properties dialog box.

3. Click the Settings tab to open the Settings page (see Figure 3.16).

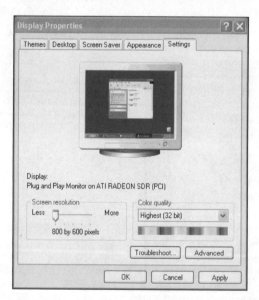

Figure 3.16   Changing the screen resolution.

4. Click the slider control in the Screen Resolution section. The values of the resolution will change, and the effect of the change will be reflected in the virtual monitor.

5. Click the drop-down list control for the Color Quality field to open the color list.

6. Click a color option to select it.

7. Click Apply. The screen will go black and then reappear with the new settings (see Figure 3.17).

8. In the dialog box that appears asking you to keep these settings, click Yes or No as you like.

NOTE: *If you do not reply to this last question, Windows will revert to the last screen settings in 15 seconds.*

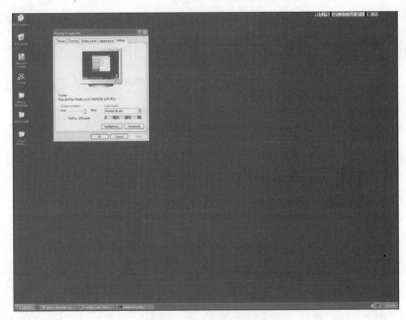

Figure 3.17   Twice the resolution of a normal screen.

Restoring "Classic" Windows

Let's say, after a whole lot of working in Windows XP, you just don't like the new look. Well, that's fair—different strokes, and all that. The good news is that you can quickly get your desktop back to a "classic" Windows look in just a few short steps:

1. Right-click the Windows XP desktop. The context menu will appear.

2. Click Properties to open the Display Properties dialog box.

3. Click the Appearance tab to open the Appearance page (see Figure 3.18).

4. Click the drop-down list control for the Windows And Buttons field to open the options list.

5. Click Windows Classic style.

6. Click the drop-down list control for the Color Scheme field to open the options list.

7. Choose a preferred color scheme.

8. Click the Effects button to open the Effects dialog box (see Figure 3.19).

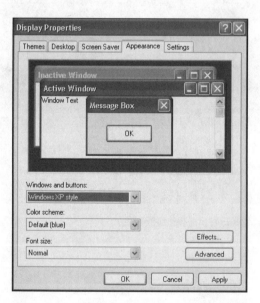

Figure 3.18   On the road back to classic Windows.

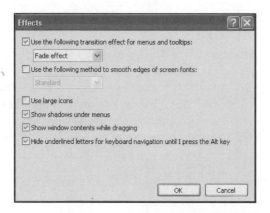

Figure 3.19   You can fine-tune the visual effects of Windows.

9.   Click the options you want to try or discontinue.

10.   Click OK to close the Effects dialog box.

11.   Click Apply to apply the changes to your desktop.

12.   If you like the changes, click OK to close the Display Properties dialog box (see Figure 3.20).

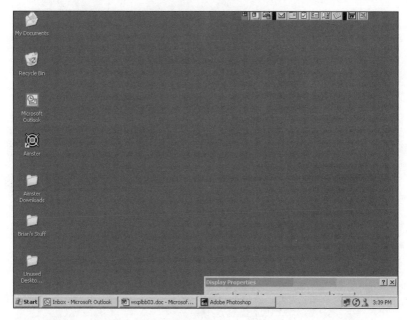

Figure 3.20   Proof that you *can* go back.

Leaving Your Computer

When all is said and done at the end of the day, you will want to leave the computer. You can choose a couple of options. You can either log off and leave the computer running for another user or shut it down altogether. Experts have different opinions on this subject, but they tend to lean toward the "leave the computer on all the time" option because many believe that shutting down the computer often is not good for it.

So, if you have to walk away for a while, the best option is to simply log off as follows:

1. Click Start|Log Off to open the Log Off window (see Figure 3.21).

2. Click Log Off. The Windows User Welcome Screen will appear.

If you want to let another user use your machine, you can quickly switch over to his or her desktop as follows, all the while leaving your current applications running unharmed:

1. Click Start|Log Off to open the Log Off window.

2. Click Switch User to open the Windows User Welcome Screen.

3. Click the User Name for the new person to load the user's desktop.

If you want to simply turn off the computer or reboot it, that's a simple process, too. Just follow these steps:

1. Click Start|Turn Off Computer to open the Turn Off Computer window (see Figure 3.22).

2. To reboot the computer, click Restart.

3. To place the computer in hibernation mode, click Stand By.

4. To turn off the computer completely, click Turn Off.

Figure 3.21   A simple Log Off screen.

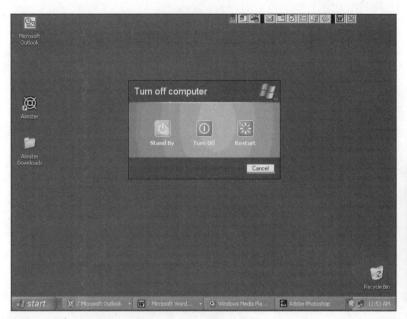

Figure 3.22   Shutting down the computer.

Chapter 4

Organize Windows XP

In Brief

It is said that a cluttered desk is a sign of a disordered mind. If that's the case, it is a wonder that anything gets done in the world. Yet, somehow, the bridges still get built, the trains still run on time, and we all get to work a 40-hour work week and still feel as though we haven't accomplished anything.

The main problem is this: What is one person's mess is another person's organized file system, and vice versa. This dilemma is all related to the fact that you can't really know what's going on in my head, and I cannot really know what's going on in yours. We can each make some pretty fair guesses based on each other's outward reactions, but to really know someone's complete motivations requires a level of intimacy that many people never achieve.

Still, this subjectivity is not absolute. We share some perceptions, it seems—just enough so that when we call a tree a tree in the same language, we each pretty much know what the other is talking about. These perceptions are called conventions, and most typically, they are based on language. Though, not always.

In the business world, conventions that are followed every day are based on mutual acceptance. Need to talk to several people right away? Call a meeting. Need to store documents? Put them into a folder and put it, in turn, into a file cabinet.

This method of handling paper has become so pervasive that the earliest computer interface designers thought it would be an easier transition for new computer users to organize data with the same metaphors they used when dealing with paper. A collection of related data became known as a file. Files were stored in directories, which later were referred to as folders.

The upshot of all this discussion is this: We are now dealing with a paper metaphor for a completely paperless system. Technology is replete with this sort of thing—we still call musical releases "albums" instead of discs. We still call a library's collection database a "card catalog."

Windows XP continues to carry on this paper and folder metaphor because, quite frankly, it is the easiest for many home and office users to understand. It's certainly a lot simpler to get your head around than "data packets located on a file allocation table." People who talk like that need to get out more.

The metaphor has never been complete, and some gaps still remain. No really good paper-related metaphor exists for file associations, shared documents, or Network Places. It is in these areas that Windows XP has really tried to smooth out the transition between familiar paper-based conventions and computer-based methods.

Examining the New XP File System

More and more, computer operating systems are trying to become as transparent as possible. The developers and designers are realizing that users are no longer interested in the novelty of working with a snazzy new interface—they just want to get some work done.

I call this the Popcorn Principle. Microwave ovens, like any electronic device, have an operating system to manage all that energy and timing. But, you and I don't have to learn how to use this new operating system to make a bag of popcorn. We just push the popcorn button and let the oven do the rest. This is an example of a truly transparent operating system: It simply presents the tools the user needs to get the job done and stays out of the way while doing so.

Windows XP is not at this level of transparency yet—no PC operating system is—but it is moving in this direction. One prime example of this movement is how the file system is presented in Windows XP.

Recall that in DOS-based file systems, series of directories are contained in the hard drive of your computer. These directories may contain files or even other directories. Nothing new here, right? In the past, storing your files in these locations could prove tedious because you often had to navigate endless directories to get where you needed to be. Files for this book, for instance, would be stored in D:\My Documents\Brian\Windows XP LBB under my old methodology of storage. With Windows XP, I no longer really care where the files are stored. I can put them anywhere and still have instant access to them by creating shortcuts or easily customizing my existing My Documents settings to point straight to this folder. Plus, now that Windows XP has better-defined multiuser tools, I no longer have to keep a "Brian" folder because my My Documents will be different from the My Documents folders of the other users on my computer.

You may be thinking that none of these capabilities are new, and you would be right. Shortcuts have been around since Windows 3.1, and

4. Organize Windows XP

the ability to alter the target folder of the My Documents icon is not new, either.

What Windows XP has done is *not* add a lot of new tools to get work done. Instead, it has changed the packaging of these tools so that easier ways to organize your files are more readily apparent. Now, it is not an arcane ritual to change the settings of all the Windows central folders to match your needs.

The result of these changes is that with just a little help from you, you will not care that your documents are actually stored in C:\Documents and Settings\John Doe\Great American Novel. For you, they are in "My Documents." No complicated folder navigation to slow you down.

Handling File Associations

The issue of transparency also comes into play in the way Windows XP manages the opening of files on your computer.

Every file on your computer can be opened by a particular application. Some files, such as plain-text files, can be opened by several applications. Others, such as Portable Document Format files, can be opened by only one application: the Acrobat Reader by Adobe. So, how does Windows tell which file can be opened by which application?

This interesting little trick is managed by file associations. Each file has various clues that can tell Windows XP what kind of file it is. The extension on the file name is usually a first sign. If a file is named Windows XP Chapter 04.doc, the .doc extension is a big clue to Windows that the application best suited to open this file is Microsoft Word because most files created by Word have this extension. Upon opening this file, Windows XP, which knows where Microsoft Word is located on your PC, starts the application for you and instructs the application to open the file at the same time.

Sometimes, a little more information is needed to figure out what kind of file you are dealing with. Perhaps someone has taken a Corel WordPerfect document and mistakenly named it with the .doc file extension instead of the default .wkb extension such documents are supposed to have. By file extension alone, Windows might try to start the document in Word. But, inside every file is a smart little code that reveals more about the file's true nature than the file extension. Called the MIME type, this universal identifier labels the file for what it really is. Word files all have the application/msword MIME type no matter what name they are given. If a DOC file is opened and does not contain the application/msword MIME type, Windows XP is going to notice this discrepancy and ask you for a little assistance.

Windows XP comes with a fairly comprehensive database of file extensions, MIME types, and application relationships, so it has a head start knowing what applications are needed to open many types of files. But, no database is truly comprehensive, so Windows XP will do a little spying on you to help build this database.

When you come to a file type that Windows XP does not recognize, it will ask you what application you want to use to open the file. It will also ask you whether you want to use that application to open files of that same type from now on. If you say yes, you have just created a new file association with Windows XP.

Again, none of this process is new to Windows. But, in Windows XP, this often-confusing process has been taken out of the user's hands as much as possible. And, when it is in the user's purview, it is now a much simpler process to manage. That is a pattern you will find repeated throughout the Windows XP operating system: The tools and capabilities that have long been a part of the Windows operating systems are now less complicated and easier to find than in past releases.

4. Organize Windows XP

Immediate Solutions

Managing Files in XP

As easy as file management has become in Windows XP, users are still going to deal with files every once in a while. Although the developers at Microsoft fervently hope that you do not have to deal with them very often, they have also made great strides in how you can manage your files when you get around to working with them.

The main component in file management is the ubiquitous file manager Windows Explorer. If you go looking for Windows Explorer on the All Programs menu, forget it. You'll find very few references to this Windows tool under that name. Apparently, the designers at Microsoft have decided to play down the concept of the Windows Explorer as a separate application and encourage the perception that this file manager is fully incorporated in the Windows XP operating system.

Whatever the reason, the Windows Explorer is still serving as the primary file manager for users. Capitalizing on the success of the Internet Explorer browser, Windows Explorer acts as a file browser more than a file manager. In fact, as of Windows 98, the two applications are practically identical, with only a few cosmetic differences to distinguish the two.

Windows Explorer can almost be referred to as the Application with No Name, but it is used in various capacities. Every time you click the My Computer link or My Music or My Pictures, you will be using Windows Explorer. Even the Control Panel is just a Windows Explorer window displaying special content.

To start the basic Windows Explorer, you can use one of these two steps:

• Click on Start|My Computer.

• Click on Start|All Programs|Accessories|Windows Explorer.

You need to learn some basics about Windows Explorer before you set out to use it. As you can see in Figure 4.1, each Windows Explorer window is made up of the same tools—some familiar, some not.

For the most part, this window looks very much like the older Windows Explorer—if it weren't for the odd-looking pane on the left side.

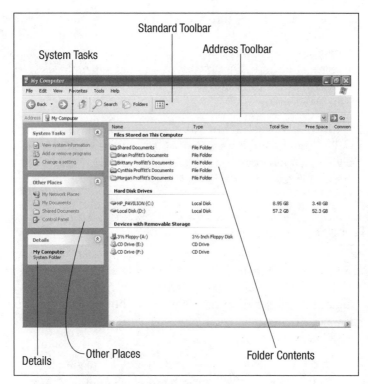

Figure 4.1   Windows Explorer looking at My Computer.

It is here that the Windows Explorer takes a sharp departure from its previous incarnations. This pane contains the task windows—small windows that contain the tools Windows XP thinks you are most likely to use.

In the window shown in Figure 4.1, for example, you can see the broad overview of an entire PC in the right pane of the Windows Explorer, and in the left pane, you can see the System Tasks, Other Places, and Details windows. The System Tasks window, which appears when the Windows Explorer is looking at a system folder, such as a hard drive or My Computer folder, has a handful of tasks you can start while looking at this folder.

Other Places displays links to alternate folder locations on your computer or (if applicable) other computers on your network. The Details window lists any applicable information about the folder or any selected drive, folder, or file you might select within the folder you are viewing.

If you were to click one of the drives listed in this broad overview of this PC, you would see a dramatic change in the contents of the left pane (see Figure 4.2). The System Tasks, Other Places, and Details windows are still there, but now their contents have changed to reflect what Windows XP believes you need to manage the files and folders in *this* window.

Notice, too, that a new window has been added in the tools pane: the File And Folder Tasks window. Now that you are looking at a location on your computer that has files and folders, this window is brought up for your convenience.

TIP: *You can open or collapse any visible window in the tools pane by clicking the expansion/ collapse icon at the top of each window.*

The tool window contents change not only when different folders are opened, but their contents also can change when you simply select a particular file or folder. This incredible flexibility ensures you should have the best tools available at your fingertips as you navigate with the Windows Explorer application.

The rest of the Windows Explorer tool should seem quite familiar to you. To open a folder or file, you can double-click it. To navigate to

Figure 4.2   Windows Explorer looking at the C: drive of a PC.

folders you have recently opened, you can use the Back or Forward buttons to shift along your navigation path, in much the same way as you would in a Web browser such as Internet Explorer.

You can also use the Up button to change to the next higher folder in the directory tree. Clicking Up in the C:\Documents and Settings\John Doe\Watergate Tapes folder would take you to the C:\Documents and Settings\John Doe folder.

Related solutions:	Found on page:
Managing Shortcuts and Folders	52
Managing Users	165
Sharing Files with Other Users	174

Copying Files

If you need to create a specific kind of file in a hurry, one of the best ways to do so is to make a copy of a similar file you have already done and then build from that point. I have tried this approach with books, but with little success because there's that pesky copyright law to deal with.

For less litigious files, copying works wonders for saving time and effort. Copying can be done with just a few quick steps:

1. In Windows Explorer, click the file you want to copy to select it.

2. In the File And Folder Tasks window, click the Copy This File link to open the Copy Items dialog box (see Figure 4.3).

Figure 4.3   Select where you want to place the copied file.

4. Organize Windows XP

3. Using the expansion icons, navigate to the folder in which you want to place the copied file.

4. Click the destination folder to select it.

5. Click Copy to copy the file to the destination folder.

NOTE: *If the file is copied to the same folder as the original's, it will automatically be renamed to "Copy of...name of file." If the file is sent to a different folder, the original file name will remain.*

You can copy files, folders, and multiple items. Although, initially, this process may seem like an extra step, recall that in the past, Windows Explorer would create only a copy of the file and make you navigate to the destination folder within Explorer before you could paste the copy into that folder. With this new method, you can simply point the new copy to the right folder and not have to leave the original folder.

That said, there is something to the diverse methods that Windows offers users to simply accomplish one thing. Besides this new technique of copying files, the old ways still work as well, as you can see in the following steps:

1. In Windows Explorer, right-click the file you want to copy. The context menu will appear.

2. Click Copy.

3. Using the Windows Explorer, navigate to the folder in which you want to place the copied file.

4. Right-click a blank spot in the destination folder. The context menu will appear.

5. Click Paste to copy the file to the destination folder.

If you are fonder of using the keyboard, here is the popular variant of this technique:

1. In Windows Explorer, click the file you want to copy to select it.

2. Press Ctrl+C.

3. Using the Windows Explorer, navigate to the folder in which you want to place the copied file.

4. Press Ctrl+V to copy the file to the destination folder.

Finally, you can use one more quick method of copying a file from one place to another. It does involve altering the look of Windows Explorer so that it displays the folder tree for your system in the left pane rather than the Windows XP tools. To make this pane appear, click the Folders button in the Standard toolbar (see Figure 4.4).

4. Organize Windows XP

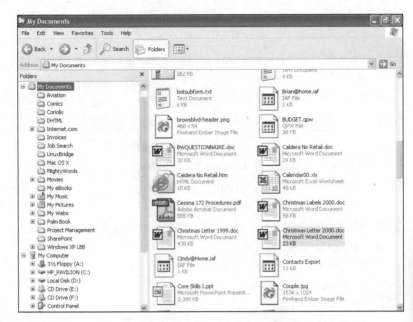

Figure 4.4   Viewing the folder tree in Windows Explorer.

When the folder tree is visible, it becomes much easier to follow these steps to copy a file:

1. In Windows Explorer, right-click and hold the file you want to copy to select it.

2. Drag the outline of the file over to the folder tree pane.

3. Place the icon outline on the destination folder and release the mouse button. The context menu will appear.

4. Click Copy Here to copy the file to the destination folder.

Moving Files

Moving a file is pretty much the same procedure as copying it. The only difference is that after the file is moved, no trace of it remains in its original folder.

With this point in mind, you should note that moving files from a read-only device—such as a CD-ROM—is not possible because the original file cannot be removed from the CD. Other than that, the sky's the limit with file moving.

To move files, follow these steps:

1. In Windows Explorer, click the file you want to move to select it.

2. In the File And Folder Tasks window, click the Move This File link to open the Move Items dialog box.

3. Using the expansion icons, navigate to the folder in which you want to place the file.

4. Click the destination folder to select it.

5. Click Move to move the file to the destination folder.

You can, of course, use the older methods to move your files from one folder to another. Here's one example:

1. In Windows Explorer, right-click the file you want to move. The context menu will appear.

2. Click Cut to remove the file from the original folder.

3. Using the Windows Explorer, navigate to the folder in which you want to place the file.

4. Right-click a blank spot in the destination folder. The context menu will appear.

5. Click Paste to place the file in the destination folder.

If you prefer to use the keyboard, this move method was made just for you:

1. In Windows Explorer, click the file you want to move to select it.

2. Press Ctrl+X to remove the file from the folder.

3. Using the Windows Explorer, navigate to the folder in which you want to place the file.

4. Press Ctrl+V to place the file in the destination folder.

If you have the folder tree in place, you can use this drag-and-drop method to move a file:

1. In Windows Explorer, right-click and hold the file you want to move to select it.

2. Drag the outline of the file over to the folder tree pane.

3. Place the icon outline on the destination folder and release the mouse button. The context menu will appear.

4. Click Move Here to move the file to the destination folder.

Deleting Files

When you are completely finished with a file, you have the option of archiving it for later use or just letting it go altogether. Most people seem to be pack rats by nature because a whole segment of the software industry out there is devoted to cleaning up your Windows machine.

Don't be afraid to delete files. Just be sure you won't need them again. Or, make sure they are saved somewhere else. Whenever I finish a project, I copy the files to a CD-ROM and then delete the files from my hard drive. Even though space is not a premium on my machine, I know it's a good habit to have; otherwise, my computer will be crammed with years-old files that are doing nothing but collecting the electronic equivalent of cobwebs and dust.

Deleting a file in Windows XP is the same two-stage process it has been since Windows 95. "Deleting" the file actually moves it to the special folder known as the Recycle Bin, which serves as a temporary safety buffer until you are 100 percent sure the files the Recycle Bin contains need to go.

With the File And Folder Tasks window, however, a new method has been added to the various ways you can delete the file or files you no longer need. Just follow these steps:

1. In Windows Explorer, click the file you want to delete to select it.

2. In the File And Folder Tasks window, click the Delete This File link to open the Confirm File Delete dialog box.

3. Click Yes to send the file to the Recycle Bin and close the dialog box.

Nothing too hard there, to be sure. Another simple method, shown here, works best on the desktop:

1. On the desktop, click and hold the file you want to delete to select it.

2. Drag the file's icon over the Recycle Bin icon.

3. Release the mouse button. The file will disappear from the desktop and be placed in the Recycle Bin.

The easiest way to delete a file in Windows XP? Here's how:

1. In Windows Explorer or on the desktop, click the file you want to delete to select it.

2. Press the Delete key. The file will disappear from its location and be placed in the Recycle Bin.

Sometimes, the simple things bring the most pleasure. But, now that the files are in the Recycle Bin, what do you do? Well, from this folder, you have the option of deleting the files altogether from your computer or restoring them to their original location on your computer. Just follow these steps:

1. Double-click the Recycle Bin to open the Recycle Bin folder (see Figure 4.5).

2. Select the item(s) you want to put back onto your computer.

3. Click the Restore This Item link to return the item to its original folder on your system.

4. After you restore everything you want, click the Empty Recycle Bin link to open the Confirm (Multiple) File Delete dialog box.

5. Click Yes to empty the Recycle Bin and close the dialog box.

Figure 4.5   Looking at the contents of the Recycle Bin.

Managing Folders in XP

Every action you can perform on files in Windows XP, you can perform on folders as well. Copy, move, delete... it's all the same in Windows Explorer. Some special tasks, however, are unique to folders.

Creating New Folders

Whenever you create a new file, odds are that it will be done within an application. For folders, however, you will need to perform this task in Windows Explorer, as shown in the following steps:

1. Open the folder in which you want to place the new folder.

2. Click the Make A New folder link. A New Folder icon will appear, with the name highlighted.

3. Type a new name for the folder.

4. Click anywhere else within Windows Explorer. The new name will be applied and the folder ready to use.

NOTE: *Many applications have Save As functions, and many of those functions can create a new folder from within the Save As dialog box. Keep an eye out for this handy feature as you use your Windows applications.*

Customizing Folders

You can customize folders within Windows Explorer in two ways: using a local "look and feel" method or a universal file settings method. In this section, we'll examine the local, aesthetic method.

To customize your folders, follow these steps:

1. In Windows Explorer, right-click the folder you want to customize. The context menu will appear.

2. Click Properties to open the Properties dialog box.

3. Click the Customize tab to open the Customize page (see Figure 4.6).

4. Click the drop-down list for the Use This Folder Type As A Template field. A list of folder type templates will appear.

5. Click the appropriate folder type to select it.

6. Click the Change Icon button to open the Change Icon For Folder dialog box.

7. Click a desired icon to select it.

8. Click OK to close the Change Icon For Folder dialog box.

9. Click OK. The Properties dialog box will close, and the changes will be made to the folder.

Related solution:	Found on page:
Accessing Files and Folders Offline	337

4. Organize Windows XP

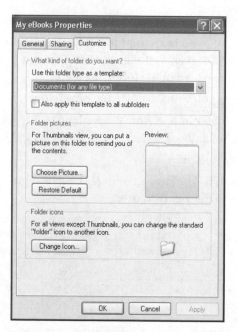

Figure 4.6   Customizing a folder.

Customizing Windows Explorer

One of the hardest lessons for Microsoft to learn was that not every good idea the developers had was necessarily all that good for everyone.

When Windows 98 came out, one of the most touted features was the Active Desktop, which was essentially the "Web page as desktop" model Microsoft was implementing. For the most part, this technology still exists within the Windows XP desktop, but Microsoft has quietly relegated elements of the Active Desktop to the background, such as the not-so-popular single-click file management.

The single-click methodology, which was to be reminiscent of the single clicks we all perform on hyperlinks within a Web page, did not prove to be wildly popular because files would spring open at each click, even if you only wanted to drag them somewhere else.

Still, some people found this method functional, and it is in deference to them I include this section on customizing all Windows folders in Windows Explorer. Just follow these steps:

Figure 4.7   Customizing all Windows folders.

1. In Windows Explorer, click Tools|Folder Options to open the Folder Options dialog box (see Figure 4.7).

2. Click the Single-Click To Open An Item option to select it.

3. Click Apply so that the settings will take effect in Windows Explorer.

If you are none too enamored of the tools pane in Windows Explorer, you can use this dialog box to restore Explorer to a more "classic" look by following these steps:

1. In Windows Explorer, click Tools|Folder Options to open the Folder Options dialog box.

2. Click the Use Windows Classic Folders option to select it.

3. Click Apply so that the settings will take effect in Windows Explorer.

One other change that many people like to make in Windows is the ability to view file extensions in Windows Explorer. By default, this setting is turned off when Windows XP is first installed, but I find it's very handy to see the extensions, particularly if Windows XP is having difficulty deducing what kind of file it is working with.

To turn on the option to see file extensions, follow these steps:

1. In Windows Explorer, click Tools|Folder Options to open the Folder Options dialog box.

2. Click the View tab to open the View page (see Figure 4.8).

3. Click the Hide Extensions For Known File Types option to uncheck it.

4. Click Apply so that the setting will take effect in Windows Explorer.

NOTE: *More fully exploring the View tab of the Folder Options dialog box will be worth your time because it is full of handy settings to really tweak your Windows XP machine.*

Related solution:	Found on page:
Restoring "Classic" Windows	64

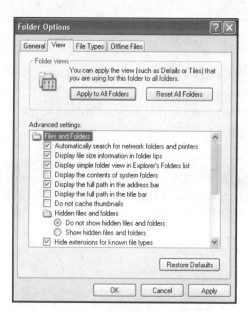

Figure 4.8   Changing the look of all folders.

Searching for Files

With all the files you have on your computer, it is a wonder you can remember where all of them are located. That's why Windows XP has a very useful Search feature to hunt down those files. You use it as follows:

1. In Windows Explorer, click the Search button to open the Search pane (see Figure 4.9).

2. Click the All Files And Folders link. The Search pane will now display this window (see Figure 4.10).

3. Click the Search In drop-down list and select where on the computer you want the search to occur:

   • If you know only the name of the file, enter the information in the All Or Part Of The File Name field.

   • If you recall a passage from the interior of the file, enter it in the A Word Or Phrase In The File field.

   • If you think you know when you last worked on the file, click the expansion icon next to the When Was It Modified? section and fill in the information in the displayed section.

   • If you remember how large the file was, click the expansion icon next to the What Size Is It? section and fill in the information in the displayed section.

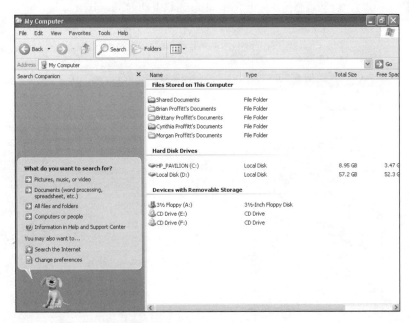

Figure 4.9   Searching for all the answers.

4. Organize Windows XP

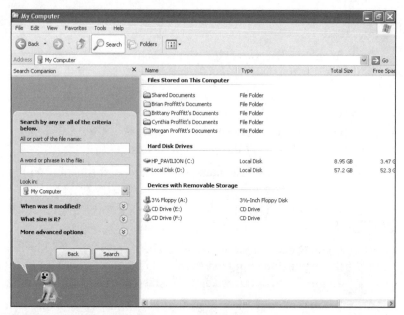

Figure 4.10   Narrow your search as much as you can.

4. After you type the information, click the Search button to display the Search results screen (see Figure 4.11).

5. If the correct file is displayed, double-click the file to open it.

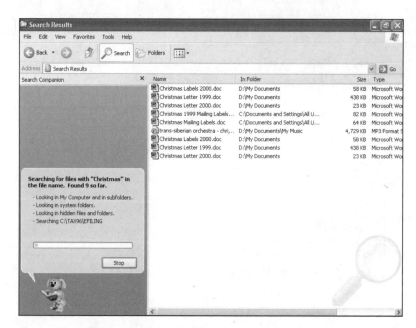

Figure 4.11   Finding the right files for you.

Automating File Compression/Expansion

As cheap as memory is, you never seem to have enough room on your computer for all the files you need. And, at no time does memory become a larger obstacle than when you're trying to send a file somewhere else. Whether you are using a floppy disk or sending an email attachment, the larger the file, the more headaches you will have.

Compressing files is a good all-around solution for this problem. One of the most popular third-party compressors is the WinZip compression tool, which will create the near-standard ZIP files that have become widely used on the Internet.

With Windows XP, you don't need WinZip to create those ZIP files. Now, you can create these files with just a few clicks of the mouse, as shown here:

1. In Windows Explorer, right-click the file or folder you want to compress. The context menu will appear.

2. Select Send To to open the submenu.

3. Click the Compressed (Zipped) Folder option. The Compression message box will appear, and a compressed form of the file or folder will appear within the same folder.

4. Organize Windows XP

TIP: Look at the bottom of the file list for the newly compressed folder.

That's really all there is to it. The file is now a compressed ZIP file that can be opened by any utility that can open such files.

Opening a ZIP file is just as easy, as you can see here:

1. In Windows Explorer, right-click the compressed folder you want to extract. The context menu will appear.

2. Click Extract All to open the Extraction Wizard.

3. Click Next to move past the Welcome screen.

4. Either by using the Browse function or by typing in the file path, enter a destination folder for the extracted files.

5. Click Next so that the files will be extracted to the destination folder.

6. Click Finish. The Extraction Wizard will close, and the Explorer window will open to the destination folder.

Configuring File Associations

File associations are one element of Windows that will always remain a bit of a bugaboo for users. The reason is a bit ironic: The very success of Windows means that so many applications and file types are out there (with more coming every day) that it is very hard for Windows to keep up with all of them.

The success of the Internet has contributed to this problem as well. In the past, if a file was on your computer, it was likely you already had the application for it. What business would it have on your computer otherwise? With files flying at your computer from all over the world, you are now likely to run across something that your computer cannot open.

Luckily for you, a new feature in Windows XP will let you track down mysterious file types, even if Windows XP has no clue what kind of file it is. To use this feature, follow these steps:

1. In Windows Explorer, double-click the file you want to open. If Windows XP cannot find the file type or proper application, the Windows dialog box will appear.

2. Click the Use Web Service To Find The Appropriate Application option.

3. Click OK. The Windows dialog box will close, and the Internet Explorer browser will open to the Windows File Associations page.

Chapter 5

Run Applications

In Brief

Hundreds of thousands of Windows applications are available out there in the software world. No one has ever made an accurate count because many of the applications are noncommercial, private applications that are hard to catalog. Even if we don't take these applications into account, the commercial base alone is more than enough to ensure Windows' standing as the most widely used computer platform.

The trouble is, not all those applications will be able to run on your Windows XP machine. Many of them were built in an earlier time, for an earlier version of Windows. You will need to find out which applications are safe for you to run and which will need some additional help from you to get started on your machine.

One thing Windows does very well is managing applications. From start to run to program termination, Windows XP is designed to protect the integrity of your application (and its data) like a mother bear protecting her cubs.

5. Run Applications

How XP Deals with Compatibility

Let's be honest: One thing Microsoft has managed to do extremely well is leverage its position in the marketplace to ensure software compatibility with all the hot new applications coming out of software development houses around the world. Some would say Microsoft has used a bit too much leverage—which is something we will leave for the courts to decide.

This is how Microsoft has essentially maintained its strength in compatibility: Each software developer logically attempts to make small improvements over its competitors, changing and enhancing various functions and then competitively marketing those enhancements. However, if the developer wants to sell its software in the largest market, then—despite fierce competition—each will adhere to Windows operating specifications.

This phenomenon, for good or ill, has left us with a lot of very similar-looking applications in today's market. The real differences between developers are apparent only when you look at the speed and methodology used by their applications.

One big monkey wrench in this situation is the constant need for all software developers (Microsoft included) to improve upon their products. This need brings about that event that many computer users dread as they groan and reach for their wallets yet again: the upgrade.

The idea behind upgrades is essentially a good one: When developers figure out ways to make their product better, they release a new version to their customers. Sometimes, this upgrade is free to existing users. And, sometimes it is not. This situation is a source of frustration for many users because no one is ever sure that the upgrade is worth the money until testing it. And then, the question becomes: Will the application work with my older files?

Backward compatibility is the technique used by many upgraded applications to ensure that files and documents created by previous versions of the application can still be used by the new, current application. This technology is what allows Word 2000 users to open and edit Microsoft Word 5.5 files if they need to.

Backward compatibility is by no means a sure thing, though many users are surprised when it's not available. If a file worked on their computer yesterday with the old version of Application X, they reason, then this fancy-schmancy new version of Application X ought to open the same file!

Alas, this expectation is sometimes not met, as in the case of Intuit's TurboTax program. Although it is an excellent piece of tax software, imagine current users' dismay when they learned that current versions of TurboTax could not open older tax files created by previous editions of TurboTax. Not necessarily a pleasant feeling, particularly if there's an audit afoot.

The reason for this lack of universal backward compatibility is a problem that has plagued all of us: a lack of time and resources. To keep the ability to open all past files created by an application, programmers must add thousands of extra lines of code to the application every time it is upgraded. After a while, all these new lines of code lead to a rather bulky and probably very slow application. Thus, software developers must sometimes leave out the ability to read all versions of the application's files. Usually, to ease the transition, a utility is sent to the customers to convert their older files to more current formats.

When an application upgrades, that is one thing. Upgrading an operating system is a far more complex operation, especially in terms of backward compatibility. Now, it's no longer a question of older files being opened—it becomes a question of whether applications will even run at all.

The official line from Microsoft is that Windows XP is more than capable of running applications built for both editions of Windows 98, though some gaps do exist in this coverage. Mostly, you will find these gaps in applications that deal with (a) hardware and (b) the outside world, because Windows XP handles these types of functions differently than Windows 9x. Windows XP, like its Windows NT line of predecessors, is much more security conscious than Windows 9x, so any application that deals directly with system hardware is going to be treated with suspicion by Windows XP. And, in the black-and-white world of Windows XP, if something is even remotely out of whack, that something is not allowed onto the system.

The very first time you will run into incompatibility issues is during the actual installation of Windows XP. As the installer runs its compatibility report, both questionable software and hardware issues will be identified. The good news is that the solution for both of these problems may be right at hand: Upgrade the errant applications and the hardware's drivers to something Windows XP will *always* be able to handle. In other words, track down the Windows 2000-compatible version of the application or driver. If it works with Windows 2000, it will definitely work for Windows XP.

For applications, the solution may be right by your computer. Dig out the discs you used to install the application in the first place and see whether the software is compatible with Windows 2000. If it is, you're in luck—just reinstall the application. The setup routine for the application should detect whether you're running a Windows 2000 (or Windows NT) type operating system and install the proper files.

At times, the software may even detect the change in the hardware and perform the necessary upgrade for you. For example, an upgrade will occur if you are using Office 2000. More specifically, Outlook 2000 needs a few more files installed if you make the switch from Windows 98 to Windows XP. The Windows Installer application for Office 2000 will detect the operating system change and implement the new file installation automatically. Just have the Office 2000 CD-ROM at the ready.

If your software is not Windows 2000-compatible, visit the developer's Web site and see whether a newer version is available and whether that version will work with Windows 2000.

For hardware drivers, you can skip a reinstall and go straight to the manufacturer's Web site. It is very probable that you will locate a Windows 2000-ready driver for your hardware. Hewlett-Packard, for instance, keeps an excellent supply of current drivers for many Windows versions on its Web site—just the ticket for getting that printer back up and running.

Run Applications on XP

An application will start every time you run an open command on the application's single executable file. The executable file is the single file in which most of the action occurs in the application. Most of the source code and other instructions are in the executable; it is literally the heart and soul of any application. The executable knows where all the shared libraries are and how to get Windows to access your processor's time and all the other hardware it needs to run properly.

But, with all this power comes a bit of a problem. Installation routines are often so Byzantine that you're never quite sure where the executable for the application is. Somewhere, buried in all those folders, are the executables to run all the applications on your machine. If you had to run them all manually, you would hardly get any work done.

For this reason, Windows—from Windows 95 on—has made it part of any installation process to note the location of installed executables and place a shortcut icon for them somewhere that's easy to find. Usually, the shortcuts are placed in the desktop or the Start menu, though some applications let you choose where to put such shortcuts.

With all this variety in locating executables, you would expect a number of ways to start applications in Windows XP. And, you would be right. You would also be correct in assuming that you can deal with applications in a number of ways after they are running in Windows XP. After all, you have multitasking, you have the monitor screen—why not make more effective use of what Windows XP has to offer? You can start finding out what Windows XP can offer in the following "Immediate Solutions."

5. Run Applications

Immediate Solutions

Starting Applications in XP

Starting an application in Windows XP is perhaps the most often performed task you will ever do. Running applications is what Windows is all about; otherwise, all you would do all day is sit around and watch the pretty colors.

Opening an application, as shown in the following steps, is also one of the easiest things for you to do in Windows XP:

1. Click Start|All Programs to open the All Programs menu.

2. Select the folder that contains the application you want to start. The folder's menu will open.

3. Click the application's icon to start the application.

Yes, opening an application is just that simple. It can be even simpler if you have recently run the application, as you can see here:

1. Click Start to open the Start menu.

2. In the recent applications section, click the application's icon to start the application.

NOTE: For more information, see the "Customizing the Start Menu" section later in this chapter.

Another method of starting an application is to execute the application file from the Run command-line utility. This utility serves as a command-line emulator, reminiscent of the old DOS operating system. Because the Windows XP operating system is based on NT, which never ran DOS, you are not really even running things in DOS. Think of the command-line interface as a utility to use if you just need to run some quick applications without the fancy windows.

The Run utility lets you issue single-line commands from its compact form. Because executable files are essentially commands, all you need to do is enter the full file name of the application you want to run as follows:

1. Click Start|Run to open the Run window (see Figure 5.1).

2. Click the Browse button to open the Browse window (see Figure 5.2).

5. Run Applications

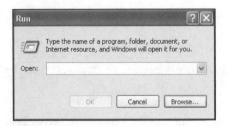

Figure 5.1   Opening the Run window.

Figure 5.2   Browsing for executable files.

3. Navigate to the folder containing the executable for your application.

4. Click the executable file to select it.

5. Click OK. The Browse window will close, and the full file path for the application will appear in the Run window's Open field (see Figure 5.3).

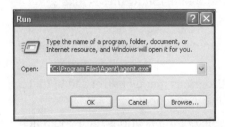

Figure 5.3   Ready to start the application.

6. Click OK. The Run window will close, and the application will start.

TIP: *To run a windowed command-line session in Windows XP, enter "cmd" in the Open field and click OK.*

Of course, one other way to easily run an application is to just double-click its shortcut on the desktop or the actual file in Windows Explorer. Whichever method you prefer, Windows can be flexible to meet your preferences.

Customizing the Start Menu

The Start menu is one of the most integral components of Windows XP because of its usefulness in running applications. Therefore, it is important to customize this menu to start your applications in the most efficient manner possible.

One of the most useful features of the Start menu is the ability to add program icons to it. Normally, icons are added automatically when the application is installed. Some older programs or programs that were on the PC when you performed a clean install may not be properly represented on the Start menu, however.

To place an application's shortcut on the menu, you must first create a shortcut for the application. Preferably, this shortcut should appear on the desktop.

Related solutions:	Found on page:
Managing Folders in XP	82
Repairing System Incompatibility	444

To place a shortcut on the Start menu, follow these steps:

1. Click and hold the application shortcut icon to select it.

2. Drag the icon to the Start menu button and hold it there. The Start menu will open.

3. Drag the icon to the All Programs menu control and hold it there. The All Programs menu will open.

4. Drag the icon through the list of applications until you reach the spot where you want the icon placed. A black horizontal

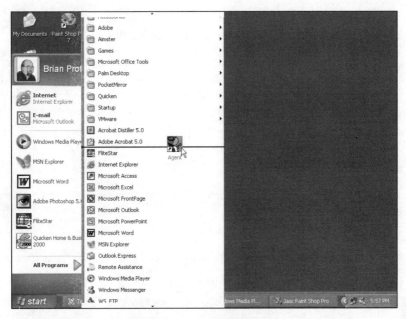

Figure 5.4   Dragging a shortcut to the Start menu.

line will act as a place marker for the icon's position on the list
(see Figure 5.4).

5. Release the mouse button so that the shortcut icon will be
   placed in the All Programs list.

6. If you wish, delete the shortcut icon that still remains on the
   desktop.

TIP: You can also use the preceding procedure for placing folders on the Start menu.

If the application is one that will get a lot of use, you can pin a shortcut for the application right into the pinned applications section of
the Start menu by following these steps:

1. In a folder, on the desktop, or in the Start menu, right-click the
   application icon you want to pin. The context menu will open.

2. Click the Pin To Start menu option. The application icon will
   appear in the pinned applications section.

Removing an application from the pinned section is just as simple.
Just follow these steps:

1. In the Start menu, right-click the application icon you want to
   remove from the pinned section. The context menu will open.

2. Click the Unpin From Start menu option. The application icon will be removed from the pinned applications section.

Some people may not be terribly fond of the myriad features contained on the Start menu. They may think that wading through all those nifty features is just slowing them down. If you are one of these people, you can alter the Start menu until it meets your needs. Or, until it just looks good. For instance, in this next task, you can change the look of the Start menu to that of the "classic" Windows, while leaving the rest of the Windows look and feel alone.

Related solution:	Found on page:
Restoring "Classic" Windows	64

To restore the "classic" Windows look and feel, follow these steps:

1. Click the Start menu button to open the Start menu.

2. Right-click an empty area of the Start menu. The context menu will appear.

3. Click Properties to open the Taskbar And Start Menu Properties dialog box (see Figure 5.5).

4. Click the Classic Start Menu option. The menu's appearance will change in the preview window.

5. Click Apply for the new setting to take effect, as shown in Figure 5.6.

Figure 5.5   The Taskbar And Start Menu Properties dialog box.

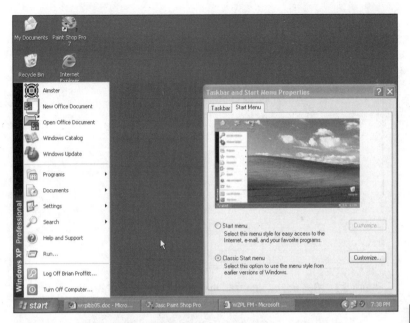

Figure 5.6 Back to the old look and feel for the Start menu.

6. Click OK to close the Taskbar And Start Menu Properties dialog box.

NOTE: *When the Windows Start menu is set to classic mode, the icons for the Windows system folders and tools (My Network Places, Internet Explorer, and so on) will be copied to the desktop.*

Whether you choose to use the new or old look for the Start menu, a wealth of options is available for this valuable Windows component. You can use them as follows:

1. Click the Start menu button to open the Start menu.

2. Right-click an empty area of the Start menu. The context menu will appear.

3. Click Properties to open the Taskbar And Start Menu Properties dialog box.

4. Click the Customize button next to the Start Menu option. The Customize Start Menu dialog box will open (see Figure 5.7).

5. Click the Small Icons option.

6. Click the spinner controls for the Number Of Programs On The Start Menu field to adjust the numeric value to something you prefer.

5. Run Applications

Figure 5.7   General customization options for the Start menu.

7. Click OK to close the Customize Start Menu dialog box.

8. Click Apply for the new settings to take effect.

9. Click OK to close the Taskbar And Start Menu Properties dialog box.

You can change many other settings in the Customize Start Menu dialog box, most of them centering on which icons will always be displayed on the Start menu. Although changing these settings may not seem like such a big deal, it certainly could be. You may have noticed the distinct lack of a Favorites menu on the Windows XP Start menu—a feature from Windows 98 that I, for one, missed. Here's how to get it back:

1. Click the Start menu button to open the Start menu.

2. Right-click an empty area of the Start menu. The context menu will appear.

3. Click Properties to open the Taskbar And Start Menu Properties dialog box.

4. Click the Customize button next to the Start Menu option. The Customize Start Menu dialog box will open.

5. Click the Advanced tab to open the Advanced page (see Figure 5.8).

6. In the Start Menu Items section, click the Favorites Menu option to check it.

Figure 5.8   Advanced customization options for the Start menu.

7. Click OK to close the Customize Start Menu dialog box.

8. Click Apply for the new settings to take effect.

9. Click OK to close the Taskbar And Start Menu Properties dialog box.

If you need more administrative tools at your fingertips, you can place the Administrative Tools folder on the Start menu, just like the Control Panel, as follows:

1. Click the Start menu button to open the Start menu.

2. Right-click an empty area of the Start menu. The context menu will appear.

3. Click Properties to open the Taskbar And Start Menu Properties dialog box.

4. Click the Customize button next to the Start Menu option. The Customize Start Menu dialog box will open.

5. Click the Advanced tab to open the Advanced page.

6. In the Start Menu Items section, scroll to the System Administrative Tools section of the list.

7. Click the Display On The All Programs Menu and the Start Menu option.

8. Click OK to close the Customize Start Menu dialog box.

5. Run Applications

9. Click Apply for the new settings to take effect.

10. Click OK to close the Taskbar And Start Menu Properties dialog box.

Managing the Taskbar

Other than the Start menu, the taskbar is likely the most visited tool in Windows. And, why shouldn't it be? Every application that runs, every folder that's opened—everything that happens in Windows XP is going to show up on the taskbar.

By now, most of us are familiar with the way the taskbar works: Open a folder and a button representing the folder appears in the taskbar. Click the button and the folder window opens. Click it again and the window closes. This method works for application windows, too. It's not exactly rocket science, but then, that's the whole point, isn't it?

Of course, Windows XP has a few extras in its taskbar that make it more efficient to use. The biggest change for users is the grouping feature in the taskbar. In previous versions of Windows, every open window got its own button. This was all well and good unless you had some ridiculous number of windows open. In this case, the taskbar buttons were too small to display their own labels, which made it a bit of guesswork to figure out which button controlled which window.

With grouping, all like windows will be grouped into a single taskbar button. Thus, all the Microsoft Word windows will appear in a single taskbar button. All the Windows Explorer buttons will do the same, and so on. Clicking a grouped taskbar icon will not open the windows, but rather a small list of the available windows for that group (see Figure 5.9). Clicking one of the window labels will bring up that window.

Like every other part of Windows, the taskbar can be modified to suit your needs. One of the first things you can do is move it to one of the four edges of the screen as follows, if that is what you need to do:

1. Right-click an empty portion of the taskbar. The context menu will appear.

2. Click the Lock The Taskbar option if it is checked. The taskbar will be unlocked.

3. Click and hold within the Notification Area (on the far right of the taskbar).

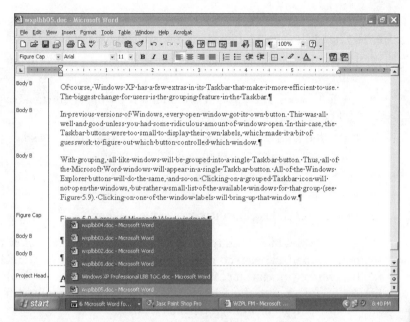

Figure 5.9   A group of Microsoft Word windows.

4. Drag the taskbar to another part of the desktop.

5. Release the mouse button so that the taskbar will be anchored in the new location (see Figure 5.10).

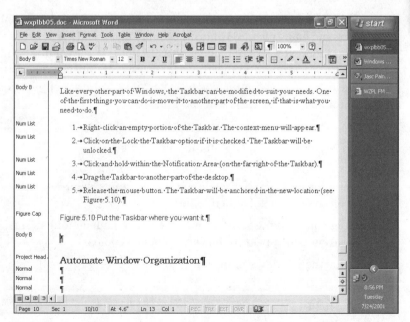

Figure 5.10   Put the taskbar where you want it.

You can use a similar method, as follows, to resize the taskbar, which is very handy if even your groups are taking up too much room:

1. Right-click an empty portion of the taskbar. The context menu will appear.

2. Click the Lock The Taskbar option if it is checked. The taskbar will be unlocked.

3. Click and hold on the top border of the taskbar. The mouse cursor will appear as a double-headed arrow.

4. Drag the border until the taskbar reaches the height or width you want.

5. Release the mouse button to resize the taskbar.

Not only can you move and resize the taskbar, but you also can add toolbars to the taskbar. The most helpful one is the Quick Launch toolbar, where you can start applications with just a single click of a button. There are also the Address, Links, and Desktop toolbars for you to utilize. You can add a toolbar as follows:

1. Right-click an empty portion of the taskbar. The context menu will appear.

2. Select Toolbars to open the Toolbars submenu.

3. Click the Quick Launch option to make the Quick Launch toolbar appear on the taskbar (see Figure 5.11).

By default, the Quick Launch toolbar displays icons for the default browser and email clients; Windows Media Player; and a handy Show Desktop icon, which, when clicked, will minimize all windows and display the desktop. Although these tools are certainly very handy to have around, wouldn't it be nice to have your most used application in this toolbar as well? You can add it like this:

1. Create a shortcut for your application on the desktop.

2. Right-click an open spot in the Quick Launch toolbar. The context menu will appear.

3. Click the Open Folder menu option. Windows Explorer will open to the Quick Launch folder.

4. Drag and drop the shortcut into the Quick Launch folder. The shortcut will appear in the Quick Launch toolbar.

5. Close the Windows Explorer window.

TIP: *You can also drag and drop an application's shortcut directly onto the Quick Launch toolbar.*

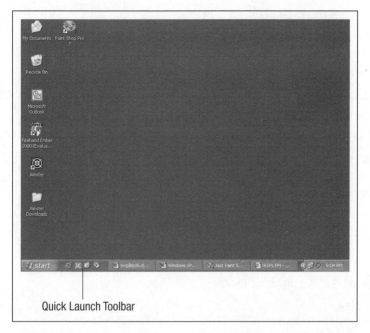

Quick Launch Toolbar

Figure 5.11   The Quick Launch toolbar gives a lot of power to the taskbar.

Besides the addition of toolbars, you can also customize the other end of the taskbar: the Notification Area. The system clock is displayed here, along with any notification icons from running applications. When email arrives, for example, the envelope icon will appear here.

To customize this section of the taskbar, follow these steps:

1. Right-click an empty portion of the taskbar. The context menu will appear.

2. Click Customize Notifications to open the Taskbar and Start Menu Properties and Customize Notifications dialog boxes (see Figure 5.12).

3. Click a Behavior for an icon to open the Behaviors list.

4. Choose from Hide When Inactive, Always Hide, or Always Show.

5. Click OK to close the Customize Notifications dialog box.

6. Click OK to close the Taskbar And Start Menu Properties dialog box.

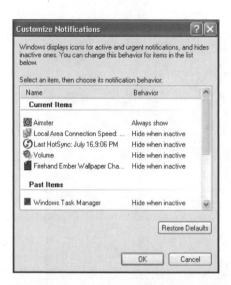

Figure 5.12   Customizing the notification area.

Finally, if you are not thrilled with the grouping function in the taskbar, you can quickly turn it off as follows:

1. Right-click an empty portion of the taskbar. The context menu will appear.

2. Click Properties to open the Taskbar And Start Menu Properties dialog box (see Figure 5.13).

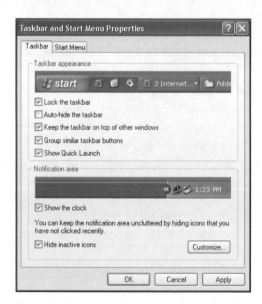

Figure 5.13   The taskbar customization options.

3. Click the Group Similar Taskbar Buttons option to uncheck it.

4. Click OK to close the Taskbar And Start Menu Properties dialog box.

Automating Window Organization

When you have all those applications up and running, your desktop can become a pretty crowded place. If you are one of those lucky people who has a gigantic plasma monitor, this may not be such a big concern. The rest of us, however, need to economize our screen space.

Windows has always enabled users to automatically place windows around the desktop, yet surprisingly this feature is little used. This is too bad because it's very handy to have around.

To automate the organization, follow these steps:

1. Right-click an empty portion of the taskbar. The context menu will appear.

2. Click Tile Windows Horizontally so that all windows on the taskbar will be tiled on the screen, as shown in Figure 5.14.

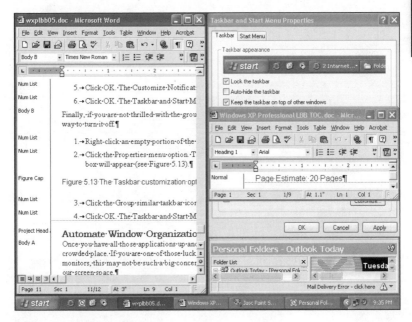

Figure 5.14   Tiled windows.

You can also automatically place windows that are within a given group as follows:

1. Right-click a grouped taskbar button. The context menu will appear.

2. Click Tile Horizontally so that all windows in the group will be tiled on the screen.

Install Applications

In Brief

I remember (in the not-so-distant past) when 19 floppy disks were needed to install Office 95. Nineteen! I also remember the sheer panic I had upon discovering one of my cats using one of the disks as a play toy.

Thankfully, such days are behind us because CD-ROMs have replaced those bulky floppy disks. In many cases, you no longer even need the CD-ROMs because downloadable software has become quite practical with secure ordering systems and higher bandwidth connections. Now, you can get robust commercial software with just a click of a link. Even if downloading takes awhile, it's usually easier than getting in the car and driving down to the local computer store.

Installing an application has become a pretty standard operation: Insert the installation medium, choose where the installed program will reside on your system, provide a security key if need be, tweak a few custom settings for that application, and let everything run!

This standardization on the user side of the equation belies the complicated mess that may be going on within the computer. In fact, installing an application is not so simple: If one file is out of place, the whole house of cards may come crashing down.

Windows XP has added some much-needed functionality to prevent problems such as this, in the hopes of making your software installations as painless as possible.

New Windows XP Installation Tools

Installing applications in a Windows environment can be a complicated venture. Not only must the application's files be placed in just the right location, but shared files such as library file components (DLLs) have to be reconciled with older versions of the same files, and everything has to be recorded in the system Registry.

When developers finish creating their masterpieces, they can't just send their compiled code out to the masses. Without formal setup applications to manage all the tasks just mentioned, their software would just sit there like a lump.

6. Install Applications

NOTE: *Programmers can bypass setup routines by sending out their code and all the attendant libraries in self-contained folders, but often these applications miss out on useful Windows features such as Registry entry and Start menu inclusion.*

Rather than make the developers figure out all these details, they can actually purchase the tools they need to automatically create setup routines. Thus, installation routines have been mostly managed by third-party software—the most popular choice being InstallShield from InstallShield Software Corporation.

InstallShield has been a good choice for programmers because it is simple to use. You tell the software what files are needed to run your application, and InstallShield will put together one really nifty package to install your software on Windows machines.

If there is one drawback to using InstallShield (or any other third-party setup routine), it is that each installation routine has to be run one at a time. Unlike Windows XP, which can be deployed simultaneously across networks, many software applications need to be installed physically on each computer in your organization. There are ways around this problem, naturally. If you are using Microsoft's Systems Management Server (SMS), you can deploy many software applications automatically. But, for smaller organizations without SMS, the Windows Installer tool is available.

Windows Installer (which actually first appeared in Windows 2000) is an installation management tool that works with pre-existing installation routines (such as InstallShield) and feeds them basic setup information so that you can perform unattended installs for nearly any software. Using this tool is analogous to using Setup Manager to install Windows XP unattended.

Windows Installer will also independently track all the changes made to your system whenever something is installed on your computer. This action has two benefits. First, if an application is ever in need of repair, Windows Installer can quickly reset the application to its original installed configuration by using the recorded settings in the Windows Installer package.

The second benefit comes into effect if you ever need to perform a rollback of your computer systems to an earlier time. Because the Windows Installer packages have monitored every change to your system, putting everything back to a previous iteration of the system is not difficult. In this respect, Windows Installer can act as a simple configuration management system.

6. Install Applications

The Saga of DLL—No More?

One of the more troubling aspects of any installation is the problem of dynamic link libraries (DLLs). For all their simple functionality—serving as shared components for applications so the applications themselves don't become bloated and cumbersome with code—DLLs have been known to cause a lot of problems in Windows.

DLLs may be simple, but they perform a vital function. They are the bricks in the structure known as your application. When one is moved or renamed, the whole structure can collapse. Even worse, DLLs are released in different versions as time goes by. And, newer versions of DLLs are not always compatible with older versions.

For instance, let's say your application needs msvideo.dll to function. This DLL provides the application with the functionality to play video files within Windows, and your application needs it to run little video clips for you. Specifically, let's state that the version of msvideo.dll your application needs is 1.8.0.1.

As time goes by, you install other applications on your system, and sure enough you install one that also uses msvideo.dll—except in this case, it's version 1.15.0.1.

Now, msvideo.dll typically resides in your Windows system folder, and in the past, only one version was available—the version sitting in the system folder. So, when the new application comes along, it re-places version 1.8.0.1 with 1.15.0.1.

Usually, a newer version of something is a good idea. But not always. For the sake of argument, let's assume that there is a marked differ-ence between these two versions—a difference profound enough to render the DLL useless to any application that needs msvideo.dll ver-sion 1.9.0.1 and before.

In reality, such a difference doesn't exist, but if it did, you could see a potential problem. As soon as the first application tried to run the video clips, it would not be able to because, from its perspective, the msvideo.dll it needs no longer exists.

Windows XP can avoid this problem altogether thanks to a better implementation of component sharing. Component sharing is a tech-nique that will keep older DLLs (and other shared components) if they need to be kept around. Programmers can stipulate this tech-nique when they set up their program installation routine, and Win-dows XP will safeguard these DLLs. If a newer version of the same

DLL file comes along, Windows XP will allow the two versions to co-exist on your computer so that all applications can have access to the exact DLL they need.

This shared system works for more than just DLL files. It works with all the Windows shared components. If such a system is implemented, a great deal of stability is lent to the system because DLL problems are a major factor in pre-Windows XP system crashes.

Giving Reboot the Boot

One of the cooler outcomes of all this new installation technology is the decreasing use of the system restart that occurs after software installation. The system restart was used in past versions of Windows for getting all the newly installed files and services started on your computer. The easiest way to do this programmatically was to simply shut down your system and have it start from zero once more. Although effective, this method is extremely bothersome to the user, who essentially has to endure a lengthy restart process just to get an application installed.

Windows XP now can forego this system restart, if it is deemed unnecessary, and can start all the needed files and services on the fly. This functionality is not comprehensive. In some instances, a system restart still will be needed. But, the frequency of these occurrences should decrease as more applications take advantage of this capability.

6. Install Applications

Immediate Solutions

Using Windows Installer to Add Applications

One of the most popular software applications made for Windows also comes from Microsoft: Office. A collection of office suite applications, Office has enjoyed immense popularity on the Windows platform in recent years.

Office is also of interest to techno-enthusiasts because Office 2000 was one of the first applications that made effective use of the Windows Installer. This use has continued with the new Office XP, as you will see in these steps to install Office XP Standard on your PC:

1. Insert the Office XP CD-ROM into your CD-ROM drive. The Windows Installer dialog box will briefly appear, followed by the Microsoft Office XP Setup dialog box.

2. When the User Information page appears, enter your name, initials, organization, and 25-character product key.

3. Click Next to move to the End-User License Agreement page.

4. Click the I Accept The Terms In The License Agreement checkbox if you have read the EULA.

5. Click Next to move to the Installation Type page (see Figure 6.1).

6. If you have Office on your system already, click the Upgrade Now option and click Next. The Begin Installation screen will appear, and you can proceed to Step 14. If you wish to customize your Office XP installation, click the Custom option and click Next. The Applications Setup page will appear (see Figure 6.2).

7. Check the applications you wish to install.

8. Click the Choose Detailed Installation Options For Each Application option.

9. Click Next to move to the Features To Install page.

10. Using the expansion icons, select those options you want to install on your computer (see Figure 6.3).

11. Click Next to move to the Remove Previous Versions page.

12. Click the options that match the application set you are about to install.

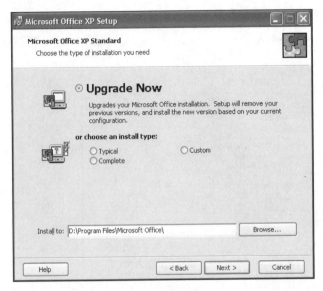

Figure 6.1   Choose your installation type.

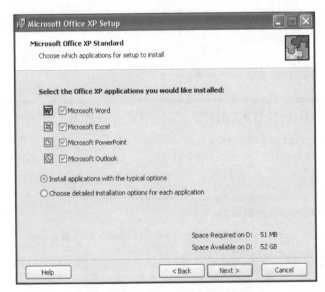

Figure 6.2   Choose which applications to install.

13. Click Next to move to the Begin Installation page.

14. Click Install to begin the installation process.

A message box will appear informing you when the installation is complete. You will not need to restart the system.

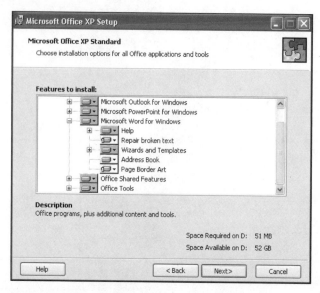

Figure 6.3   Choose the options for each application.

Related solution:	*Found on page:*
Starting Applications in XP	96

Using Windows Installer to Repair Applications

Windows Installer is not just something to use for installation. With its software management capabilities, Windows Installer can let you repair an application in just these few short steps:

1. In Windows Explorer, locate the Windows Installer package file (.msi) for your application.
2. Right-click the package file. The context menu will appear.
3. Click Repair so that Windows Installer will start the repair function (see Figure 6.4).

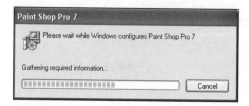

Figure 6.4   Repairing an application.

4. The Windows Installer tool will close after the repair of the installation is complete.

NOTE: *Some application repairs will start the application's own repair tool. Follow the steps outlined in these tools to complete the repair.*

Using Third-Party Installers

Even if your software does not come from Microsoft, you should take one extra step to ensure full compliance with the Windows Installer tool.

By using the Windows Installer tool in the Control Panel to initiate a third-party installation, you can ensure that the entire installation procedure will be tracked and recorded. This procedure will ultimately create a Windows Installer package file that you can use to repair, install, or uninstall your application later.

Before beginning this procedure, insert your application's CD-ROM or floppy disk into the appropriate drive and then follow these steps:

1. Click Start|Control Panel to open the Control Panel window (see Figure 6.5).

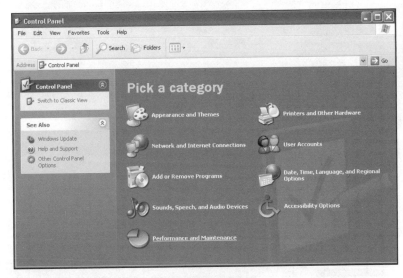

Figure 6.5 **The new Windows XP Control Panel.**

6. Install Applications

119

2. Click the Add Or Remove Programs link to open the Add Or Remove Programs window.

3. Click the Add New Programs link (see Figure 6.6) to open the Add Programs page.

4. Click the CD Or Floppy button to open the Install Program From Floppy Disk Or CD-ROM dialog box.

5. Click Next to search for the application's setup file.

6. When the file is found, click Finish. The Install Program From Floppy Disk Or CD-ROM dialog box will close, and the application's setup will begin.

Every application's installation routine is different, but they all follow pretty much the same pattern: Click through a series of dialog boxes and fill in what information is asked for. At the end of the process, click an Install or Finish button to complete the automated installation.

As one example, you can use this installation routine for Netscape 6, which is definitely not a Microsoft application:

1. In the Welcome dialog box, click Next to move to the Software License Agreement dialog box.

2. Read the license agreement.

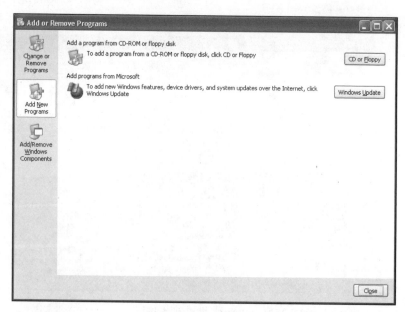

Figure 6.6   Adding a new program starts with this window.

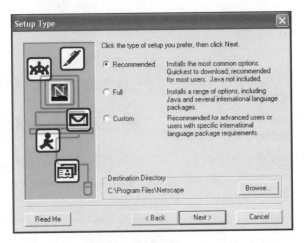

Figure 6.7   Most applications give you choices on how much or how little you want to install.

3. Click Next to move to the Setup Type dialog box (see Figure 6.7).

4. Click the options you want to use for the setup.

5. Click Next to move to the Download Options dialog box.

6. Select the download location nearest you.

7. Click Next to move to the Start Install dialog box.

8. Click Install to download the Netscape software to your computer in the location you specified.

9. When the installation is finished, click Close in the Add Or Remove Programs window to close it.

10. Click the Close control to close the Control Panel.

Related solution:	Found on page:
Managing Peripherals with the Control Panel	136

Adding Windows Components

Besides adding whole installations to your system, you can add even more components from your Windows XP CD-ROM that may not have been installed when you installed Windows XP on your system.

To add them, insert the Windows XP CD-ROM into the CD-ROM drive and follow these steps:

1. Click Start|Control Panel to open the Control Panel window.

2. Click the Add Or Remove Programs link to open the Add Or Remove Programs window.

3. Click Add/Remove Windows Components to open the Windows Component Wizard (see Figure 6.8).

4. Click a category to select it.

5. Click the Details button to display the applications within that category in a new dialog box.

6. Click the checkbox for the application you want to install.

7. Click OK to close the category dialog box.

8. Click Next. The Windows Component Wizard will analyze the changes you requested and begin installing the new components.

9. Click Finish to close the Windows Component Wizard.

10. Click Close to close the Add Or Remove Programs window.

11. Click the Close control to close the Control Panel.

NOTE: *You can also use this procedure to uninstall Windows components.*

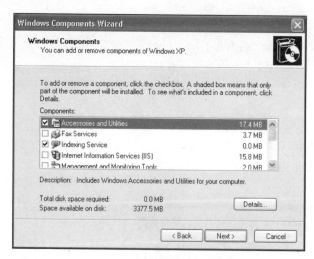

Figure 6.8   Add or remove Windows components.

Uninstalling Applications

Uninstalling applications is something you would think would be easy to do, at first glance. Just erase the files that were added to your computer, and you're all set!

Well, not exactly.

Remember, software installation does more than just add files to your computer. Some applications deliberately use shared components that are already on your system and being used by other applications. Your installed application is also recorded in the Registry and presumably has certain files associated with it.

All these settings have to be carefully undone whenever you uninstall a software program. Otherwise, you could leave gaping holes in the functionality of many other applications on your computer.

Most applications have their own uninstaller tools. (Unwise is a popular one.) But, as with installing, you should use the Windows Installer tool to initiate the process. If you used the Windows Installer to begin the program's installation way back when, you will have the benefit of knowing that your system will be cleaner when all is said and done than if you just leave it to the devices of the third-party uninstaller.

The second benefit is much more pragmatic: Even if you never used Windows Installer on this application, using it at the beginning of the uninstall will save you a very tedious step—locating the application's uninstaller routine.

To use the Windows Uninstaller, follow these steps:

1. Click Start|Control Panel to open the Control Panel window.

2. Click the Add Or Remove Programs link to open the Add Or Remove Programs window (see Figure 6.9).

3. Click the application you want to remove. The application will be highlighted, and the Change/Remove button will appear.

4. Click the Change/Remove button to open the Confirm File Deletion dialog box.

5. Click Yes. The Confirm File Deletion dialog box will close, and the Uninstall window will open (see Figure 6.10).

6. When the uninstall is complete, click the OK button to close the Uninstall window.

6. Install Applications

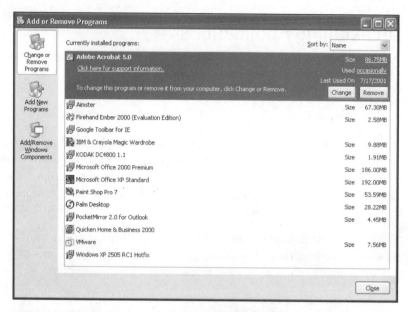

Figure 6.9   Add or remove applications from this window.

7. Click Close to close the Add Or Remove Programs window.

8. Click the Close control to close the Control Panel.

NOTE: *After running some uninstaller routines, you will need to restart your system.*

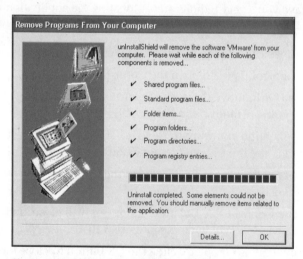

Figure 6.10   Uninstall processes are often fully automated.

Chapter 7

Hardware Issues

In Brief

Adding new hardware to a system consists of two phases: the hardware phase and the software phase. You need to add the hardware device to the system and tell your operating system how it should be managed.

The hardware phase is machine-dependent, and the software phase is operating system-dependent. Assuming you are working on an Intel-based PC, regardless of its brand (AT, ATX, IBM, Compaq, and so on), installing new hardware is straightforward and is the same whether you are using Windows or some other operating system. The interface of the PC system is made in such a way that any device can be accessed in a standard and documented method.

Although the hardware phase has not changed in recent years, Windows XP handles the software phase in a much better manner than Windows past. You may have installed new devices such as printers or sound cards in the past, but you may be surprised with the way Windows XP handles them.

Before beginning any installation, you should check the Windows XP hardware compatibility list (HCL) to see whether your device is XP-compatible. In theory, any device conforming to the standards in PC technologies should work. However, in recent years, many companies have started to make devices that were missing several important chips and then using proprietary drivers to do their work. Although this strategy makes devices less expensive to the public, it has resulted in two big side effects. First, the drivers are published for mostly Windows 9x and, because the hardware devices cannot work without the special Windows drivers, they could be incompatible with Windows XP or its predecessor, Windows 2000.

Second, the drivers need to do much more work, which means that your CPU will be busy doing what the chips were supposed to do. Hence, your system could feel much slower. The sad thing is that most of these components, commonly called *winmodems* and *winprinters*, are not identified as such on the packages. Often, the only way you can be sure is to check the HCL and contact the manufacturer.

If your device is not on the HCL, checking the manufacturer's Web site is often a very good idea. Many hardware manufacturers are recognizing the market strength of the Windows 2000 platform and have released new hardware drivers to accommodate this platform. And, as you know, if something works for Windows 2000, it will work for Windows XP.

Hardware Management Tools in XP

If computers were alive, we would almost have to feel sorry for them. Machines that were originally built to perform mathematical calculations, computers are now being asked to accomplish tasks far beyond their original purpose.

To their builders' credit, personal computers have risen to these diverse tasks remarkably well. Now, they can play games and music, use telephone lines to communicate, and talk to devices that didn't even exist a few years ago. To be sure, a lot of this ingenuity should be credited to the makers of these devices, who built the hardware and the software to make everything work together cohesively.

Today, because so many types of devices can be connected to your PC, it's important that the operating system knows how to use them effectively. Windows XP has inherited many previous versions of Windows' capabilities to deal with hardware on your computer. Besides a huge base of software driver support, Windows XP continues the use of Plug-and-Play technology (which enables your PC to at least fake it creatively with a generic plug-and-play device driver).

Windows XP does more than just carry on technology; some significant improvements have been added to this platform. Some are new and some are from Windows 2000, but the net effect of these tools for a former Windows 9x user is rather stunning.

The first tool that you will run across with hardware is the Device Driver Verifier. This component continuously monitors the devices on your computer and checks to see whether new devices are being added at any time. If a new device is added, the Device Driver Verifier will pop up with a notification and, with your permission, automatically seek out the proper driver for the device within the Windows XP pantheon of drivers or on the Windows XP driver database on the Web. If the right driver is found, the Verifier will install the driver immediately so you can get to work with the device right away.

Another hardware management tool is Windows Update. This feature keeps an inventory of the devices on your system and periodically polls the Windows XP database for updated drivers for your hardware. When they are found, Windows Update will notify you and ask whether you want to download the new driver or even download and install it in one quick operation.

The third tool in Windows XP's hardware repertoire is the rollback function. A rollback is the process by which you can revert your hardware drivers back to the last saved version. This capability is particularly handy when you have upgraded a device driver only to find out that it is driving your machine completely insane.

Rollbacks actually show up in two Windows XP functions: individual device driver rollbacks and the Last Known Good function. Last Known Good is sort of like a global "do-over" for your PC that can be implemented during a restart of the system. If you use Last Known Good, the system will automatically shift back to the configuration it last had before all the trouble started.

TIP: *To use Last Known Good, press the F8 key during the system restart. When the list of operating system choices appears, choose the Last Known Good option from the list.*

The Device Driver Rollback function is similar in operation but much smaller in scope. This function will shift back only the single device driver you select—presumably the one causing all the hullabaloo.

The Microsoft Management Console (MMC) is a fancy name for all the system administrative tools Windows XP contains. These tools monitor security and performance of your system, among other things. The Management Console's primary purpose is not hardware management, but enough tools within it do work directly with hardware (specifically your hard drive) that it earns a place in this list.

Last but not least, there is the Control Panel—the ubiquitous Windows tool that contains management tools for nearly every major device type Windows can use. But, if you think the Control Panel is still the same old set of neat little icons, think again. The Windows XP Control Panel is another animal entirely.

A Look at the New Control Panel

Windows XP has been touted as a "task-oriented" operating system, based on the premise that users don't want to have to remember multiple steps to do something—they just want it done.

You have already seen one aspect of this task-driven interface while working with the Windows Explorer. In the Control Panel, this new interface is very apparent, bringing a whole new way of working with the Control Panel and its component tools.

This new look for the Control Panel (shown in Figure 7.1) is known as the Category View, a name that gives some hints to its function. In the Category View, you no longer manage the system and peripherals by opening individual icons. Now, specific tasks for working with your computer are grouped together within categories.

This new organization makes it a lot easier for newcomers to Windows to figure out what they need to do. Of course, there's no exclusion of those users who prefer the old way of working with the Control Panel. A quick click of the Switch To Classic View link will shift the Control Panel to its older look and feel (see Figure 7.2).

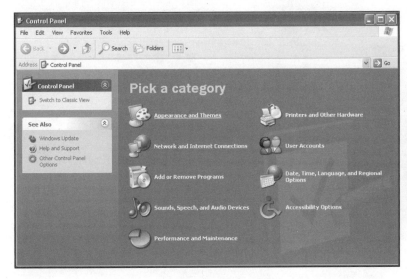

7. Hardware Issues

Figure 7.1   The Category View of the Control Panel.

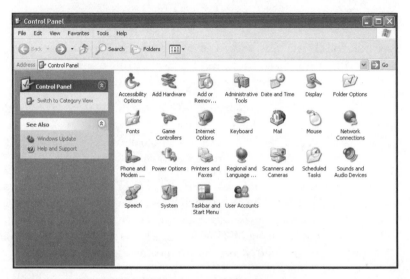

Figure 7.2   The Classic View of the Control Panel.

Immediate Solutions

Installing New Hardware

The promise of Plug-and-Play software has not been truly realized, despite the assurances of the Windows development community. The concept of buying a piece of hardware and installing it just by the simple act of plugging it in worked only rarely in earlier versions of Windows. Now, finally, that promise is being realized, as Windows XP begins to bring true Plug-and-Play functionality to your PC.

For those of us who have fought with hardware drivers and conflicting interrupts, having true Plug and Play functionality may seem to be an impossible dream. But, Windows XP, although not perfect, has managed to take a huge number of configuration tasks away from the user who, frankly, should not have to worry about this sort of thing anyway.

When you plug a new piece of hardware in to your Windows XP machine, one of two things will happen: Either Windows XP will recognize the hardware, or it won't. If the hardware is recognized, you won't have to lift a finger to install the hardware. Windows XP will automatically step through the process to get your device up and running. This is not a pokey process either—one camera I plugged into the computer was fully installed in less than 15 seconds.

If Windows XP does not recognize the hardware, you're going to have to take a hand in the installation process by following these steps:

1. Plug or otherwise physically install the hardware onto your PC.
2. Power on your system if necessary and log in to an administrator account.
3. Soon after Windows XP starts, a Found New Hardware message will appear in the Taskbar's Notification Area, followed by the Found New Hardware Wizard dialog box (see Figure 7.3).
4. Insert the software media that came with your hardware into the appropriate drive.
5. Click the Install Software Automatically (Recommended) option.
6. Click Next. The Found New Hardware Wizard will begin to look for the hardware drivers on the software supplied by the manufacturer.

7. Hardware Issues

Figure 7.3   The Found New Hardware Wizard.

When the software driver is located, the automatic installation process will begin, and the Found New Hardware Wizard dialog box will close.

Implementing Device Driver Rollback

This problem has probably happened to you at one time or another: You innocently install a new driver on your PC, and suddenly nothing on your computer works. Maybe it's a driver for a new hardware component. Maybe it's an upgrade driver for an existing piece of equipment.

Whatever the situation, you will need to get that software off your system as soon as possible. But, if it's for an existing component, removing the software completely will only leave you with a driverless piece of equipment. Performing a rollback would be better—reverting the driver to the version that was on your machine before you upgraded it.

To perform this task, you need to be logged in to an administrator account. Then, follow these steps:

1. Click Start|Control Panel to open the Control Panel.

2. Click the Performance And Maintenance link to open the Performance And Maintenance window (see Figure 7.4).

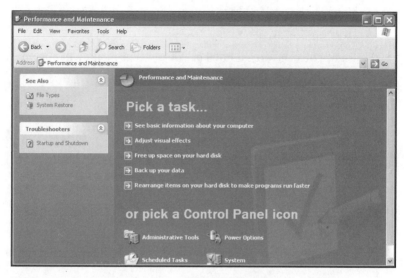

Figure 7.4   Performance and maintenance tasks for your system.

3. Click the See Basic Information About Your Computer link to open the System Properties dialog box.

4. Click the Hardware tab to open the Hardware page (see Figure 7.5).

Figure 7.5   Hardware configuration tools.

7. Hardware Issues

5. Click the Device Manager button to open the Device Manager (see Figure 7.6).

6. Right-click the errant device. The context menu will appear.

7. Click Properties to open the device's Properties dialog box.

8. Click the Driver tab to open the Driver page (see Figure 7.7).

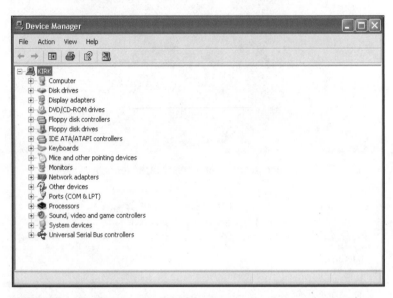

Figure 7.6   The Windows Device Manager.

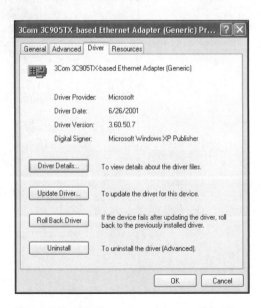

Figure 7.7   Configure your driver on this page.

9. Click the Roll Back Driver button. The Confirm Roll Back dialog box will appear.

10. Click Yes. The Confirm Roll Back dialog box will close, and the driver will be reverted to the older version.

11. Restart the system if the system requests it.

Uninstalling Hardware

If you need to remove hardware from your computer, you could just physically remove it and be done with it. Your computer probably will not suffer any ill effects from this crude form of uninstall, but removing the hardware this way is really not a good idea.

By leaving obsolete driver software on your system, you clutter your system and increase your chances of creating driver conflict if you ever try to install a similar device on your PC in the future.

The best method to uninstall hardware is to uninstall the drivers first, then power down the machine, and physically remove the hardware. Uninstalling the drivers is an easy process, though you must be logged in as an administrator. Then you can follow these steps:

1. Click Start|Control Panel to open the Control Panel.

2. Click the Performance And Maintenance link to open the Performance And Maintenance window.

3. Click the See Basic Information About Your Computer link to open the System Properties dialog box.

4. Click the Hardware tab to open the Hardware page.

5. Click the Device Manager button to open the Device Manager.

6. Right-click the errant device. The context menu will appear.

7. Click the Uninstall menu option. The Confirm Device Removal message box will appear.

8. Click OK. The Confirm Device Removal message box will close, and the device will be removed.

9. Power down the computer and physically remove the device.

Managing Peripherals with the Control Panel

Much of the hardware you have on your computer is easy to take for granted. Devices such as the keyboard and mouse are so integral to the operation of the system that you can easily forget that they really aren't a part of the PC; they're separate hardware components with their own drivers.

The fact that they are separate components is not a bad thing, either. If a device has a driver, then the driver has settings. And very often, those settings can be changed and improved.

Keyboard Management

As peripherals go, the keyboard is the oldest type on record. The earliest personal computers had some form of keyboard, usually based on (in the U.S.) the QWERTY keyboard layout.

In actuality, keyboards come in all shapes and sizes because obviously computers are not always used in the U.S., and not everyone has a standard keyboard. The thing you take for granted can be completely different for someone else's machine.

The Control Panel has some useful settings for you to tweak, regardless of what type of keyboard you have. You can make these changes by following these steps:

1. Click Start|Control Panel to open the Control Panel.
2. Click the Printers And Other Hardware link to open the Printers And Other Hardware window (see Figure 7.8).
3. Click the Keyboard link to open the Keyboard Properties dialog box (see Figure 7.9).
4. Using the slider controls, adjust the Character Repeat rates.
5. Test the rates in the test entry field.
6. Adjust the cursor blink rate. The preview cursor will change to reflect your changes.
7. Click Apply to make the changes take effect.
8. Click OK to close the Keyboard Properties dialog box.
9. Click the Close control to close the Printers And Other Hardware window.

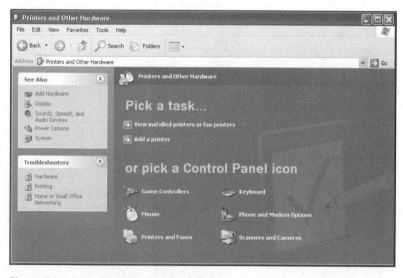

Figure 7.8   Many hardware devices can be configured from this page.

Figure 7.9   The Keyboard Properties dialog box.

Mouse Management

If keyboards seem ubiquitous, the mouse really never does. That's because so many different types of pointing devices (not counting just the mouse pointing device) are available that it's usually a surprise moving from one computer to another.

137

All these pointing devices have something in common, though: They all move the cursor around the screen. Because they all have this capability, you can change a common set of properties to reflect your needs. For instance, you can actually activate a feature that will let you drag items without holding down the mouse button.

To change mouse properties, follow these steps:

1. Click Start|Control Panel to open the Control Panel.

2. Click the Printers And Other Hardware link to open the Printers And Other Hardware window.

3. Click the Mouse link to open the Mouse Properties dialog box (see Figure 7.10).

4. Click the Turn On ClickLock option to check it.

5. Click the Settings button to open the Settings For ClickLock dialog box.

6. Using the slider control, adjust the length of time you need to hold down the mouse button to activate ClickLock.

7. Click OK to close the Settings For ClickLock dialog box.

8. Click Apply to make the changes take effect.

9. Click OK to close the Mouse Properties dialog box.

10. Click the Close control to close the Printers And Other Hardware window.

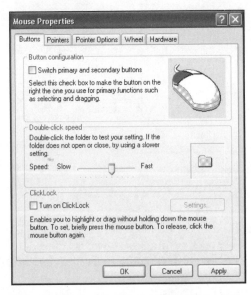

Figure 7.10   The Mouse Properties dialog box.

You also can enhance other features for the mouse, including highlighting its visibility on the screen—something that's very useful on laptop computers. To do so, follow these steps:

1. Click Start|Control Panel to open the Control Panel.

2. Click the Printers And Other Hardware link to open the Printers And Other Hardware window.

3. Click the Mouse link to open the Mouse Properties dialog box.

4. Click the Pointer Options tab to open the Pointer Options page.

5. Click the Display Pointer Trails option to check it.

6. Click Apply to make the changes take effect.

7. Click OK to close the Mouse Properties dialog box.

8. Click the Close control to close the Printers And Other Hardware window.

If you are left handed, you will definitely appreciate the feature described next. To switch the functionality of the mouse buttons for left-handed use, follow these steps:

1. Click Start|Control Panel to open the Control Panel.

2. Click the Printers And Other Hardware link to open the Printers And Other Hardware window.

3. Click the Mouse link to open the Mouse Properties dialog box.

4. Click the Switch Primary And Secondary Buttons option to check it.

5. Click Apply to make the changes take effect.

6. Click OK to close the Mouse Properties dialog box.

7. Click the Close control to close the Printers And Other Hardware window.

Sound Management

The sense of hearing is second only to sight in the human psyche—and some would argue that it's a tie. The importance of hearing is right up there with seeing, so audio cues from your computer are just as necessary as visual cues.

Windows XP has incorporated sound management into its task-oriented methodology, as you will see in the task outlined in this section. To adjust the system volume, follow these steps:

7. Hardware Issues

1. Click Start|Control Panel to open the Control Panel.

2. Click the Sound, Speech, And Audio Devices link to open the Sound, Speech, And Audio Devices window (see Figure 7.11).

3. Click the Adjust The System Volume link to open the Sound And Audio Devices Properties dialog box (see Figure 7.12).

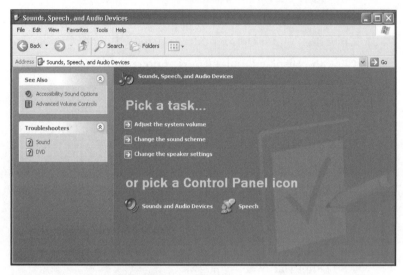

Figure 7.11   Sound controls are located here.

Figure 7.12   The Sound And Audio Devices Properties dialog box.

4. Adjust the slider control in the Device Volume section.

5. Click Apply to make the changes take effect.

6. Click OK to close the Sound And Audio Devices Properties dialog box.

7. Click the Close control to close the Sound, Speech, And Audio Devices window.

TIP: If you click the Place Volume Icon In The Taskbar option in the Sound And Audio Devices Properties dialog box, you can have a ready-to-use volume control. Just single-click the volume control icon to view the master volume control slider.

Scanner and Camera Management

A relatively new device type on the peripheral scene is the digital image device. Hardware that falls into this category includes scanners and digital cameras—two popular devices on both the home and business fronts.

Although both devices are superficially very different (try getting a scanner into a camera bag), their goal is essentially the same: to make an image of the world that can eventually be stored on your PC.

The Control Panel has a Scanner And Camera tool, just as it has tools for other peripherals. But, the similarity this tool has with the others pretty much ends with this statement. The Scanner And Camera tool does not exist to change the settings of the aforementioned devices. It is there to help facilitate the migration of the imagery from the device to the PC.

This facilitation is done with the Scanner And Camera Wizard, which automatically pops up when a camera is connected or a scanner is activated. You can see how the wizard works in the following steps, in which you download some pictures from a camera:

1. Connect the device to the PC and activate it in connection mode. The Scanner And Camera Wizard will appear.

2. Click Next to move to the Choose Pictures To Copy page (see Figure 7.13).

3. Click the pictures you want to download from the camera to check the images. By default, all the images are selected for download.

TIP: Although rudimentary rotation tools are available at this point, you might want to forego using them here, especially if you have hooked up your battery-powered camera directly to the PC. The more time you spend in this wizard, the more battery power is lost!

141

Figure 7.13   Select the pictures to pull off your camera.

4. Click Next to move to the Picture Name And Destination page (see Figure 7.14).

5. Type the name for this group of pictures. A similarly named folder will be chosen to store the pictures in your My Pictures folder.

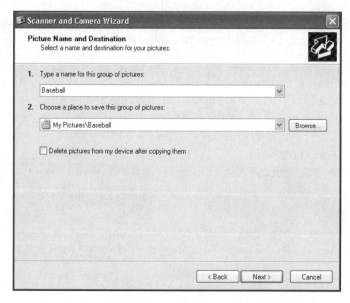

Figure 7.14   Decide where to store the pictures.

6. Click the Delete Pictures From My Device After Copying Them option to check it.

7. Click Next. The Copying Pictures page will appear, and the photos will be downloaded to the appropriate folder on your PC.

8. Click Next to move to the Other Options page.

9. Click the option you wish to pursue to select it.

10. Click Finish to close the Scanner And Camera Wizard.

Related solution:	Found on page:
Burning Music CDs	318

Chapter 8

Manage Printers

In Brief

Human beings experience a phenomenon called social inertia, which is a process in which people keep doing something or using something even when they may not need to do so.

The use of paper is a classic example of this social quirk. Despite the prevalence of computers in many countries, people have a marked predilection for having paper versions of documents created on a computer. They use several arguments to justify their use of paper. Paper, they say, is portable; you don't have to be tied to a screen to read it. Paper is self-sustaining; you don't need batteries or electricity to turn it on. Paper is easier to read; no flat-plane focusing problems to bother your eyes when you look at a monitor screen.

I think the real reason we try to keep paper around is that it is real to us. It's comfortable and something we can control on a very basic level. It means more to us than a collection of pixels on a screen, which explains why adults will spend a thousand dollars on an expensive digital camera and then agonize over how to make prints of the photos on their printer. Even though the imagery is the same, the prints are what are important, because paper is perceived as timeless and electrical impulses are not.

Printer Management Tools in XP

The universal need for paper is all good news for the printer manufacturers, of course, who have worked mightily to develop faster and higher-quality printers that perfectly mimic what's on the computer screen.

Ironically, printer connectivity was (until recently) relegated to the slowest port on a personal computer: the parallel port. The familiar 25-pin Centronic parallel port was, in its day, appropriate for the job it had to do: handling the data stream for printing simple black-and-white documents.

When photos and desktop publishing got into the picture, so to speak, printers were upgraded to handle the new load. The connection, however, was not. Nor was the parallel port upgraded when color was added to the equation. This left users with mind-churningly slow printers trying to eke out as much data from the PC as they could through pitifully slow parallel ports.

Some improvements are on the horizon, however. Recently, a new type of parallel port connection, the Enhanced Parallel Port (EPP), was made available to PCs. Physically identical to the older parallel ports, the EPP can handle data up to 10 times faster than the previous technology—a welcome relief for the printer bottleneck.

The proliferation of universal serial bus (USB) ports has also led many printer manufacturers to accommodate USB connections for their printers. USB connections are not very fast, but they are still faster than the old parallel port connections and they are more numerous. Newer PCs typically have only one parallel port but usually sport two USB ports.

Windows XP has improved upon the printer management found in Windows 98, bringing much of the management technology over from Windows 2000. Improving this technology was a good idea because now Windows XP has excellent local printer support and superior network printer connectivity.

The Printers And Faxes tool is a part of the Control Panel, but the use of printers is so critical to many users that it deserves its own special discussion. Windows XP has heavily automated the task of installing a new local printer and connecting to existing networked printers. The printer settings tools are also easily accessed though the new Printer Task tools.

8. Manage Printers

Immediate Solutions

Setting Up a New Local Printer

You add a new printer in much the same way you add any other piece of hardware to a Windows XP computer: You plug it in, connect it to the computer, and wait for Windows XP to automatically detect and install the printer.

You might have to tackle one additional choice, however, when installing a printer: Should you install the extra software that comes with the printer? Answering this question involves two steps.

First, did Windows XP detect and install the right printer drivers? If the answer to this question is yes, you can probably forego installing the manufacturer's software. Typically, this software is redundant to the drivers found on Windows XP and may even be older versions that could diminish your printing performance.

The only other thing this software adds to your computer is a snazzy GUI print manager that might pop up every time you print something. It could be helpful, or it could be very annoying. Read the manual that came with the printer to see whether your printer has this kind of interface and ask yourself "Do I really need it?"

The second concern to address is this: Does your printer have any special features? For instance, is it an "all-in-one" printer that has a scanner and fax machine? Does it have double-sided printing capabilities that your driver does not support? If your printer has any of this type of functionality, and the native Windows XP drivers do not support it, you will clearly need to install the extra software.

To install a local printer to your PC, follow these steps:

1. Connect the printer to the PC using the appropriate port and turn on the printer. If the printer is connected through a USB or Firewire port, the printer will automatically be detected and installed immediately.

2. If the printer is not detected, click Start|Printers And Faxes to open the Printers And Faxes window (see Figure 8.1).

3. Click the Add A Printer link to open the Add Printer Wizard's welcome screen.

Figure 8.1   The Printers And Faxes window.

4. Click Next to move to the Local Or Network Printer page (see Figure 8.2).

5. Click the Local Printer Attached To This Computer option to select it.

6. Confirm the Automatically Detect And Install My Plug And Play Printer option is checked.

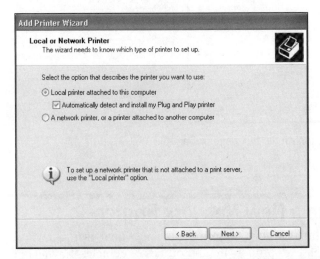

Figure 8.2   Clarify whether your printer is connected directly to the PC or is out on the network.

8. Manage Printers

7. Click Next. The New Printer Detection page will appear as Windows searches for the connected printer.

   If the detected printer is not recognized by Windows XP, the Add New Hardware Wizard will appear. Use this tool to install your printer's software.

   If the detected printer is recognized by Windows XP, the New Printer Detection page will display a message asking you to print a test page.

8. Click the Yes option to select it.

9. Click Next to move to the Completing The Add Printer Wizard page.

10. Click Finish. The Add Printer Wizard will close, the test page should be printed on your new printer, and a notification dialog box for the test page will appear (see Figure 8.3).

11. If the page printed correctly, click OK to close the notification dialog box.

Related solution:	Found on page:
Installing New Hardware	131

Figure 8.3   Confirm the test page has printed.

Setting Up a New Network Printer

In many of today's work environments, individual users do not usually have their own printers in their offices or cubicles. Having fewer printers makes sense business-wise because the costs of maintenance and upkeep of all those individual printers would be outrageous.

So, to the grumbling discontent of the masses, several people share printers. Actually, this setup isn't so bad because getting up to go to the printer is also an excellent excuse to swing by the coffee room.

Groups can use two kinds of printers. The first is the shared printer, which is hooked directly to a user's machine that the user has made available to everyone in his or her workgroup. The second type is the network printer, which is not connected to anyone's PC but rather has its own network card and is connected directly to the network. This latter type is the most often used in larger corporate environments.

Windows XP has streamlined the procedure for locating and config-uring shared and network printers, as you can see in the following steps:

1. If the printer is not detected, click Start|Printers And Faxes to open the Printers And Faxes window.

2. Click the Add A Printer link to open the Add Printer Wizard's welcome screen.

3. Click Next to move to the Local Or Network Printer page.

4. Click the A Network Printer, Or A Printer Attached To Another Computer option to select it.

5. Click Next to move to the Specify A Printer page (see Figure 8.4).

6. Click the Browse For A Printer option to select it.

7. Click Next. The Browse For Printer page will appear with a list of known printers in your workgroup, followed by a list of all

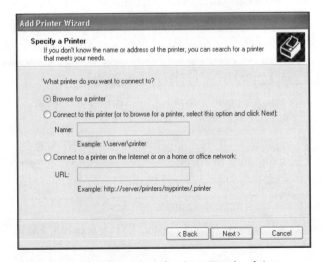

Figure 8.4   Start the search for the network printer.

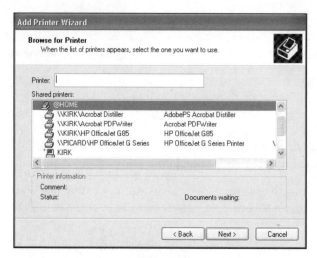

Figure 8.5   A list of detected network printers.

known PCs and printers connected directly to the network (see Figure 8.5).

8. Click the desired printer from the known printers list or from the devices list to select it.

9. Click Next to move to the Default Printer page.

10. If you want to make this printer your default printer, click Yes.

11. Click Next to move to the Completing The Add Printer Wizard page.

12. Click Finish to close the Add Printer Wizard.

Sharing a Printer with Other Users

Connecting to a network printer is easy. But, what if you want other users to connect to your printer from the network?

This process is simple as well. The only thing you have to do is share your printer. Sharing makes the printer available on the network for others in your workgroup to access and use.

Here's how to set your printer as shared:

1. Click Start|Printers And Faxes to open the Printers And Faxes window.

2. Click the printer you want to share to select it.

3. Click the Share This Printer link to open the printer's Properties dialog box (see Figure 8.6).

4. Click the Share This Printer option to select it.

5. Enter a Share Name for the printer. This name will identify your printer on the network.

6. If other users on the network are not using Windows XP exclusively, click the Additional Drivers button to open the Additional Drivers dialog box (see Figure 8.7).

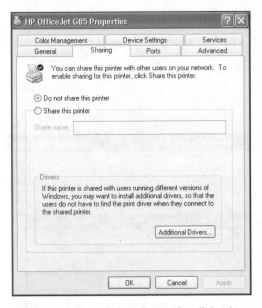

Figure 8.6   The printer's Properties dialog box.

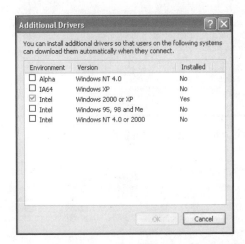

Figure 8.7   You can load drivers for other operating systems.

7. Click the operating systems you know other users have to select them.

TIP: *Have the drivers for the other operating systems ready to install before the next step.*

---

8. Click OK to open the Operating System Printer Drivers dialog box.

9. Provide the location of the additional printer drivers.

10. Click OK. The drivers will be installed, and the Additional Drivers and Operating System Printer Drivers dialog boxes will close.

11. Click Apply to apply the settings changes.

12. Click OK to close the printer's Properties dialog box.

In the Printers And Faxes window, you can tell the printer is now shared when you see the special extended hand icon for the printer (see Figure 8.8).

Related solutions:	*Found on page:*
Sharing Files with Other Users	174
Sharing Applications	288

Figure 8.8   A shared printer is marked by a gentle hand.

Managing an Existing Printer

After you connect printers to your PC, you can adjust their settings as needed. Mostly, you do so with a local printer, but you can handle remote printers in this manner as well because you are just altering how your computer is sending commands to the printer.

One of the most common printer practices is to change the type of paper you are going to use. This change can usually be made from job to job by the user, but if you are anticipating many jobs using legal-sized paper rather than letter size, a quick change of the default paper properties will save you from changing this setting every time you run a print job.

To quickly alter the default paper settings for a printer, follow these steps:

1. Click Start|Printers And Faxes to open the Printers And Faxes window.

2. Click the printer you want to configure to select it.

3. Click the Select Printing Preferences link to open the printer's Printing Preferences dialog box.

4. Click the Paper/Quality tab to open the Paper/Quality page (see Figure 8.9).

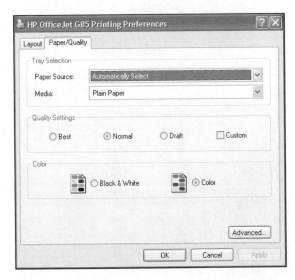

Figure 8.9   Configuring the printer's paper settings.

5. Click the Advanced button to open the printer's Advanced Options dialog box.

6. Click the Paper Size drop-down list control to see a list of paper sizes.

7. Click the desired paper size to select it.

8. Click OK to close the printer's Advanced Options dialog box.

9. Click Apply to apply the changed setting.

10. Click OK to close the printer's Printing Preferences dialog box.

Another handy trick is to change the order in which pages are printed. If your printer sends out its output facedown, the default Front To Back setting on many printers is just dandy. If the output is faceup, you are left with recollating the pages on every print job because they come out in reverse order.

Here's how to quickly change this setting for major convenience:

1. Click Start|Printers And Faxes to open the Printers And Faxes window.

2. Click the printer you want to configure to select it.

3. Click the Select Printing Preferences link to open the printer's Printing Preferences dialog box (see Figure 8.10).

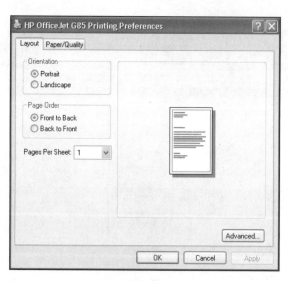

Figure 8.10   Changing the print order.

4. Click the Back To Front option to select it.

5. Click Apply to apply the changed setting.

6. Click OK to close the printer's Printing Preferences dialog box.

Removing a Printer

There comes a time in every printer's life when the printer just has to go. This time is typically gleeful for many users because it usually means getting a new printer. So much for sentimentality.

When the old printer is sent to that Great Recycling Warehouse in the Sky (or to some underling's cubicle), you will need to get rid of the printer's software on your machine. You do so for neatness' sake but more so to eliminate any drivers that might conflict with the new printer's drivers.

To quickly remove your printer's drivers, follow these steps:

1. Click Start|Printers And Faxes to open the Printers And Faxes window.

2. Click the printer you want to delete to select it.

3. Click the Delete This Printer link to open the Printers dialog box.

4. Click Yes to confirm the deletion. The Printers dialog box will close, and the printer will be removed from the Printers And Faxes window.

8. Manage Printers

Work with Multiple Users

In Brief

Because I was an only child, my first exposure to the concept of sharing came from watching *Romper Room* on television. I am sad to say that unlike many of the show's other lessons, the sharing part didn't take.

Nowhere is this lack of sharing more prevalent than with my personal computers. I know, intellectually, that my family needs to use these machines for their own work or entertainment, but every time it happens, I revert to the selfish little three-year-old hugging the monitor and crying "mine!"

There is a little more to my irritation than single-minded selfishness, mind you. Allowing multiple users on your Windows 95 or Windows 98 computer is always an exercise in hoop-jumping. Either you let everyone have access as a single user (always dangerous when one of your users is a curious four-year-old who likes to push buttons labeled Delete), or you have to somehow muddle through the murky multiple-user tools in Windows 9x.

Neither option had much appeal for me, nor would they for other users. The problem with multiple-user functionality in Windows 9x was that it was there but tantalizingly out of reach for all but the most serious power users.

In Windows XP, that problem has been neatly solved, as the multi-user policies are much clearer and simpler to create and manage. This functionality, available in both the Home Edition and Professional, makes dealing with multiple users in your home or corporate environment so much easier that you may actually learn to share your PC!

Understanding Multi-user Profiles

What are some of the key advantages to having multiple-user management on your computer? Multi-user support is nothing new for users of Windows NT 4 or Windows 2000, naturally, but for users coming from Windows 9x, this new functionality will offer some heady benefits.

Perhaps the most noticeable advantage is the ability for users to manage the desktop's look and feel exactly the way they want without interfering with other users' configurations. This ability may not seem all that important, but for many users it is a very big deal.

User accounts also let users keep their own files separate from the other users. This is a transparent effect, too, as all users are (from their perspective) storing their files in the My Documents folder and yet not intermingling with other users' files.

User accounts also can let the owner/administrator of the computer breathe a little bit easier because most user account scenarios will have one administrative account with the real power, and everyone else will have limited accounts. Limited accounts will let users view and modify their own data files but will not let them do anything silly like uninstall an application they didn't install in the first place. That scenario may seem rather far-fetched to some, but IT managers are painfully aware of the new and creative ways users can damage a computer's software, so any little extra security will be a big help.

Applications that have profiles that vary from user to user will be easier to use. The Internet Favorites from one user will be maintained separately from another. So will the email profiles for individual users. When Jane Doe pulls up her mail in Outlook under her account, she will see her messages rather than her fellow users'. Any application settings that can vary from user to user will be tracked and maintained, leading to a better sharing experience for all the users.

Immediate Solutions

Setting Up New Users

When Windows XP is first installed, one user is immediately created: the Administrator account. This type of account holds all the important power within Windows XP: All the software installation, user management, and security policies must be implemented from this type of account.

It is important to note that the Administrator account is not the same as the first user account that is also created during the Windows XP installation, though it is difficult to tell the difference.

During a clean install of Windows XP, the installation routine will ask for a password for the Administrator account. After that password is given, the next screen will ask for the name of the primary user account. This is *not* the Administrator account—it is the user who is the "owner" of the machine. Very often, the people who own these accounts are one and the same person, but not always.

When the primary user account is created, by default, it is categorized as a Computer Administrator type account. Notice the word *type*. This first user account has all the capabilities of the Administrator account, but it is a completely separate entity from that account.

The reason for this hair-splitting distinction is actually pretty sensible. In a home environment, you would want one of the regular users (Mom, Dad, or the brainy eight-year-old) to have a Computer Administrator type account because that user would be making all the important configuration changes to the home computer. The Administrator account becomes superfluous, but it's not like the account is taking up space.

In a corporate environment, however, there is a strong case for letting *none* of the system's users have a Computer Administrator type account. If IT management decides the computer needs some form of protection from careless or malicious users, you can give all the users a Limited type account.

In this situation, you would need the Administrator account because it would have to be available any time you needed to install software for all the users or make some other kind of sweeping system-level configuration change.

When you perform a system upgrade to Windows XP, the installation lets you choose which of any existing user accounts on your system should have the Computer Administrator rating. Or, you can create a new one of that type.

After the initial setup of the primary user, that user then has the option of creating new users for the system. Table 9.1 lists the three types of user accounts that can be created in Windows XP.

Creating a user account is easy. Remember, you must be logged in as the Administrator or a Computer Administrator type account before you can follow these steps:

1. Click Start|Control Panel to open the Control Panel window.
2. Click the User Accounts link to open the User Accounts window (see Figure 9.1).
3. Click the Create A New Account link. The Name The New Account page will appear.
4. Enter the user's given name or username into the Type A Name For The New Account field.
5. Click Next to move to the Pick An Account Type page (see Figure 9.2).
6. Click the Limited radio button to select it.
7. Click Create Account. The User Accounts page will reopen with the new user added to the list.

Table 9.1   User account types.

Type	Description
Computer Administrator	This user has full rights to install applications, manage files, manage users, and set security policies for the Windows XP system.
Limited User	This user can view all the files he or she has created, as well as any in the Shared Documents folders. This user can also make changes to his or her own account settings, such as passwords, pictures, and desktop settings.
Guest	This very limited account lets a user have rudimentary access to the computer. It is useful for tasks such as surfing the Web or checking email messages without giving the guest a full user account.

9. Work with Multiple Users

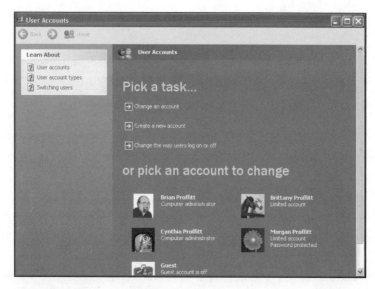

Figure 9.1   The central User Accounts window.

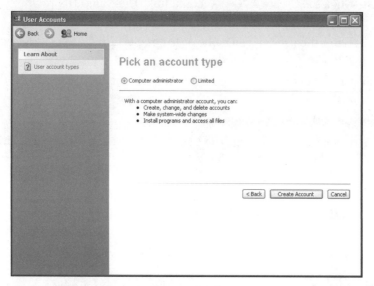

Figure 9.2   Assigning an account type.

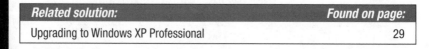

Related solution:	*Found on page:*
Upgrading to Windows XP Professional	29

Setting Up a Guest User

A nifty feature of the Windows XP multi-user system is the capability to add a Guest user account. This account would serve as a catch-all account for those users who might need some use of your computer, but not a Limited type user account.

Microsoft's online documentation provides a good example of this kind of situation: A visiting relative who just needs a quick peek at her email while she's away from home. Or, how about the coworker who's visiting from the branch office and borrowing your cubicle for the day?

The interesting thing about the Guest user account is that you don't have to create it. It's already made, in fact. You just have to activate it, as shown in the following steps:

1. Click Start|Control Panel to open the Control Panel window.

2. Click the User Accounts link to open the User Accounts window.

3. Click the Guest account icon. The Do You Want To Turn On The Guest Account? page will appear.

4. Click the Turn On The Guest Account button. The User Accounts page will reopen with the Guest account indicated as turned on.

When you no longer need a Guest account, you should turn it off again, by following these steps, to increase system security:

1. Click Start|Control Panel to open the Control Panel window.

2. Click the User Accounts link to open the User Accounts window.

3. Click the Guest account icon. The What Do You Want To Change About The Guest Account? page will appear.

4. Click the Turn Off The Guest Account link. The User Accounts page will reopen with the Guest account indicated as turned off.

Managing Users

After a non-guest user account has been set up on the Windows XP system, you can change any number of settings for the account: the account type, the password, the logon method, even the picture that's displayed on the Welcome screen and Start menu.

9. Work with Multiple Users

Managing all these settings is simple, given that they are presented in Windows XP's task-oriented fashion. All you need to do is visit the User Accounts window from the Control Panel to begin.

Administering Account Type

There are only two account types for Windows XP user accounts, and you can easily switch a user from one type to the other by following these steps:

1. Click Start|Control Panel to open the Control Panel window.

2. Click the User Accounts link to open the User Accounts window.

3. Click the account icon you want to change. The What Do You Want To Change About The [User]'s Account? page will appear, where [User] is the name of the account (see Figure 9.3).

4. Click the Change The Account Type link. The Pick A New Account Type For [User] page will appear.

5. Click a different account type radio button to select it.

6. Click the Change Account Type button. The What Do You Want To Change About The [User]'s Account? page will appear, with the new type assigned to the user.

Related solution:	Found on page:
Implementing Ctrl+Alt+Delete Logon	399

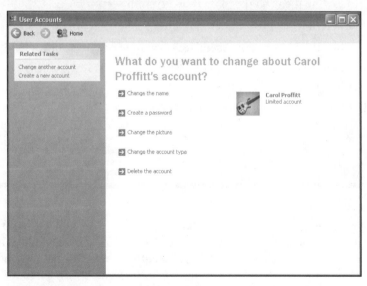

Figure 9.3   A user's central account management screen.

Managing Passwords

Of all the potential bugaboos that come with user management, none are more problematic than passwords. Passwords represent a mentality that not a lot of users seem to understand. Passwords, they acknowledge, are important, but they also seem to leave them out where anyone can see them. Still, administrators try to get the use of these valuable tools across to their users. With practice, slowly the password mentality is starting to sink in.

Interestingly enough, as security conscious as Windows XP is, passwords are *not* required for any account other than Administrator. This point is very surprising and not something you should relax about. Even if you are using your Windows XP Professional machine at home with the family, protecting your system from outside access is critically important, especially in today's environment of always-on broadband connections.

In Windows XP, passwords are also necessary if you want to use such features as the encrypted file system or privacy settings.

You should implement passwords for every user account on your system, using the following steps from a Computer Administrator account:

NOTE: *Passwords can also be set up from within the user's account.*

---

1. Click Start|Control Panel to open the Control Panel window.
2. Click the User Accounts link to open the User Accounts window.
3. Click the account icon you want to change. The What Do You Want To Change About The [User]'s Account? page will appear.
4. Click the Create A Password link to open the Create A Password For [User]'s Account page (see Figure 9.4).
5. Enter a new password in the Type A New Password field.

TIP: *Remember that passwords in Windows XP are case sensitive.*

---

6. Enter the same password in the Type The New Password Again To Confirm field.
7. Enter a word or phrase to help you remember the password in the Type A Word Or Phrase To Use As A Password Hint field.
8. Click the Create Password button. The What Do You Want To Change About The [User]'s Account? page will appear with the account now listed as Password Protected.

9. Work with Multiple Users

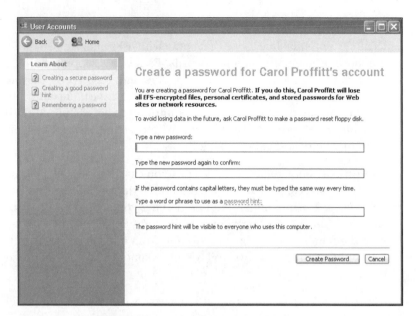

Figure 9.4   Making a new password.

When users have passwords in place, they can use them to their heart's content. Or, until they need to change passwords, whichever comes first. Passwords can be changed by the users themselves. This method is much safer. If passwords are altered by a Computer Administrator, the users will be heavily penalized. All previous access to safeguarded files, certificates, and Web sites will immediately be lost.

It is imperative, therefore, that users manage their own passwords, to ensure smooth and secure transitions. To manage passwords, follow these steps:

1. Click Start|Control Panel to open the Control Panel window.

2. Click the User Accounts link to open the User Accounts window.

3. Click your account icon. The What Do You Want To Change About Your Account? page will appear.

WARNING!   If you change another user's password as a Computer Administrator, the user will lose all access to any password-protected files, security certificates, and passwords for Web sites.

4. Click the Change My Password link to open the Create Your Password page (see Figure 9.5).

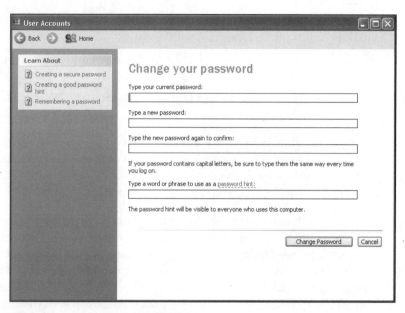

Figure 9.5   Altering your password.

5. Enter the current password in the Type Your Current Password field.

6. Enter a new password in the Type A New Password field.

7. Enter the same password in the Type The New Password Again To Confirm field.

8. Enter a word or phrase to help you remember the password in the Type A Word Or Phrase To Use As A Password Hint field.

9. Click the Change Password button to return to the What Do You Want To Change About Your Account? page.

Users also have the option of removing their passwords altogether. Doing so may not be such a great idea security-wise, but the capability is there. Just remember to let the users perform the action on their own accounts, to prevent loss of access problems. To remove a password, follow these steps:

1. Click Start|Control Panel to open the Control Panel window.

2. Click the User Accounts link to open the User Accounts window.

3. Click your account icon. The What Do You Want To Change About Your Account? page will appear.

9. Work with Multiple Users

4. Click the Remove My Password link to move to the Are You Sure You Want To Remove Your Password? page.

5. Enter the current password in the To Verify Your Identity, Type Your Current Password field.

6. Click the Remove Password button to return to the What Do You Want to Change About Your Account? page.

Because changing or removing a user's password can be a traumatic event for the user's data access, what can you do when the inevitable occurs: A user comes to you and sheepishly admits he's forgotten his password? If you reset it, you have a potential disaster.

The best solution to this problem is to take a proactive approach: Create a password reset disk that will (in an emergency) reset the user's password to something he can use to access the account. This method, however, does have a huge drawback. The password reset disk will enable anyone with that disk to access the user's account, so it is important the disk is stored under strict security. If you are willing to take this chance, follow these steps to create a password reset disk:

1. Click Start|Control Panel to open the Control Panel window.

2. Click the User Accounts link to open the User Accounts window.

3. Click your account icon. The What Do You Want To Change About Your Account? page will appear.

4. Click the Prevent A Forgotten Password link to open the Forgotten Password Wizard.

5. Click Next to move to the Create A Password Reset page.

6. Insert a blank, formatted disk into your floppy drive.

7. Click Next to move to the Current User Account Password page.

8. Type the account's password in the Current User Account Password field.

9. Click Next. The Creating Password Reset Disk page will appear and display the progress of the disk's creation.

10. When the process is finished, click Next to move to the Completing The Forgotten Password Wizard page.

11. Click Finish to close the Forgotten Password Wizard.

12. Store the password reset disk in a secure location.

Changing Logon/Logoff Method

The Windows XP Welcome screen is a pretty neat way of signing on to your system—with an emphasis on the word *pretty*. If, for whatever reason, you don't like to use the Welcome screen, you can switch the logon scheme to a more classic arrangement where the username is typed in. Just follow these steps:

1. Click Start|Control Panel to open the Control Panel window.
2. Click the User Accounts link to open the User Accounts window.
3. Click the Change The Way Users Log On Or Off link to open the Select Logon Or Logoff Options page.
4. Click the Use The Welcome Screen checkbox to deselect it.
5. Click Apply Options. The User Accounts window will reappear.

The next time you log on to the system, the "classic" logon screen will appear.

Changing the Picture

Every user account has a little picture that users can use to display a little visual icon that represents the user. A number of stock pictures are included with Windows XP, but you can use any compatible graphic file for the task.

To implement the following steps, be sure you have a Windows bitmap (.bmp), GIF89 (.gif), JPEG (.jpg), or Portable Network Graphics (.png) graphics file ready:

1. Click Start|Control Panel to open the Control Panel window.
2. Click the User Accounts link to open the User Accounts window.
3. Click your account icon. The What Do You Want To Change About Your Account? page will appear.
4. Click the Change My Picture link to open the Pick A New Picture For Your Account page (see Figure 9.6).
5. Click a picture from the displayed samples or, if you have a picture of your own, click the Browse For More Pictures link. The Open dialog box will appear in thumbnail mode (see Figure 9.7).
6. Navigate to the picture you want to use and click it to select it.
7. Click Open. The Open dialog box will close, and the What Do You Want To Change About Your Account? page will reappear.

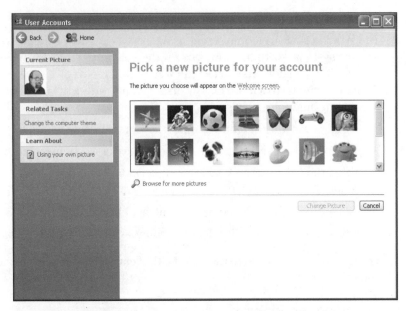

Figure 9.6   Choose a sample picture for your account.

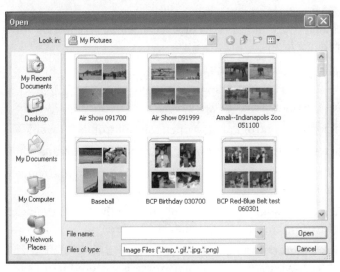

Figure 9.7   Or, pick a picture of your own.

Implementing Fast User Switching

This situation has probably happened to you before: You're sitting at your computer, minding your own business, when another person comes along and asks you if she can quickly log on and edit a file on the network. Not wanting to appear rude (though you're certainly feeling like it on the inside), you close down all your open applications, log off your account, and move aside to let the other user on to your machine.

Or, how about this home scenario: You walk into your den to check for an urgent email only to find your oldest child deeply engrossed in a very important game. The fate of the whole universe (or at least the Federation) hangs on what your little starship pilot does next, and there's no way to save the game at this point.

In both of these situations, a new feature in Windows XP called Fast User Switching will be your savior. Fast User Switching is a process that will let one user suspend operations *without shutting down any applications* and allow another user to log on and accomplish what he or she needs to do. When the second user is finished, the first user can log on and start right back where he or she was—even if it was in the middle of a game.

Performing a Fast User Switch is a piece of cake, too, as these steps demonstrate:

1. The first user should click Start|Log Off to open the Log Off Windows window.

2. Click Switch Users. All the current operations will be suspended, and the Windows XP Welcome screen will appear.

3. The second user can click another user account to log on to that account.

4. When the work is completed by the second user, he or she should click Start|Log Off. The Log Off Windows window will reappear.

5. The second user should click Log Off. He or she will be logged off, and the Windows XP Welcome screen will reappear.

6. The first user should click the original user account to log back in to the account. All the previous applications will be open, ready for you to continue.

If, for some reason, Fast User Switching has not been activated on your system, these few short steps will turn it on for you:

1. Click Start|Control Panel to open the Control Panel window.

2. Click the User Accounts link to open the User Accounts window.

3. Click the Change The Way Users Log On Or Off link to open the Select Logon Or Logoff Options page.

4. Click the Use Fast User Switching checkbox to select it.

5. Click Apply Options. The User Accounts window will reappear.

Sharing Files with Other Users

Even though users will want to have their own little fiefdoms of data, the modern workplace (and modern family) dictates that in some instances some files will need to be shared. Windows XP has an interesting feature called the Shared Documents folder.

The Shared Documents folder is much like the My Documents folder in design: a universal folder for documents that contains Music and Pictures subfolders. In this case, however, these folders can be seen by *every* user on the system. And, you can copy, move, and delete files into the Shared Documents folder just like any other folder.

To open the Shared Folder, follow these steps:

1. Click on Start|My Computer. The My Computer window will open.

2. Click on the Shared Documents link. The Shared Documents folder will appear.

TIP: To share a folder that is not in the Shared Documents folder with users on your system, you can move the folder into the Shared Documents folder.

If you want to share something more widely, you can share folders so that users across the entire network can view and edit the contents, using these steps:

1. In Windows Explorer, navigate to the folder you want to share.

2. Click the Share This Folder link. The folder's Properties dialog box will open (see Figure 9.8).

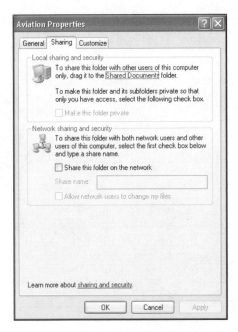

Figure 9.8   Sharing a folder with network users.

3. Click the Share This Folder On The Network checkbox to select it.

4. To allow users to edit files in this folder, confirm the Allow Network Users To Change My Files option is checked.

5. Click Apply to apply the settings.

6. Click OK to close the folder's Properties dialog box.

Related solutions:	Found on page:
Copying Files	77
Moving Files	79
Deleting Files	80

9. Work with
Multiple Users

Chapter 10

Connect to the Internet

In Brief

A friend of mine once wrote: "The Internet is the most erroneously capitalized word in the English language."

This sweeping statement makes a bit more sense when you consider his reasons for writing it. The Internet is not one single entity that exists for its own sake. The Internet is, rather, a collection of hundreds of thousands of networked machines, all working together in a loose form of organization to pass information between one another. Of course, this description is a bit long, so instead, we call this conglomeration of networked computers the Internet.

The Internet is one of those inventions that has been around for a long time but has only recently been noticed by the Public Eye; therefore, it still falls under the label "new." This is the same Public that thinks living in suburbs of identical homes is a good thing, so it can be excused for making a slight error in timing.

In truth, the Internet has been around since the sixties. In those heady days, the network was in the hands of two widely different groups: the military and the universities. Despite this mix, the network actually survived, serving as a conduit of information for academics and soldiers alike.

By the early 1990s, the Internet was being sponsored by the National Science Foundation, which could not afford to pay the bills for maintenance and upkeep of this vast network. Thus, a monumental decision was made: Let private industry foot the bill and allow commercial traffic on this heretofore noncommercial network.

That was when we, the Public, first started seeing glimmerings of the Internet as we know it today. Private content providers such as CompuServe, Delphi, and Prodigy made access to the Internet part of their connectivity packages.

These were the wild and wooly days of the Internet—when Web sites could be numbered in the hundreds, not the millions. When megasearch engines such as Yahoo and Google were only distant dreams and the entire list of known Web sites could be listed on a single Web page. When Spam was something you ate.

That was then, and this is now. The Internet has so quickly permeated our lives that it's hard to believe that only 15 percent of U.S. households have regular access to the Internet. This slow growth after nearly 10 years of public use mirrors the growth rate of another invention at the turn of the last century: the telephone.

The telephone also experienced slow growth in the first decade of its use, as only the wealthy and risk-takers were venturing to use this technology. Soon after, the proliferation of telephones in U.S. households skyrocketed, thanks to less expensive models and a better infrastructure. In less than 10 more years, 80 percent of U.S. households had telephones.

Will the Internet duplicate this pattern of growth? Perhaps. It is interesting to note that today many consumers are considering Internet connectivity as part of their criteria for buying a new computer. And, some people are even considering the location of their new home based on broadband availability.

How Best to Connect?

You just bought your new computer, and you are wondering how to go about connecting to the Internet. The simple answer? Get the fastest connection you can reasonably afford.

This response may seem like a devil-may-care answer to a serious issue, but the fact is you can't afford not to have the biggest pipe you could possibly have to connect to the Internet. This is true because the Internet has changed its content in recent years to include more multimedia, which translates into very large files. Video and audio compression technology has made the situation more tolerable, but there's no getting around the fact that the latest Britney Spears video clip or weekly database upload is going to be a multi-MB download— a lot of time to spend using a 56K modem.

If broadband is available in your area, I strongly recommend you get it. If you need some numbers, try this exercise. If you use a dial-up connection, the best way to optimize this connection is to get a second phone line for your home so that you don't tie up the first line for your teenager. If you consider that the average cost of a local Internet service provider (ISP) account is about $20/month, and the average cost of a second phone line is about $30, you will be spending $50 for just a dial-up connection. Compare this number with the average cost of a cable broadband connection, which is about $40/month, and you can see a real savings.

Even if you don't have a second phone line, the speed alone will save you enough time to justify the expense. A broadband connection may cost twice as much as a dial-up connection, but it certainly delivers far more than twice a dial-up connection's speed. For many people, the extra cost per month is worthwhile just to avoid babysitting a long download to make sure there are no disconnects.

If broadband is not available in your area or if you're just not willing to pay for it, that's okay because many alternatives for dial-up Internet connectivity are available for you.

Essentially, you can choose from two kinds of dial-up Internet connections: direct and indirect. Indirect Internet connections are provided from online media content providers, such as MSN or America Online (two little companies you may have heard of). When using one of these online services, you get more than just the Internet. Private messaging and original content are just part of the package, with Internet connectivity touted as a "feature."

AOL users make up a huge percentage of new online users every day. AOL, along with MSN, is ideal for those users who like everything in nice, neat packages. Their mail is here, their buddies are there, and so on.

If you are not as interested in packaged content and want the Internet pure and unfettered, a direct connection might be for you. This type of connection lets you dial straight into a server that is directly hooked to the Internet. No original content, nothing packaged for you. If you want email, you need to get the software and configure it yourself. Want instant messaging? Download a chat client and configure away.

Using this type of connection may sound rather bothersome, but the advantages are clear: You get to set up your window to the Internet in your way—not some other company's. You can use whatever tools you want and visit for as long as you like on any site you choose.

Direct dial-up connections can be found at the local or national level. Local Internet service providers are usually better for service and support because they are in your hometown, whereas national ISPs can provide connectivity to rural areas at an inexpensive rate.

NOTE: *For a great list of local and national ISPs that you can search by area or country code, visit* ***http://thelist.internet.com/****.*

The good news is, no matter which type of connection to the Internet you choose to obtain, Windows XP will be able to handle it thanks to its superior collection of Internet connectivity tools.

Dial-Up Networking Tools

Dial-up connectivity to the Internet is an amazing thing, if you think about it. Here, you are shoving signals from a digital device down a phone line designed to carry analog sound information and getting a coherent response in return.

It is this conversion from digital to analog and back again that enforces the speed limit many of our modem connections must endure. Regular telephone lines were not built for a huge amount of clarity, and because of that, sometimes the analog signal gets distorted and dropped. When we're talking to Mom in Topeka, it's not a big deal— we may hear a few pops and static for a second or two.

If the same distortion happens in a modem transmission, the data that was masked by that brief burst of static is lost. In a slower modem transmission, less data is lost and the redundancies built into the TCP/IP transmission protocol are usually sufficient to recover what was lost.

Imagine, though, a modem operating at twice the speed of the first modem. The same static burst occurs at the same time and duration. This time, because of the faster modem, twice the data is lost. The TCP/IP safeguards may be able to recover the data—then again, they may not.

After a certain transmission speed, the benefits of a fast connection are canceled out by all the backtracking that has to be done to recover dropped data. In most parts of the country, this speed is around 56.6 Kbaud (kilobits per second). This is why you won't find many reliable modems broadcasting faster than this speed. The problem is not the modems—it's the line on which they must broadcast.

TCP/IP has been the *de facto* transmission protocol on the Internet for many years now and has been improved to a degree that you don't need a large mainframe computer and a dedicated network line to implement it. Windows XP has done a good job in integrating TCP/IP into its toolset, too. Historically, users regarded TCP/IP as a cranky and contentious piece of software, so this is a welcome change.

The Dial-Up Connection tools can do more than dial up an ISP for an Internet connection. These tools can also connect your computer directly to a private network, which is useful when you need to contact the office and don't want to run the connection through the Internet.

Internet Connection Tools

The best connectivity tool in the Windows XP toolset is certainly the Internet Connection Wizard. This one tool will let you establish connections with established national ISPs, a local ISP, and a private network anywhere in the world, either through dial-up or Virtual Private Network (VPN).

The Internet Connectivity Wizard is a major nod to all those users who don't want to worry about all this protocol and bandwidth stuff. They just want to get connected and do all that cool stuff their friends and family are doing on the Internet. This is an admirable goal. But, before you can leap onto the Internet, you will need to figure out a few things after you establish the type of connection (dial-up or broadband) you want to use.

First, you will need to set up an account with the ISP or content provider. Most ISPs can handle account setup over the phone (which is a good thing because presumably you don't have a connection yet). When you get your account, the phone representative will tell you exactly how to connect to the Internet. Here's the basic information you will get:

• Your logon username

• Your password

• The phone number to dial

The representative may give you other information, such as mail server settings, but you can hold on to it for later.

Content providers such as AOL and MSN have very likely already sent you the means to connect in the form of those CD-ROMs you get in the mail or with the Sunday paper. Now, you can do something with those CD-ROMs other than use them as coasters!

Most of the information you would need from an ISP will be config-ured by the setup software on the CD-ROM, so you don't need to call the content provider and get things started. Just slip the disk into the drive and off you go.

If you decide to get a broadband connection, it is almost a sure bet that you will get a technician to come out to your house to install the connection because cable and DSL lines have to be physically run to your dwelling. Cable and DSL modems differ from regular modems in that they are physical components of the service provider's network and need to be registered by the provider upon installation.

When the technician comes out, he or she will configure your com-puter for you to connect to the Internet, usually through a software application that will do most of the work automatically.

In recent months, some of the larger providers have put together do-it-yourself kits for cable and DSL connections, using PPP over Ethernet (PPPoE) connectivity.

TIP: *Right after Windows XP comes out, you will need to bear with all the Internet service providers (of either type) as they come to terms with the new operating system. In many cases, there is a delay of a few weeks while the support staff members get their ducks in a row regarding how to handle a new operating system. If your ISP gives you a little grief, ask whether the company supports Windows 2000. If the representative says yes, tell him or her to help you because XP shares many of the same connectivity tools.*

Armed with this information, you can set out to connect your lonely PC to the vast and powerful Internet.

Immediate Solutions

Setting Up a Dial-Up Internet Account

You have the modem and all the information from the ISP. Now, you just need to get connected. Before getting started, you need to make sure the modem (if it's external) is connected to the computer and that the phone line is connected to the wall jack. And, make sure your modem is turned on and all the drivers are loaded.

If all that is accomplished, it's time to set up the connection. Don't be daunted by the number of steps in this procedure; this is just Windows XP's way of making sure all the correct information is supplied:

1. Click Start|Control Panel to open the Control Panel.

2. Click the Network And Internet Connections link to open the Network And Internet Connections page (see Figure 10.1).

3. Click the Set Up Or Change Your Internet Connection link to open the Internet Properties dialog box (see Figure 10.2).

4. Click Setup to open the New Connection Wizard.

5. Click Next to move to the New Connection Type page (see Figure 10.3).

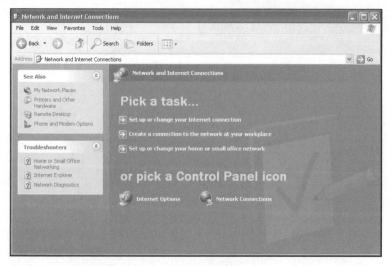

Figure 10.1   The Control Panel's networking page.

Figure 10.2   The Internet Properties dialog box.

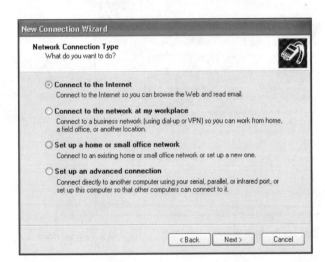

Figure 10.3   Choose the type of connection to create.

6. Click the Connect To The Internet radio button to select it.

7. Click Next to move to the Getting Ready page (see Figure 10.4).

8. Click the Set Up My Connection Manually radio button to select it.

9. Click Next to move to the Internet Connection page (see Figure 10.5).

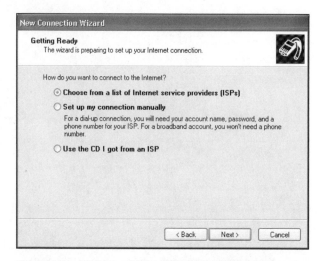

Figure 10.4   Decide which connection path to take.

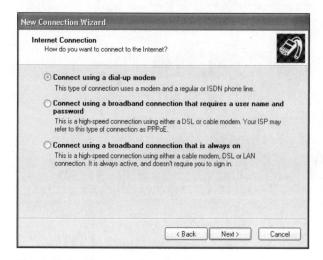

Figure 10.5   Dial-up or broadband connection setups are started here.

10. Click the Connect Using A Dial-Up Modem radio button to select it.

11. Click Next to move to the Connection Name page.

12. Enter the proper name of the ISP connection in the ISP Name field.

13. Click Next to move to the Phone Number To Dial page.

14. Enter the phone number your modem needs to contact the ISP's modem in the Phone Number field.

15. Click Next to move to the Internet Account Information page (see Figure 10.6).

16. Enter the username provided by the ISP in the User Name field.

17. Enter the password provided by the ISP in the Password field.

18. Enter the password again in the Confirm Password field.

19. Confirm the selected options for connection.

20. Click Next to move to the Completing New Connection Wizard page.

21. Click the Add A Shortcut To This Connection To The Desktop checkbox to select it.

22. Click Finish. The New Connection Wizard and Internet Properties dialog boxes will close, and a shortcut for the connection will appear on the desktop.

23. Click the Close button in the Network And Internet Connections page to close the Control Panel.

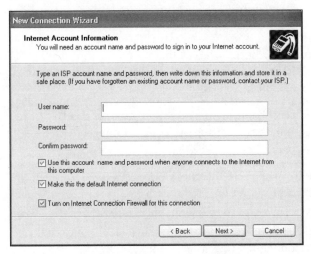

Figure 10.6   Supply the information the ISP gave you about your account.

Setting Up a Dial-Up Networking Account

Telecommuting has become a billion-dollar investment for companies around the world, as more managers and employees are discovering the benefits of working out of the home.

One key IT issue for telecommuters is how to establish connectivity to computers at the workplace. The Internet provides one easy answer, especially for messaging, because email has become ubiquitous in recent years.

But, issues such as file transfers are a bit trickier to handle. Telecommuters could send in their work via email, but problems arise with this scenario almost immediately. For instance, what if a telecommuter needs a file from the office right away? That person has to depend on the kindness and efforts of someone in the office to send the file out. Or, what if the telecommuter has sent in a file to someone who is out of the office that day but other coworkers need the file anyway?

The solution seems readily apparent: Use File Transfer Protocol (FTP) to move the files back and forth. This solution has problems, too, particularly because FTP servers sit outside the company's firewall and the office worker's network is inside—as any secure setup should be. This means that someone in the office will have to spend the time to pull down the files from the FTP server to get them inside the firewall.

Two solutions apply here: a direct dial-up connection to the office servers and a VPN connection that encrypts transmissions over existing Internet connections to establish connectivity.

Setting up a direct dial-up connection, as you can see from the following steps, is similar to setting up a dial-up Internet connection:

1. Click Start|Control Panel to open the Control Panel.
2. Click the Network And Internet Connections link to open the Network And Internet Connections page.
3. Click the Create A Connection To The Network At Your Workplace link. The New Connection Wizard will open to the Network Connection page (see Figure 10.7).
4. Click the Dial-Up Connection radio button to select it.
5. Click Next to move to the Connection Name page.
6. Enter the name of the connection in the Company Name field.
7. Click Next to move to the Phone Number To Dial page.
8. Enter the phone number your modem needs to contact the company's modem in the Phone Number field.
9. Click Next to move to the Completing New Connection Wizard page.

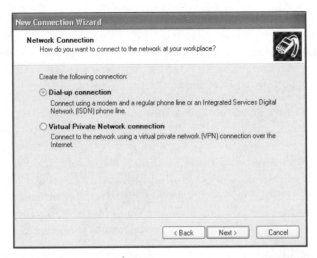

Figure 10.7   You can choose to set up a dial-up or VPN connection.

10. Click the Add A Shortcut To This Connection To The Desktop checkbox to select it.

11. Click Finish. The New Connection Wizard will close, and a shortcut for the connection will appear on the desktop.

12. Click the Close icon in the Network And Internet Connections page to close the Control Panel.

Related solution:	Found on page:
Setting Up VPN	233

Setting Up a Broadband PPPoE Internet Account

One major problem confronting broadband suppliers and users is the difficulty involved with actually setting up such an account. The process—which can involve the configuration of static IP addresses, Dynamic Host Control Protocol (DHCP), or Network Address Translation (NAT)—can be tedious and time-consuming, something which neither party wants to deal with. And, let's face it, these techniques are really best used within corporate environments, not out in the field. This point especially becomes apparent when more and more households and small businesses are using more than one computer and they all need Internet connections.

In the remote client environment that our suburbs have become, Point-to-Point Protocol (PPP) works much better. PPP was designed, after all, to establish sessions between millions of dial-up subscribers and ISP networks. PPP can authenticate users, dynamically assign IP addresses, and negotiate other connectivity parameters.

So, now some of the broadband providers are catching on to a new protocol, PPP over Ethernet (PPPoE). In a nutshell, PPPoE provides the capability to connect multiple clients at a remote site through a common device such as a cable or DSL modem. And, it does so in a way that allows access control and billing functionality in a manner similar to dial-up services using PPP. In other words, the broadband provider can now bill all the machines for the traffic they're generating.

If your broadband provider has implemented PPPoE protocols, you're in luck because Windows XP supports this technology natively. PPPoE has been deliberately made to mimic dial-up connectivity, to make it easier for users to handle. This mimicry is even apparent in the setup of PPPoE, shown in the following steps:

1. Click Start|Control Panel to open the Control Panel.
2. Click the Network And Internet Connections link to open the Network And Internet Connections page.
3. Click the Set Up Or Change Your Internet Connection link to open the Internet Properties dialog box.
4. Click Setup to open the New Connection Wizard.
5. Click Next to move to the New Connection Type page.
6. Click the Connect To The Internet radio button to select it.
7. Click Next to move to the Getting Ready page.
8. Click the Set Up My Connection Manually radio button to select it.
9. Click Next to move to the Internet Connection page.
10. Click the Connect Using A Broadband Connection That Requires A User Name And Password radio button to select it.
11. Click Next to move to the Connection Name page.
12. Enter the proper name of the ISP connection in the ISP Name field.
13. Click Next to move to the Internet Account Information page.
14. Enter the user name provided by the ISP in the User Name field.

15. Enter the password provided by the ISP in the Password field.

16. Enter the password again in the Confirm Password field.

17. Confirm the selected options for connection.

18. Click Next to move to the Completing New Connection Wizard page.

19. Click the Add A Shortcut To This Connection To The Desktop checkbox to select it.

20. Click Finish. The New Connection Wizard and Internet Properties dialog boxes will close, and a shortcut for the connection will appear on the desktop.

21. Click the Close icon in the Network And Internet Connections page to close the Control Panel.

Related solution:	Found on page:
Setting Up VPN	233

Using a Dial-Up or PPPoE Account

After you configure a dial-up account, it's a snap to use. If the dial-up connection is your system's default account to the Internet, the simple act of surfing to a Web page in Internet Explorer or requesting your email messages in Outlook Express will be enough to automatically activate the connection.

To manually start any dial-up connection, follow these steps:

1. On the desktop, double-click the shortcut icon for the connection to open the Connection dialog box.

2. Click Connect to begin the dial-up process.

After you successfully connect, the Connection dialog box will be minimized to a network icon in the notification area.

When you are finished with the connection, follow these steps:

1. Right-click the network icon in the Taskbar's notification area. The context menu will appear.

2. Click the Disconnect option. The connection will be closed, and the network icon will be removed.

Optimizing a Connection

Having dial-up connectivity on a mobile computer is pretty nice because you don't have to be tied to a single location to connect to the Internet. All you need is a phone line, and in the case of a wireless modem, not even that.

Of course, when you are traveling, your dial-up connection may run into some problems. Specifically, the first thing to go is the phone number you are dialing into. When you were at home, you just clicked the connection, and a local number was dialed. But, if you're now in Kuala Lumpur (and this is not where you live), dialing a local number isn't going to help a bit.

The bludgeon solution to this problem is to manually change the phone number to be dialed to establish the connection every time you relocate the computer. But, life is too short to be doing this all of the time.

Enter the *dialing rules*, a neat way to accommodate the different dialing needs you are likely to encounter while you and your computer are out and about. And, they're not too hard to set up, as you'll see in the following steps:

1. Click Start|Control Panel to open the Control Panel.
2. Click the Network And Internet Connections link to open the Network And Internet Connections page.
3. Click the Phone And Modem Options link to open the Phone And Modem Options dialog box (see Figure 10.8).
4. Click the New button to open the New Location dialog box (see Figure 10.9).
5. Type a name for the dialing rule in the Location Name field.
6. Click the drop-down list control for the Country/Region field to see the list of countries.
7. Click the country from which you plan to use this dialing rule to select it.
8. If the office or hotel where you will be staying uses a code to get an outside line, enter that numeric code in the appropriate fields.
9. Click Apply to apply the settings.
10. Click OK. The New Location dialog box will close, and the activated dialing rule will appear in the Locations list.

Figure 10.8 Setting dialing options.

Figure 10.9 No matter where you roam, you can always phone home.

10. Connect to the Internet

11. Click your home dialing rule if you are not actually in the new location yet to activate it.

12. Click Apply to apply the settings.

13. Click OK to close the Phone And Modem Options dialog box.

Dialing rules can assist you even when you are not using a laptop computer. One of the prolific features of twenty-first century phones is the lovely call-waiting feature. Well, it's lovely for callers. Not so wonderful for ongoing connections to the Internet, which tend to choke and die when a call-waiting notification occurs. The solution is to turn it off for the duration of the call by following these steps:

1. Click Start|Control Panel to open the Control Panel.

2. Click the Network And Internet Connections link to open the Network And Internet Connections page.

3. Click the Phone And Modem Options link to open the Phone And Modem Options dialog box.

4. Click the home dialing option to select it.

5. Click the Edit button to open the Edit Location dialog box.

6. Click the To Disable Call Waiting, Dial checkbox to select it.

7. Enter the code for disabling call waiting in the adjacent field.

8. Click Apply to apply the settings.

9. Click OK to close the Edit Location dialog box.

10. Click Apply to apply the settings.

11. Click OK to close the Phone And Modem Options dialog box.

Another modern feature of the telephone is the capability to use a phone card and bill someone else for every call you make, even (if need be) local calls. You can program this capability into the dialing rules and get every call billed to the right person (and with any luck it's not you) by following these steps:

1. Click Start|Control Panel to open the Control Panel.

2. Click the Network And Internet Connections link to open the Network And Internet Connections page.

3. Click the Phone And Modem Options link to open the Phone And Modem Options dialog box.

4. Click the dialing option to which you wish to add calling cards to select it.

5. Click the Edit button to open the Edit Location dialog box.

6. Click the Calling Card tab to open the Calling Card page (see Figure 10.10).

7. Click a calling card option from the list presented or click the New button. The New Calling Card dialog box will appear (see Figure 10.11).

8. Enter a name for the calling card in the Calling Card Name field.

9. Using the instructions from your calling card, enter the commands and codes necessary to use this card for long-distance, international, and local calls in the appropriate pages of this dialog box.

10. Click Apply to apply the settings.

11. Click OK. The New Calling Card dialog box will close, and the new calling card will be selected in the Card Types list.

12. If you have not done so, enter the Account Number and Personal ID Number for your card in the appropriate fields.

13. Click Apply to apply the settings.

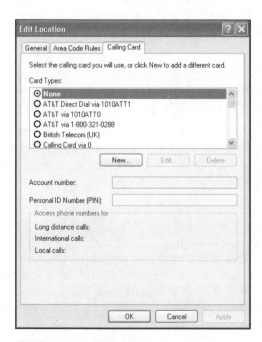

Figure 10.10   Charge those calls away!

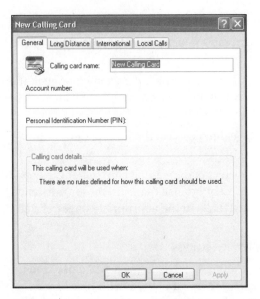

Figure 10.11   Set up any calling card for your dial-up connection.

14. Click OK to close the Edit Location dialog box.

15. Click Apply to apply the settings.

16. Click OK to close the Phone And Modem Options dialog box.

Sharing an Internet Account

More and more homes and small businesses are using multiple computers every day. This phenomenon has been brought about by recent strong economies and the sheer need for everyone in the home
or business to work on a computer at any given time.

Despite this trend, however, still only one pipe is running out to the
Internet from any given home or business. This statement may gener-
alize too much, but it is true enough for this discussion. The fact of
the matter is, the economics of having a separate connection to every
PC at a particular location rules out this possibility for all but the
wealthiest users. And, even the wealthiest users would decline this
method when they saw how easily they could share a single connection to the Internet between all computers.

Sharing an Internet account used to involve strange and arcane ritu-
als in IP configuration and network card management. The Network
Setup Wizard will set up a shared connection in just minutes.

You do need to do some preparation before running the Network Setup Wizard. First, you need to be connected to the Internet—ideally, through a broadband connection, though a dial-up connection will work just as well.

If you have a dial-up connection, the connection to the Internet must be live when you start the wizard. Also, your computer must be connected to the others on the network, and all networking equipment must be on. Don't worry if you can't see the other computers on the network in My Network Places; that's what the Network Setup Wizard is going to fix.

If you are connected to the Internet through a broadband connection (for instance, a cable modem), you will need to add some additional equipment to the PC that is directly connected to the cable modem. Specifically, you will need to add a second network card to that PC. Here's why: To connect to your cable modem, you have been using a network card and cable. Because you are also going to be part of a network, you need a second card to connect to the other computers, most likely through a hub.

TIP: *You should carefully note which card is connected to the network and which is connected to the cable or DSL modem. This information will be useful during the following procedure.*

After you install the second network card and connect it to the rest of the home network, you can start the Network Setup Wizard.

TIP: *For ease of use, you should try to run this wizard first on the PC connected to the Internet directly. By making this computer the "core" of your network, you will simplify the setup of the other computers.*

To set up a shared Internet connection, follow these steps:

1. Click Start|Control Panel to open the Control Panel.
2. Click the Network And Internet Connections link to open the Network And Internet Connections page.
3. Click the Network Connections link to open the Network Connections page (see Figure 10.12).
4. Click the Set Up A Home Or Small Office Network link to open the Network Setup Wizard.
5. Click Next to move to the Before You Continue page.
6. Review the instructions and click Next. The Select A Connection Method page will appear (see Figure 10.13).

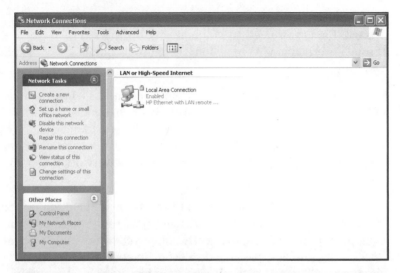

Figure 10.12   All the network connections on your computer are listed here.

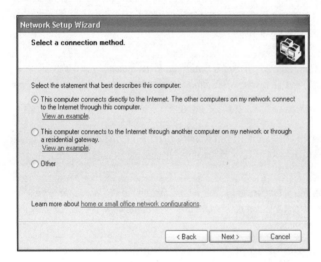

Figure 10.13   Inform Windows XP how your network is physically configured.

7. Click the option that is appropriate to your setup.

TIP: *If you're not clear what these options signify, click the View An Example link to see a diagram of what the options mean.*

---

8. Click Next to move to the Select Your Internet Connection page.

9. Select the connection tied to the network card that is connected to the cable modem or represents the primary dial-up Internet connection.

10. Click Next to move to the Give This Computer A Description And Name page.

11. Enter a descriptive phrase for the computer in the Computer Description field.

12. Enter a network name for the computer in the Computer Name field.

13. Click Next to move to the Name Your Network page.

14. Enter a name for your network in the Workgroup Name field.

15. Click Next to move to the Ready To Apply Network Settings page (see Figure 10.14).

16. Review the settings and click Next. You will need to wait as the network settings are applied, and then the You're Almost Done screen will appear (see Figure 10.15).

17. Click the Create A Network Setup Disk radio button to select it.

18. Click Next to move to the Insert The Disk You Want To Use page.

19. Insert a blank, formatted floppy disk into the disk drive.

20. Click Next. The network setup file will be copied to the floppy disk, and the Completing The Network Setup Wizard page will appear.

21. Click Finish to close the Network Setup Wizard.

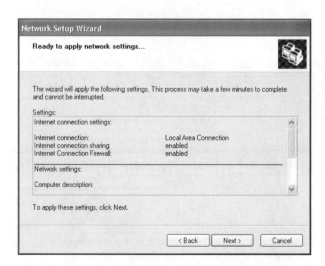

Figure 10.14   Review these settings carefully before continuing.

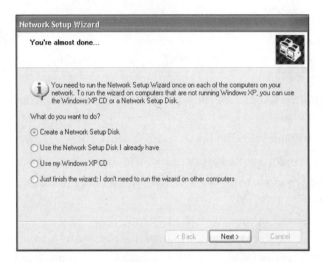

Figure 10.15   After the first computer is configured, you have to pass these
settings to the other computers on the network.

With the Setup Disk, you can now go around to all the different computers on your network and set up the shared connection by following these few easy steps:

1. Insert the disk into the client Windows computer's floppy drive.

2. Using Windows Explorer, open a window for the floppy drive.

3. Double-click the Netsetup.exe file. The Network Setup will be started and the settings on the Windows computer automatically configured.

Related solution:	Found on page:
Installing New Hardware	131

Configuring the Internet Connection Firewall

By default, the Internet Connection Firewall (ICF) will be enabled any time you create a connection to the Internet. Firewalls have become a necessary part of conducting business on the Internet, thanks to the efforts of a few demented people who enjoy nothing more than trying to take over machines for their own purposes.

Firewalls basically work on the principle that every incoming signal hitting your computer has to be requested by you first or come from a trusted source. Unsolicited calls to your machine are immediately killed off because they might be something you won't like.

This description is a drastic oversimplification of what a firewall does, but it's accurate nonetheless. Firewalls are not perfect and they can be fooled. The good news is, the average Internet user has nothing on his or her system that a cracker (a hacker with less-than-pure intentions) would want anyway.

Basically, crackers are looking for computers running Internet services, such as a Web, FTP, or mail server. Getting their electronic hands onto one of these babies is the real goal for crackers because they can subvert them to their own ends.

NOTE: *During the writing of this book, I had to set an FTP server to anonymous logon status for a few hours to accommodate a client. I received the files I was waiting for—and discovered no fewer than five users had sniffed out my server and were using it as a dumping ground for some illicit files.*

If you are not running any of this kind of software on your Windows XP machine, you should have nothing to worry about from active attacks. (Email viruses are another story.) It's still a good idea to keep the firewall in place, just in case.

If you do decide to run an Internet service on your computer, you will have to open the firewall to allow unsolicited traffic to hit your server. Otherwise, the firewall will still keep everything out.

You can change the firewall configuration by following these simple steps:

1. Click Start|Control Panel to open the Control Panel.
2. Click the Network And Internet Connections link to open the Network And Internet Connections page.
3. Click the Network Connections link to open the Network Connections page.
4. Click the connection for which you want to alter the firewall settings to select it.
5. Click the Change Settings Of This Connection link to open the connection's Properties dialog box.

6. Click the Advanced tab to open the Advanced page (see Figure 10.16).

7. Click the Settings button to open the Advanced Settings dialog box (see Figure 10.17).

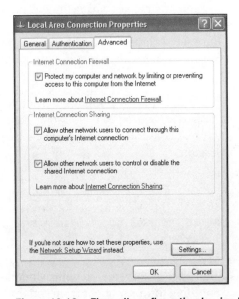

Figure 10.16   Firewall configuration begins here.

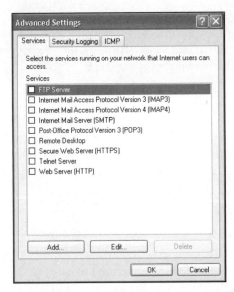

Figure 10.17   Choose the services you want to allow through the firewall.

8. Click a service checkbox. The service is selected, and the Service Settings dialog box will open.

9. Confirm the settings and click OK to close the Service Settings dialog box.

10. Click OK to close the Advanced Settings dialog box.

11. Click OK to close the connection Properties dialog box.

Chapter 11

Network XP for Small Businesses

In Brief

The age of the middle-sized business is waning in these, the early days of the twenty-first century. The pattern is clear: Either businesses are becoming gargantuan in size, through growth and acquisition, or they are breaking up into smaller and smaller units, such as sole proprietorships and limited partnerships. Mid-sized organizations are a slowly dwindling breed.

Technology has made this divergence possible because individual workers no longer need a larger organization to provide the resources required to do their jobs. In the past, only a company of a certain size could afford to put computers on all the employees' desks because the computers were big, slow, and expensive. When computers became less expensive and were no longer tied to big, expensive mainframes, a more independent type of worker began to emerge. Now, more types of work could be done on the same machine. Programming different mainframe applications became unnecessary.

The success of the Internet has made workers even more independent. Now, their machines can not only perform most kinds of tasks that are thrown at them, but they also can perform those tasks in any physical location.

But, moving the location of a computer still does not preclude the need to keep that machine connected to others. As more computers leave their centralized office locations, the need for better and smaller networks steadily grows.

Why Networks Aren't Just for the Giants Anymore

Here's a statistic for you: As of late 2000, 660,000 homes had added computer networks. According to the Yankee Group, that number will grow to about 1.6 million homes by the end of the year 2001, and to 9.5 million homes by 2003. Nearly 10 million home networks in the space of the next two years. That's quite a level of growth, one that Windows XP has clearly been designed to capitalize on.

The reason for all this prolific growth of networks is, of course, the Internet. Because PCs can readily communicate with the world, people want to make sure that all their PCs can connect to this wonderful tool.

Beyond that desire for connection, there is the simple "teenager's phone" effect. For the same reason parents wind up getting an additional phone (and perhaps even an additional phone line) for their teenaged children, people are becoming compelled to purchase second PCs for their homes. The reason for this need is not just teenagers, mind you. Perhaps one machine has to be designated as work-only for tax purposes. Maybe one PC is a desktop unit, and the other is a more portable laptop with a wireless connection so that someone can work while watching TV in the family room.

The reasons for getting a second PC are as varied as the families who own them, but one common purpose draws these people to creating a network with these multiple-home computers: All the users want to connect to the Internet. They want to share printers. They want to share.

Home users are now learning what business users have known for quite some time: The easier it is to share information, the faster they can get work done.

The way computers can talk to each other has improved in recent years as well. Computers, locked away in their little metal cases, were never really built to talk to each other very easily. Networking computers was less a problem of physically connecting the computers than actually getting the computers to speak with each other. Common protocols had to be established. The language in which the computers spoke to each other had to be the same; otherwise, the whole connection was pointless.

Naturally, protocols still exist today. Instead of removing this particular problem, recent operating systems have found ways to make protocol management much easier and more transparent for the user to manage. In some cases, the networking tools in the operating system can set up all the protocols and network addresses for you. This is most definitely the case in Windows XP. Using the Network Setup Wizard, you can put together just about any kind of small network you can think of. Just plug everything in and tell the wizard how you would like things to work. This one simple tool has taken away a lot of the mystery surrounding network setups. But, you still need to do some work. If you are going to put together a small network, what kind of network will it be?

Initial Network Preparation

Networks are also becoming more prolific because they are so easy to set up. No longer do you need a master's degree in computer science to figure out how to hook computers together. Most new PCs have preinstalled network cards, and those that don't can usually accept one with ease.

After you get the network cards in place, the hard part is over. A simple connection of Category V network cable from one computer to another is all you need to complete the network.

Ah, but you have some choices here. You can't just connect the cables to all the computers like a giant spider web and hope everything works. No, you must do some planning so you know what kind of network you're going to have.

The most basic kind of network you can set up with Windows XP's Network Setup Wizard is the peer-to-peer network. In this network, each computer is connected to a central Ethernet hub, forming a sort of star with its physical layout. Each computer shares an equal status on the network—no one computer is in charge.

Peer-to-peer networks are becoming a very popular configuration option for configuring networks, even across the Internet. File-sharing services such as Aimster and BearShare are macro examples of efficient peer-to-peer network configurations. If your computer is running Aimster, it essentially becomes just one more peer in the Aimster network, allowing others to share specific files on your PC while you go out and acquire files from them.

On the much smaller scale of your small network, one computer might be connected to another network, so this computer will act as a bridge to that separate network and coordinate communications between the two networks. If this configuration sounds vaguely familiar to you, it should. It is exactly the same configuration described for Internet Connection Sharing, which was reviewed in Chapter 10. If you followed the steps to share an Internet account in the preceding chapter, you have also set up a peer-to-peer network.

Another small network setup you can configure with Windows XP is one with multiple Internet connections. This configuration is useful if you need every machine on your network to have an independent connection to the Internet and have made such arrangements with your ISP. The main advantage to this kind of configuration (and the reason that many small businesses need it) is that you don't have to leave the computer connected to the Internet turned on all the time for the others on the network to access the Internet.

Interestingly enough, even though Windows XP will support this kind of network, Microsoft does not really recommend you do so. There are security risks and you will have to implement workarounds to make it work.

Because each computer is directly connected to the Internet, you have to make sure every computer is firewalled. Besides the extra time and effort in configuring all these firewalls, this safety precaution will come with another price of its own: File and printer sharing will be difficult with all these individual firewalls. You can find a way around this problem, fortunately. In Windows XP, file and printer sharing is accomplished through the TCP/IP protocol, which is exactly the protocol a firewall is going to try to stop. You can configure another protocol (Microsoft recommends IPX/SPX) to handle the duties of file and printer sharing, which the firewall will cheerfully ignore.

Physically setting up this kind of network is pretty much the same as setting up a peer-to-peer network. Each computer is connected to a central Ethernet hub. Instead of being connected to a single computer on the network, the cable or DSL modem is connected directly to the hub as well, becoming a component of the network that everyone can see.

A third approach to setting up a small network would be to use a device called a residential gateway. Residential gateways serve two functions: They let multiple computers share a single Internet connection and can also act as hardware-based firewalls, which will let you have extra security. This sort of setup also lets you connect to the Internet without leaving one computer always turned on and lets you use Universal Plug and Play to configure the Internet connection from any computer in the network. The physical setup for this type of network is identical to that for multiple Internet connections—except that between the hub and the DSL/cable modem is the residential gateway device.

To use this configuration, you have to go out and buy a new device, so it will hit your wallet a bit, but the cost is not too bad. Prices start at $89 U.S. for baseline models, which can support 32 computers and up to 128 users right out of the box.

You can see that none of these setups are particularly complex, which is all part of the plan. Complexity is something all of us could do without.

You can choose other types of networks, too, using different mediums of transmission than twisted-pair wiring. Wireless networks are becoming very popular, especially in the home, where people are reluctant to knock holes in walls to string CatV wires. Wireless networks solve the problem of computer portability within a home, but they also add their own share of quirks. Distances, walls, and electrical interference all have to be taken into account.

Windows XP makes the use of wireless quite a bit easier with its wireless management tools. After a wireless network card is installed on your computer, Windows XP has an automatic wireless configuration tool to get you up and running.

Another networking medium that garners little attention but is nonetheless useful is an infrared (IR) connection. Infrared has been used to transmit and receive information for quite some time. We use it daily in our television remote controls. In the IT world, IR has gained popularity due to its widespread use in handheld personal digital assistants (PDAs), such as the PalmPilot or PocketPC.

Using IR can still be a cantankerous affair, and it won't set any speed records. But, for systems running low on ports to connect to, IR is a nice option to fall back to.

Immediate Solutions

Setting Up Multiple Internet Connections

When we talk about Internet Connection Sharing and other methods to share a pipe to the Internet, we are making the assumption that this is all well and good with your ISP. Many ISPs actually frown on using one Internet account for multiple computers because you are essentially increasing the amount of traffic on their network for the price of one account.

On the other hand, there is typically very little way this sort of setup can be detected. If your connected computer is assigned an IP address from your ISP, any traffic coming out of your network is going to appear to come from that one IP address. All the other computers are essentially invisible to the Internet. Most ISPs realize that strictly enforcing a one-account-per-computer policy is really a fool's game, so they usually take the approach that if any user decides to configure a network in this manner, as far as service and support goes, the user is on his or her own.

You should take this situation into account when you decide to set up your network. If you're not comfortable with losing service and support from your ISP, or whatever other penalty the ISP might have in store, you can choose to get an account for every computer.

Running multiple accounts through a single Internet connection device such as a cable or DSL modem is not as scary a proposition as Microsoft wants you to believe. Doing it this way raises two main concerns: Make sure every computer in the network is individually firewalled, and make sure you can implement some kind of file and printer sharing through these firewalls.

Knowing that file and printer sharing is a big marketing strategy for Microsoft, of course, you would expect it to be a bit squeamish with any network configuration that might inadvertently preclude this option.

First, let's step through the procedure to get the network set up. Then, we'll discuss how to get around that file and printer sharing sand trap. These first steps (which mirror those used to set up Internet Connection Sharing) are shown here:

1. Click Start|Control Panel to open the Control Panel.

2. Click the Network And Internet Connections link to open the Network And Internet Connections page.

3. Click the Set Up Or Change Your Home Or Small Office Network link to open the Network Setup Wizard.

4. Click Next to move to the Before You Continue page.

5. Review the instructions and click Next to move to the Select A Connection Method page.

6. Click the Other radio button to select it.

7. Click Next to move to the Other Internet Connection Methods page (see Figure 11.1).

8. Click the This Computer Connects To The Internet Directly Or Through A Network Hub radio button to select it.

9. Click Next to move to the Select Your Internet Connection page.

10. Select the connection tied to the network card that is connected to the cable modem or represents the primary dial-up Internet connection.

11. Click Next to move to the This Network Configuration Is Not Recommended page (see Figure 11.2).

12. Read the warnings (which repeat the issues outlined at the beginning of this section) and click Next. The Give This Computer A Description And Name page will appear.

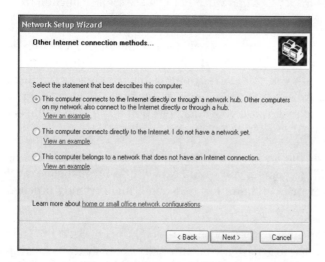

Figure 11.1 More connection methods to choose from.

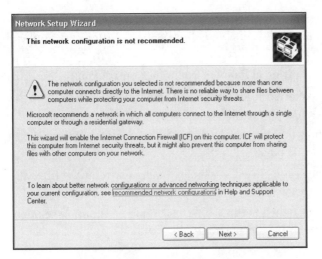

Network Setup Wizard

This network configuration is not recommended.

⚠ The network configuration you selected is not recommended because more than one computer connects directly to the Internet. There is no reliable way to share files between computers while protecting your computer from Internet security threats.

Microsoft recommends a network in which all computers connect to the Internet through a single computer or through a residential gateway.

This wizard will enable the Internet Connection Firewall (ICF) on this computer. ICF will protect this computer from Internet security threats, but it might also prevent this computer from sharing files with other computers on your network.

To learn about better network configurations or advanced networking techniques applicable to your current configuration, see recommended network configurations in Help and Support Center.

[< Back] [Next >] [Cancel]

Figure 11.2   Don't let this screen give you the heebie-jeebies.

13. Enter a descriptive phrase for the computer in the Computer Description field.

14. Enter a network name for the computer in the Computer Name field.

15. Click Next to move to the Name Your Network page.

16. Enter a name for your network in the Workgroup Name field.

17. Click Next to move to the Ready To Apply Network Settings page.

18. Review the settings and click Next. You will need to wait as the network settings are applied, and then the You're Almost Done screen will appear.

19. Click the Create Setup Disk radio button to select it.

20. Click Next to move to the Insert The Disk You Want To Use page.

21. Insert a blank, formatted floppy disk into the disk drive.

22. Click Next. The network setup file will be copied to the floppy disk, and the Completing The Network Setup Wizard page will appear.

23. Click Finish to close the Network Setup Wizard.

Using the Network Setup disk and the steps you learned in Chapter 10, you can now set up the necessary network configurations on the other computers in your network.

For Windows XP machines on your network, make sure your Internet Connection Firewall is enabled after the new settings are applied by using these steps:

1. Click Start|Control Panel to open the Control Panel.
2. Click the Network And Internet Connections Link to open the Network And Internet Connections page.
3. Click the Network Connections link to open the Network Connections page.
4. Click the connection for which you want to alter the firewall settings to select it.
5. Click the Change Settings Of This Connection option to open the connection's Properties dialog box.
6. Click the Advanced tab to open the Advanced page.
7. Confirm the Protect My Computer And Network By Limiting And Preventing Access To This Computer From The Internet checkbox is selected.
8. Click OK to close the connection's Properties dialog box.

If computers on your network use another version of Windows, you will need to enable the firewalls on those systems accordingly, even if you need to purchase and install third-party firewall software.

As Microsoft warned you, you will immediately notice an inability to share files and devices on your network after this configuration is in place because file and printer sharing uses the TCP/IP protocol by default—the one protocol that firewalls are going to try their hardest to cut off.

The solution to this problem is not too difficult: Just use another protocol to handle the file and printer sharing. IPX/SPX is a good one because most firewalls are going to ignore it. Getting this protocol to carry the file and printer sharing duties is a bit involved, but nothing you can't handle, as you can see in the following steps:

1. Click Start|Control Panel to open the Control Panel.
2. Click the Network And Internet Connections Link to open the Network And Internet Connections page.
3. Click the Network Connections link to open the Network Connections page.
4. Click the connection for small network to select it.

5. Click the Change Settings Of This Connection option to open the connection's Properties dialog box.

6. Click the Install button to open the Select Network Component Type dialog box (see Figure 11.3).

7. Click Protocol to select it.

8. Click the Add button to open the Select Network Protocol dialog box (see Figure 11.4).

9. Click NWLink IPX/SPX/NetBIOS Compatible Transport Protocol to select it.

10. Click OK to close the Select Network Protocol and Select Network Component Type dialog boxes.

11. Click Close to close the connection's Properties dialog box.

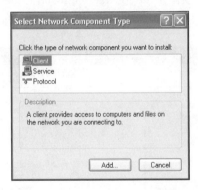

Figure 11.3   You can add different components to your network here.

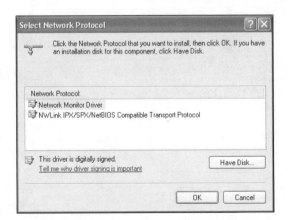

Figure 11.4   Choose the new network protocol.

Now that the IPX/SPX protocol is installed on this computer, you will need to give the file and printer sharing duties to it, as shown in the following steps:

1. In the Network Connections page, click Advanced|Advanced Settings to open the Advanced Settings dialog box (see Figure 11.5).

2. Click the connection in which you want to change the File and Printer Sharing protocol to select it.

3. Click the Internet Protocol (TCP/IP) checkbox under the File And Printer Sharing For Microsoft Networks category to clear the option.

4. Click OK to close the Advanced Settings dialog box.

You will have to repeat the procedures to add IPX/SPX protocols to every other machine in your network. After you accomplish this task, you will have file and printer sharing despite the multiple firewalls.

Related solution:	*Found on page:*
Sharing an Internet Account	196

Figure 11.5   Assigning tasks to protocols.

Using a Residential Gateway

Between the two extremes of Internet Connection Sharing and multiple Internet connections lies the configuration compromise of using a residential gateway. Despite the name, the residential gateway is an affordable solution for small businesses that want to share a single connection to the Internet. By offering native support within Windows XP for these devices, Microsoft has made installing them a breeze.

Ironically, given their label, it is not at all clear whether you should use residential gateways in the home. For a network of two to four PCs, a gateway might be a bit of overkill. There's no harm in getting one, though, if you are determined not to leave a computer on 24/7.

When the gateway is installed on your network, you'll need to run the Network Setup Wizard as you did in setting up multiple and shared Internet connections. This time, you will be configuring your network in a different way with the same tool, as seen in the following steps:

1. Click Start|Control Panel to open the Control Panel.

2. Click the Network And Internet Connections link to open the Network And Internet Connections page.

3. Click the Set Up Or Change Your Home Or Small Office Network link to open the Network Setup Wizard.

4. Click Next to move to the Before You Continue page.

5. Review the instructions and click Next. The Select A Connection Method page will appear.

6. Click the This Computer Connects To The Internet Through Another Computer On My Network Or Through A Residential Gateway radio button to select it.

7. Click Next to move to the Give This Computer A Description And Name page.

8. Enter a descriptive phrase for the computer in the Computer Description field.

9. Enter a network name for the computer in the Computer Name field.

10. Click Next to move to the Name Your Network page.

11. Enter a name for your network in the Workgroup Name field.

12. Click Next to move to the Ready To Apply Network Settings page.

13. Review the settings and click Next. You will need to wait as the network settings are applied, and then the You're Almost Done screen will appear.

14. Click the Create Setup Disk radio button to select it.

15. Click Next to move to the Insert The Disk You Want To Use page.

16. Insert a blank, formatted floppy disk into the disk drive.

17. Click Next. The network setup file will be copied to the floppy disk, and the Completing The Network Setup Wizard page will appear.

18. Click Finish to close the Network Setup Wizard.

Configuring Wireless Networking

Wireless connectivity is becoming more and more prevalent in home and small office settings because the technology is getting more stable and easier to use than stringing wire. Most wireless hardware settings come with their own protocol software, and for the most part, you should use it to implement the communication between your computer and the rest of the network.

If your wireless connection device supports the Wireless Zero Configuration Service, you can use Windows XP to configure your wireless device instead; doing so will give you more seamless control of your network.

NOTE: *For an excellent explanation of Zero Configuration, visit **www.isoc.org/inet2000/ cdproceedings/3c/3c_3.htm**.*

What's also interesting to note is that Windows XP now supports the IEEE 802.1x wireless protocol, which means that you can move your computer into any wireless network that supports 802.1x and be instantly part of that network!

If you decide to use Windows XP to handle your wireless network instead of third-party tools, you will need to turn on the automatic configuration tools, as shown here:

1. Click Start|Control Panel to open the Control Panel.

2. Click the Network And Internet Connections link to open the Network And Internet Connections page.

3. Click the Network Connections link to open the Network Connections page.

4. Click the connection that reaches the wireless network to select it.

5. Click the Change Settings Of This Connection option to open the connection's Properties dialog box.

6. Click the Wireless Networks tab to open the Wireless Networks page.

7. Click the Use Windows To Configure My Wireless Network Settings checkbox to select it.

8. Click OK to close the connection's Properties dialog box.

If you need to add a new wireless network to your settings, you continue working with the connection's Properties dialog box and add the new settings as follows:

1. In the Wireless Networks page, click Add to open the Wireless Network Properties dialog box.

2. Enter the network's name in the Service Set Identifier field.

3. Enter the wireless network key in the Wired Equivalent Privacy field.

4. Click the type of wireless network you desire to select it.

5. Click OK to close the Wireless Network Properties dialog box.

6. Click OK to close the connection's Properties dialog box.

Implementing Infrared Networking

If you are fortunate enough to have an infrared port on your computer (and if that port is easily accessible by other devices and not hidden under a desk like mine), you can use it to communicate with various devices that use IR—cameras, printers, even other computers.

Setting up IR support is easy. When Windows XP was first installed, the infrared transceiver on your computer was likely found and attached to a specific communications port (COM1 or COM2). If you have added a transceiver recently, use the Add New Hardware Wizard to install the device on your system. The only difference in installing this device is that you need to be sure to assign a communications port to the device so it will function properly.

After the transceiver is installed, connecting to IR devices is simply a matter of aligning the devices' IR ports (about 2 to 3 feet apart) so they are inline with each other. The IR ports will detect each other, and the connection will be established. In the case of an infrared printer, the connection is automatic if the printer is installed. For transferring photos from a digital camera, you will need to change one setting as follows to allow the photos to be downloaded:

1. Click Start|Control Panel to open the Control Panel.

2. Click the Network And Internet Connections Link to open the Network And Internet Connections page.

3. Click Wireless Links to open the Wireless Link dialog box.

4. Click the Image Transfer tab to open the Image Transfer page.

5. Click the Use Wireless Link To Transfer Images From A Digital Camera To Your Computer checkbox to select it.

6. Click OK to close the Wireless Link dialog box.

If you plan to use your IR link to transfer files you will need to implement the following steps:

1. After you align your computers' IR ports, open the Windows Explorer.

2. Navigate to the files you wish to transfer.

3. Click the files to select them.

4. Drag the selected files to the Wireless Link icon in the Notification Area of the taskbar.

5. Release the mouse button to transfer the files to the other computer.

TIP: *You can also use the Send To option in the file's context menu to transfer the file via infrared link.*

Related solution:	Found on page:
Installing New Hardware	131

Incorporating Network Bridges

If your computer is part of a larger network, chances are good that your computer may be connected to one node of the network with one connection and to another node with another connection. Perhaps one of the nodes is wired, and the other is wireless.

If you need to connect these two nodes, you can bridge them through your computer and create one larger integrated network by following these steps:

1. Click Start|Control Panel to open the Control Panel.

2. Click the Network And Internet Connections link to open the Network And Internet Connections page.

3. Click the Network Connections link to open the Network Connections page.

4. Holding the Ctrl key, click the connections you want to bridge to select them.

5. Right-click one of the connections. The context menu will appear.

6. Click the Bridge Connections menu option. The connections will be bridged.

Migrating Users with the Files And Settings Transfer Wizard

If one constant exists in the universe, it is that there is always change. Even when you think change will never occur. A good example is Niagara Falls, which conveys a sense of permanence in its sheer size and power. The Falls themselves have only been in existence for a mere 12,000 years, which is not very long on the geologic time scale. As time goes by, the Falls are eroding the top of the Niagara Escarpment, a huge sheet of cap rock that has made the water flow over the huge falls instead of creating a less dramatic flow of water through the softer shale below. Even that cap rock is not impervious to the constant effect of the Falls, and little by little, the Falls have slowly moved south, farther and farther up the Niagara River.

In around 900 years, scientists predict, the American Falls will no longer exist, as the neighboring Horseshoe Falls erodes itself farther south and cuts off the flow of water to the American Falls. And, some-day this singular Falls will eventually back itself far enough to the south that it will no longer have the hard cap rock to contend with and will create for itself a much less dramatic slope in the softer shale and mud of the Upper Niagara region.

If even Niagara Falls is not a constant, what chance will you have to keep your users in one place for very long? If change is a part of life, then it is certainly the motto of small and big businesses. Users are promoted. Offices are relocated. IT managers have major headaches.

One tool of Windows XP that can help break the cycle of pain that comes with every user change is the File And Settings Transfer Wizard. This wizard will record every important setting that exists on your current computer and allow you to transfer those settings to a new computer. Even your personal files located in My Documents and the other Windows folders will be copied to the new machine, as you will see in the following steps:

1. Click Start|All Programs|Accessories|System Tools|Files And Settings Transfer Wizard. The Files and Settings Transfer Wizard will open.

2. Click Next to move to the Which Computer Is This? page (see Figure 11.6).

3. Click the Old Computer radio button to select it.

4. Click Next. The wizard will begin to gather your settings, and the Select A Transfer Method page will appear (see Figure 11.7).

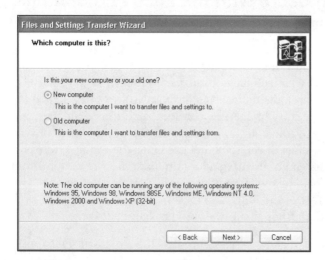

Figure 11.6   Old or new computer?

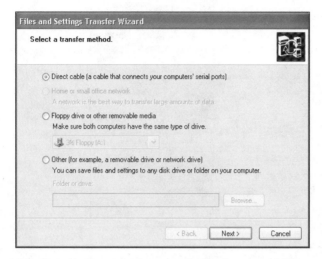

Figure 11.7   Choose how to transfer the files and settings.

5. Click the option appropriate for your situation to select it.

6. Click Next to move to the What Do You Want To Transfer? page (see Figure 11.8).

7. Click the transfer option you want to affect to select it.

8. Click Next to move to The Install Programs On Your New Computer page.

9. Review the list of applications the wizard has indicated you will need to install on your new computer.

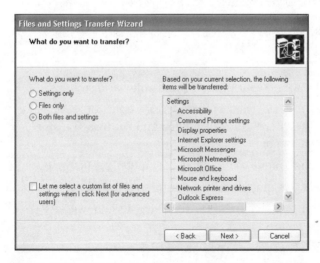

Figure 11.8   Selecting the files and settings to transfer.

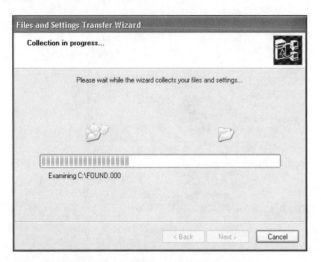

Figure 11.9   Collecting the data for transfer.

10. Click Next. The Collection In Progress page will appear, marking the progress of the data gathering (see Figure 11.9).

11. When the Completing The Collection Phase page appears, click Finish to close the Files And Settings Transfer Wizard.

Now that the settings and files have been gathered, you can run the same wizard on the new computer and apply them on the new machine.

TIP: *If you are transferring files and settings from a non-Windows XP machine, run the Files And Settings Wizard on the destination machine first and tell the wizard you need a Wizard disk. The wizard will then step you through the procedure to create a Wizard disk that can be run on Windows 98, 98SE, ME, or 2000.*

To install settings on your new machine, follow these steps:

1. Click Start|All Programs|Accessories|System Tools|Files And Settings Transfer Wizard. The Files And Settings Transfer Wizard will open.

2. Click Next to move to the Which Computer Is This? page.

3. Click the Old Computer radio button to select it.

4. Click Next to move to the Do You Have A Windows XP CD? page (see Figure 11.10).

5. Click the I Don't Need The Wizard Disk radio button to select it.

Files and Settings Transfer Wizard

Do you have a Windows XP CD?

You will also need to run this wizard on your old computer. You can either create a wizard disk to use on your old computer, or use the wizard from the Windows XP CD.

To create a Wizard Disk, insert a blank, formatted disk into this computer's disk drive. Make sure the old computer has the same type of drive.

◉ I want to create a Wizard Disk in the following drive:

3½ Floppy (A:)

○ I already have a Wizard Disk

○ I will use the wizard from the Windows XP CD

○ I don't need the Wizard Disk. I have already collected my files and settings from my old computer.

< Back   Next >   Cancel

Figure 11.10   You can choose how you want to set up the network
              configuration on other computers in the network.

6. Click Next to move to the Where Are The Files And Settings? page.

7. Click the option that matches the location of your gathered files
    and settings.

8. Click Next. The Transfer In Progress page will appear, the
    settings will be applied, and the files will be transferred.

9. When the Completing The Collection Phase page appears, click
    Finish to close the Files And Settings Transfer Wizard.

11. Network XP for
Small Businesses

Chapter 12

Network XP for Large Businesses

In Brief

Much has been said here and in other quarters regarding the ease of use Windows XP will offer home and small-office users. Although no one would fault the accolades Windows XP seems to be garnering in those areas, the operating system's impact on the large-scale corporate level should not be ignored.

In Chapter 11, I speculated that the age of the mid-sized business may be waning, as recent evidence seems to support the notion that technology can enable businesses to become much smaller or much larger. The rest of that chapter investigated the possibilities Windows XP has for those systems being used on the small end of the spectrum.

But, what about the large businesses, the giant companies that have been euphemistically labeled "enterprise-level corporations?" Where does Windows XP fit within these organizations?

In this chapter, we'll look at Windows XP's role in the enterprise and the reasons it may be the solution many IT managers have been waiting for—if they can just get over their dread of upgrading to another Windows system.

What XP Can Offer Over NT

Let's face it: Windows 2000 was not the screaming success it was expected to be. The fact that it was two years late didn't help matters any.

With the revamp of Windows NT 4 to 5 came a whole host of problems that Microsoft had somehow allowed itself to forget during the evolution of the NT and Windows 9x operating kernels—problems that would not go away with the wave of a magic wand. Bug after show-stopping bug kept cropping up as the developers at Redmond frantically worked to get the next version of NT (and the first unified version of both Windows kernels) up and running.

In the end, pressure to get Windows NT 5 out the door became too great. Too many other Microsoft products—Active Directory, BackOffice 2000, Office 2000, Commerce Server, and BizTalk Server—depended on the release of the new Windows. Windows NT 5 was named Windows 2000—probably for marketing reasons as well as incentive reasons for the developers to get the product out the door on the new schedule—and shipped February 17, 2000.

This mad rush to deliver Windows 2000 led to some more compromises than just the name. The product never became the unifying platform for the two Windows kernels; that task would fall to Windows XP. The lateness of Windows 2000 also affected its cousin Windows 98 in another way. The huge delay prompted the Windows 98 product managers to release another update of their venerable OS: Windows ME.

In the meantime, Windows 2000 had to convince its potential customers, many of whom were still content with Windows NT 4, that the late delivery of the product had been worth the wait. To Microsoft's dismay, many of these potential clients balked, not because of the lateness of the product so much as their reluctance to use the very piece of technology that Windows 2000 was late in delivering: Active Directory.

With Active Directory, Microsoft was finally offering its customers a complete directory solution. This area of technology had been under the purview of third-party vendors such as Novell. Microsoft (and many other observers) felt that even with this head start, Novell's hold over directory services would be given a serious challenge just by the pervasiveness of Windows. But, this was not to be the case because many IT managers were reluctant to move to an entirely new and unfamiliar directory service. Given that Windows 2000's interface was in many respects similar to Windows NT 4, many IT managers were wondering why it would be necessary to migrate to Windows 2000. If they needed a directory service, they told themselves, they could just keep on using the third-party services.

IT managers were also concerned about the new OS's much-vaunted reliability. Windows 2000 had been revamped to improve stability, but not with simple patches. Windows 2000 had been written from the ground up—40 to 60 million lines of new code. That's a lot of new code to entrust with your organization's data. The bug argument has been settled somewhat, with the release of two service packs for Windows 2000.

A third issue that slowed deployment was the scarcity of Windows 2000-optimized applications available early in its release life. Most existing NT (and 9x) applications ran just fine on Windows 2000, but few were able to take advantage of Active Directory or other Windows 2000 enhancements. Applications that took full advantage of the operating system would not ship until late 2000.

12. Network XP for Large Businesses

In February 2001, Microsoft announced the sale of its one millionth license for Windows 2000, but now Windows 2000 may face its greatest hurdle: Windows XP.

Many observers, including myself, initially dismissed Windows XP as little more than a desktop upgrade for Windows 2000 that would not be a serious upgrade for the Windows 2000 user base. After looking at Windows XP's ease of use, better application compatibility, and lower hardware requirements, however, I now strongly advocate serious consideration of a move to Windows XP for Windows 2000 shops. This statement is based on the firm belief that if corporations want to reduce their operating costs, they must align their platforms to create as much uniformity as they possibly can. If this means an entire shop of Windows 2000 machines, then so be it. If this means a completely Linux-based organization, then that's what should be done.

In the case for Windows XP, the organizations that migrated to Windows 2000 are still very client-heavy with Windows 9x-based machines. Part of this situation was simple economics: It was too expensive to purchase Windows 2000 licenses for *every* machine in a given organization. This situation was compounded by the fact that the hardware requirements for Windows 2000 made the entry threshold rather high to justify physically upgrading machines just so they would run Windows 2000.

Many of these same hardware requirements exist for Windows XP, but they are not as stringent as Windows 2000's. Furthermore, the less-expensive Windows XP licenses and ease-of-migration tools may have at last balanced these costs of migration with the payoff of upgrading.

Shops that are predominantly Windows 98–driven should give serious consideration to moving to Windows XP Professional to finally gain the affordable stability that was not completely delivered by Windows 2000. And, if the clients migrate to Windows XP, rolling the servers to this platform as well is an easy matter.

From a configuration management standpoint, such a uniform platform would serve to immediately lower maintenance and upkeep costs, not to mention training costs for all those different platforms. One platform—be it Windows, Mac, or Linux—is always better for an organization than many.

Remote Access: Direct or VPN?

One of the many solutions that are unique to larger organizations is the need for employees to contact servers in faraway offices for the purpose of information sharing. Certainly, the rise of telecommuting has highlighted this need, but even on a day-to-day intra-office basis, connectivity needs are increasing at a tremendous rate.

Windows XP can aid your organization in solving this connectivity issue in a couple of different ways. The first, and perhaps the simplest, is the direct dial-up solution. Direct dial-up connections are simple to use and set up. You dial up the server computer with your client. The connection passes through some security procedures, and the connection is made. What could be easier?

Some drawbacks come to mind right away. First, because you are limited by analog telephone lines, speed is a concern. Dial-up connections are often painfully slow compared to an organization's basic Internet connectivity speed. The telephone line itself is also a concern. Dial-up connections tie up a line where a line would not ordinarily be needed, and some kind of toll charge is likely to be charged for the call.

Until a few years ago, the only way users could establish direct connections was to use dial-up connections—that is, until the advent of the Virtual Private Network (VPN). VPNs are regarded as a perfect mesh of private encryption traffic with a public network. They are far from perfect, but they can do a great job for your organization if they are a good fit.

VPNs use encryption and tunneling technology to move data around the very public Internet, essentially turning the worldwide network into a private wide area network (WAN) for your company. Tunneling protocols, such as the Point-to-Point Tunneling Protocol (PPTP) help ensure the data packets being moved about are invisible to all except your organization's systems. Encryption ensures that even in the unlikely event the packets are seen, they will be scrambled enough to be useless.

Because VPNs use just the Internet, they can easily be routed through an existing Internet connection. For many companies, this means a lot more speed than a dial-up connection. And, of course, there are the associated benefits to having freed up telephone lines and decreasing telephone charges.

Because they are typically very secure and fast, VPN connections can let you do a lot more remotely than would be efficient with a dial-up connection. In particular, you can create a high-speed remote access account with VPN access, enabling the users to control their desktop systems as if they were typing directly into it instead of sitting in a hotel room in Albuquerque.

VPNs are not, however, without their drawbacks. Though they are highly secure, they are often highly frowned upon by many Internet service providers—particularly from home accounts. If you have visions of telecommuting 75 percent of your workforce from their cozy little home offices, you had better research their home ISPs' policies carefully because many residential accounts prohibit VPN usage.

This restriction is only fair from the ISPs' point of view. VPNs are, by their very nature, going to be carrying commercial traffic and therefore should be billed under a commercial account. This is bad news for the few hobbyists out there who might want a VPN for gaming or noncommercial use, but the ISPs figure it's worth the effort.

If none of the ISPs being affected by the VPN have a concern about VPN usage, you're in luck. The ease in which you can set up a VPN account in Windows XP should make it a very attractive alternative to dial-up connections.

12. Network XP for Large Businesses

Immediate Solutions

Setting Up VPN

VPN access to a remote computer can be accomplished in one of two ways. The first method is to use a dial-up connection to an Internet service provider that will automatically seek out the remote server as soon as the link to the Internet is established.

The second method presumes you have already established a link to the Internet (perhaps through a dedicated connection) and just connects directly through the remote server using PPTP or Layer Two Tunneling Protocol (L2TP).

PPTP and L2TP are roughly similar in capabilities, though L2TP supports transmission only over IP networks such as the Internet and cannot tunnel through frame relay, ATM, or X.25 networks like PPTP can. PPTP can only use a single tunnel at a time, whereas L2TP can handle multiple tunnels. Only L2TP can natively provide tunnel authorization; if you are using PPTP, the IP Security (IPSec) protocol must be used to handle the authorization duties. Interestingly enough, if you choose to use IPSec in conjunction with L2TP, L2TP's authorization functions are supplanted by IPSec's authorization functions.

Whichever method you choose to use, the setup is identical because Windows XP always tracks your default connection to the Internet and will use it for any VPN connection. The result of this handy feature is that you will have to worry only about configuring your settings based on the remote server.

When you connect to a remote server through a VPN connection, you will need to know the IP address of the server or its *full domain name*, which refers to the domain and machine name for the server. Thus, **somewhere.com** would not be enough, but **jupiter.somewhere.com** might be enough.

Follow these steps to set up a VPN connection:

1. Click Start|Control Panel to open the Control Panel.
2. Click the Network And Internet Connections link to open the Network And Internet Connections page.

12. Network XP for Large Businesses

3. Click the Create A Connection To The Network At Your Workplace link. The New Connection Wizard will open to the Network Connection page (see Figure 12.1).

4. Click the Virtual Private Network Connection radio button to select it.

5. Click Next to move to the Connection Name page.

6. Type the name of your company in the Company Name field.

7. Click Next to move to the VPN Server Selection page (see Figure 12.2).

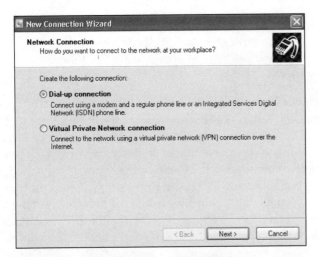

Figure 12.1   Choosing the connection type.

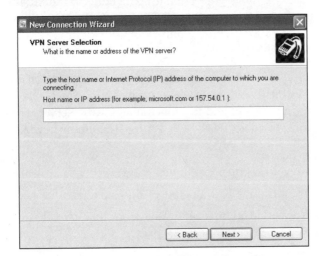

Figure 12.2   Enter the name of the remote server.

NOTE: *You may be asked to verify that the public network is connected. If this occurs, follow the instructions on the Public Network page.*

8. Type the IP address or hostname in the Host Name Or IP Address field.

9. Click Next to move to the Completing New Connection Wizard page.

10. Click the Add A Shortcut To This Connection To The Desktop checkbox to select it.

11. Click Finish. The New Connection Wizard will close, and a shortcut for the connection will appear on the desktop.

12. Click the Close button on the Network And Internet Connections page to close the Control Panel.

Related solution:	Found on page:
Setting Up a Dial-Up Networking Account	187

Using a VPN Connection

After a VPN connection has been created, you can use it to connect to the remote computer with just a few clicks, as shown in the following steps:

1. On the desktop, double-click the icon for the VPN connection to open the Connect dialog box (see Figure 12.3).

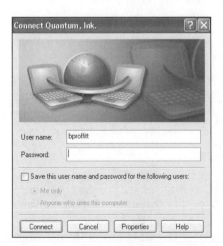

Figure 12.3   Starting the VPN connection.

2. Type the username to be used for the connection in the User Name field.

3. Type the password in the Password field.

4. Click Connect. The Connecting dialog box will appear, indicating the status of the connection.

When your network is connected, a Network Connection icon for the VPN connection will appear in the Notification Area. You can now use file management tools such as Windows Explorer to access files, folders, and other computers from the remote server.

NOTE: *You may be prompted for additional share-level passwords when accessing files, printers, and computers because VPN connections do not pass them along.*

Configuring a VPN Connection

After a VPN connection is established, you can take several measures to improve and secure the connection. One of the first things you can do to improve the convenience of making the VPN connection is to save the username and password so that you don't have to keep typing it in. You can even handle this task on a per-user basis, so the other users on your computer cannot access a remote server with your credentials.

To save the logon settings, follow these steps:

1. On the desktop, double-click the icon for the VPN connection to open the Connect dialog box.

2. Type the username to be used for the connection in the User Name field.

3. Type the password in the Password field.

4. Click the Save This User Name checkbox to select it.

5. Click the Me Only radio button to select it.

6. Click Connect. The Connecting dialog box will appear, indicating the status of the connection.

If you are using a VPN system that uses the IP Security (IPSec) protocol, you can make some changes that will take advantage of this secure protocol. The IPSec protocol supports two encryption modes: Transport and Tunnel. Transport mode encrypts only the data portion of each packet but leaves the header untouched. The more secure Tunnel mode encrypts both the header and payload. An IPSec-compliant remote server can decrypt each packet.

To use the IPSec protocol, you must establish a VPN connection using the L2TP protocol. When the VPN connection is first made, one of the handshaking procedures made during the initial connection figures out which protocol (PPTP or L2TP) the remote machine is using. You can shave off a little of the connection time by configuring the connection to be L2TP only. Also, if a shared encryption key is used in your IPSec configuration, you will need to enter it in the connection's properties.

The steps to complete both of these operations are simple:

1. On the desktop, double-click the icon for the VPN connection to open the Connect dialog box.

2. Click the Properties button to open the connection's Properties dialog box.

3. Click the Networking tab to open the Networking page (see Figure 12.4).

4. Click the drop-down list control for the Type Of VPN field to see the list of options.

5. Click the L2TP IPSec VPN option to select it.

6. Click the Security tab to open the Security page (see Figure 12.5).

Figure 12.4   VPN network settings.

Figure 12.5   VPN security settings.

7. Click the IPSec Settings button to open the IPSec Settings dialog box (see Figure 12.6).

8. Click the Use Pre-shared Key For Authentication checkbox to select it.

9. Enter the shared encryption key in the Key field.

10. Click OK to close the IPSec Settings dialog box.

11. Click OK to close the connection's Properties dialog box.

Encryption comes in many forms, and it is pretty much a given that the more encrypted a connection is, the less chance the data has of being intercepted. You can lend some additional encryption support to the VPN connection by determining just how encrypted you want a successful connection to be. To do so, follow these steps:

1. On the desktop, double-click the icon for the VPN connection to open the Connect dialog box.

Figure 12.6   VPN IPSec settings.

2. Click the Properties button to open the connection's Properties dialog box.

3. Click the Security tab to open the Security page.

4. Click the Advanced (Custom Settings) radio button to select it.

5. Click the Settings button to open the Advanced Security Settings dialog box (see Figure 12.7).

6. Click the drop-down list control for the Data Encryption field to see the list of options.

7. Click the Maximum Strength Encryption (Disconnect If Server Declines) option to select it.

8. Click OK to close the Advanced Security Settings dialog box.

9. Click OK to close the connection's Properties dialog box.

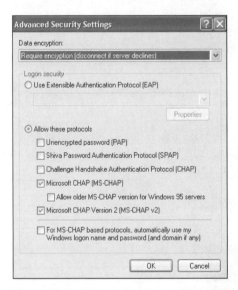

Figure 12.7   Enhance your security settings.

Diagnosing Network Connections

One of the more demanding tasks for network administrators is dealing with the many help-desk issues that cross their desk every day. Although IT administrators' main duty is to be proactive in maintaining the network and machinery, too many times they find themselves placed in a reactionary mode—fighting fires wherever they crop up.

Complicating this often Herculean task is the fact that many IT customers have no real idea what's going on with their machines. To them, it's usually point and click in a rote fashion on a daily basis. If something goes awry, they may not have any idea what they did just prior to failure.

Windows XP's Task Manager does a good job in shutting down errant applications that have crashed on the user. If the problem persists, error logs will allow IT personnel to see where the error occurred.

For network-related problems, the situation may be a little harder to pin down. Network transactions are inherently transient, so real-time monitoring may be needed to deduce the cause of any problems.

Again, the Task Manager can help IT personnel figure out what's going on, thanks to the new Networking page in this useful control. You can view and configure the networking tools in the Task Manager by following these few short steps:

1. Press Ctrl+Alt+Delete simultaneously to open the Windows Task Manager window.

2. Click the Networking tab to open the Networking page (see Figure 12.8).

Each connection available on your machine, whether it is on or off, will be monitored on this page. You can easily change the information that is displayed on these monitors by following these steps:

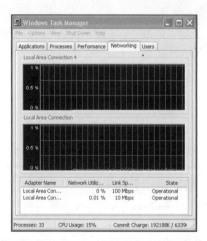

Figure 12.8   Scoping out the network connections.

1. Press Ctrl+Alt+Delete simultaneously to open the Windows Task Manager window.

2. Click the Networking tab to open the Networking page.

3. Click View|Networking Adapter History|Bytes Received (Yellow). The option will be selected, and a yellow line will appear in the monitors to show the number of bytes received.

4. Click View|Networking Adapter History|Bytes Sent (Red). The option will be selected, and a red line will appear in the monitors to show the number of bytes sent.

You can also change the information displayed below the monitors, as shown in these steps:

1. Press Ctrl+Alt+Delete simultaneously to open the Windows Task Manager window.

2. Click the Networking tab to open the Networking page.

3. Click View|Select Columns to open the Select Columns dialog box (see Figure 12.9).

4. Click the options you want to be displayed to select them.

5. Click OK to close the Select Columns dialog box.

6. Click the Close icon to close the Windows Task Manager window.

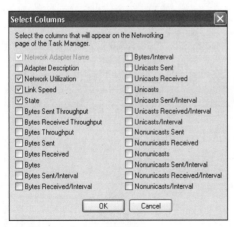

Figure 12.9   Display the information you need to monitor.

On the off chance that live monitoring does not solve the problem, there is a way to actively probe current networking settings to find some problems. The findings from this diagnostic probe can then be saved for later examination by an IT staff member.

Called the Network Diagnostic tool, this Web-based application can easily discover gross errors on your system, as shown in the next steps:

1. Click Start|Control Panel to open the Control Panel.

2. Click the Network And Internet Connections link to open the Network And Internet Connections page.

3. Click the Network Diagnostics link. The Help And Support Center window will open to the Network Diagnostics page (see Figure 12.10).

4. Click the Set Scanning Options link to open the Options section of the page (see Figure 12.11).

5. Click the options you want to be scanned to select them.

6. Click the Save Options button to store the options for later diagnostic scans.

7. Click the Scan Your System link. The system will be scanned based on your set parameters and the results displayed in the Computer Information and Modems And Network Adapters sections (see Figure 12.12).

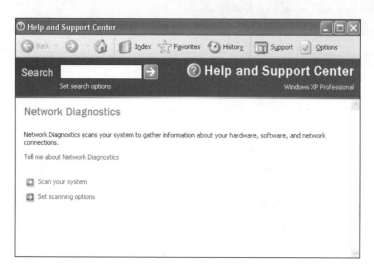

Figure 12.10   The Network Diagnostics tool.

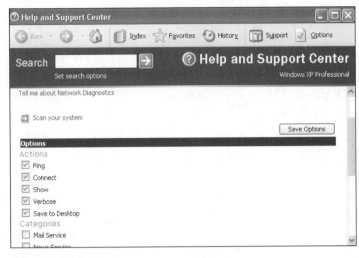

Figure 12.11   Choose what you want to scan.

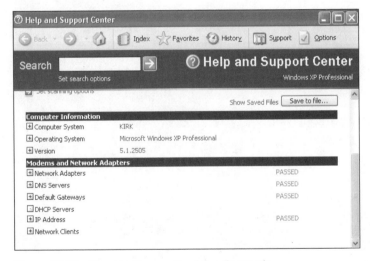

Figure 12.12   Viewing the results of the diagnostic.

8. Click the Save To File button. A file with all the results will be saved in the user's Documents and Settings folder.

9. Click the Close icon to close the Help And Support Center window.

After the results are saved, a network administrator can examine the file to determine what, if any, errors were detected.

Related solution:	*Found on page:*
Using the Task Manager	452

Chapter 13

Internet Explorer 6: One-Stop Browsing

In Brief

In the mid-nineties, two topics seemed to be at the forefront of party conversation: What new wackiness would President Clinton get himself involved in next and what (among the geek set) did we think about the Browser Wars?

Here is what I thought at the time: Didn't these people have anything better to do than play around with the standards of the Internet? Apparently not, because history shows this kind of thing has happened before.

If you missed the infamous Browser Wars, or have blocked it out of your mind, here's a quick summary.

After Marc Andressen left the NCSA in 1994 and founded Netscape Communications, the company's first browser, Navigator 1.1, surpassed Mosaic in many important ways—not the least of which were the added HTML extensions that Netscape alone would support, such as tables, colors, text size, and (saints preserve us) blinking text. None of these functions were included in the original HTML specifications, mind you. Netscape added them because they looked good. And, they did look good and led to the adoption of these new extensions by Web developers, who in turn encouraged visitors to pick up Netscape and see how cool its pages really looked. This viral marketing had its effect. Soon, Netscape controlled more than 90 percent of the browser market.

About this time, Microsoft realized that this Internet thing was a good idea, and it was clearly missing the boat. To lure people away from the Web and proprietary services such as CompuServe and Prodigy, it started the Microsoft Network. MSN 1.0 was a flop, however, which then prompted Microsoft to go head to head against the Netscape megalith.

Netscape was about to get hit from another side, as well. Fearful of a complete lack of standards for the Internet's newest subsection, the World Wide Web Consortium was established to implement standards for the HTML language, which was the sole tool for building Web pages. The W3C took too few innovative steps while working on the HTML 3 specifications in 1995, because right at the beginning of 1996, Navigator 2 was released, supporting just a few of the HTML 3 specs and quite a few of its own. In as pure a case of market-driven events as you will ever see, the W3C threw up its collective hands and released HTML 3 soon after. These specifications incorporated many of the extensions Navigator 2 had introduced.

One of these new extensions was the support of the new programming language JavaScript, which, along with its parent language Java, offered Netscape users a platform-less way of accessing innovative tools on any Web page with any version of Netscape.

Soon after, Microsoft released Internet Explorer (IE) 2, which was very similar to Navigator 1.1, and contained some of its own extensions, such as background music and scrolling text. As far as releases went, it would have been no big thing—save for the fact that IE 2 was released free of charge. Microsoft didn't let up either, as it banged out several upgrades of 2. Then, Microsoft announced it would implement only "true" standardized HTML from that point on. In the first half of 1996, Web designers started to make sites that were "optimized for Netscape" or "optimized for MSIE."

Critics of IE (and there were plenty) knew that the only way Microsoft would ever be on an equal footing would be if IE supported something like JavaScript. In August 1996, the pundits got what they asked for, when Navigator and IE 3 were released within one week of each other, and IE 3 included a newfangled technology called ActiveX. ActiveX went beyond the scripting model of JavaScript and the plug-in methodology of Netscape. Now, users could pick up the tools they needed to read any special Web media automatically—they didn't need to find and install any helper apps.

No one at Netscape was laughing anymore.

The next targeted release of the Big Two browsers would be 4, and each company had its own plan for changing the face of the desktop. IE would be integrated directly into the Windows desktop, and Navigator would become so powerful and versatile that it would essentially become the platform from which everything would run—at least that's what was announced at a Netscape Conference in 1997. But still, Netscape's market share was dropping like a rock. By the end of 1997, it held anywhere from 10 to 20 percent of the overall browser share.

There was no clear end to the Browser War conflict, though many believe it was brought to a halt in December 1997, when the U.S. government levied charges of unfair competitive practices against Microsoft because of the decision to integrate IE into the upcoming Windows 98. It is widely speculated that Netscape had a hand in blowing the whistle on its chief competitor.

It may have been too late for Netscape, until Andressen announced in 1998 the release of the source code for Communicator 5. Thus began the Mozilla Project and a whole new era for Netscape.

But, was this really the end of the Browser Wars? Perhaps not, if only because historically things like this keep happening again and again.

The recent evolution in the status of the Big Two browsers may change the pattern of open warfare somewhat. Instead of a winner-take-all ending that other standards wars have had in the past, what we are now seeing is a complete and utter shattering of IE and Netscape into a whole host of competing browsers. And, the peculiar thing is that these two companies may have done it to themselves.

Clearly, the U.S. government's almost decision to break up Microsoft and the States continuing desire to punish the Redmond company could do the most damage to IE because a fragmented Microsoft will clearly not be able to integrate the browser into the desktop. If IE becomes a standalone product again, seeing how it competes with old rival Netscape and new powerhouse Opera will be interesting.

Microsoft's newest browser, MSN Explorer, may even be edging out IE as the company's flagship browser. There are hints that Microsoft is considering releasing MSN Explorer in the Personal version of its newest operating system, the beta code-named Whistler. IE would come only with the Professional and Server versions of Whistler, which would become Windows XP.

And then, we must consider the myriad companies that have licensed the IE browser engine for their own browser creations. One example is NeoPlanet, a browser that gets quite a bit of use (1.3 million downloads from CNET's **download.com**) due to its aesthetic look and feel, plus an aggressive brand marketing strategy. These browsers have growing user bases and may be "stealing eyeballs" from IE itself.

Netscape's fragmentation started the instant its code became open source. When that happened, developers all over the world began building their own homegrown Mozilla-based browsers. K-Meleon and Galeon are just two of the latest browsers joining Netscape 6 in the ranks of Mozilladom.

So now, instead of one superpower versus another, scattered collections of minor and major browsers are all squabbling to grab users from the ever-growing new user community and from the ranks of those disenfranchised with IE or Netscape.

The Browser War has become a Brush War, replete with alliances, hidden deals, and outright skullduggery. The situation becomes even more complicated when you throw in the arrival of a whole new platform of browsers: embedded and personal digital assistant (PDA) browser applications.

The arrival of this new platform does not mean the Big Two browsers have gone away, mind you. On the contrary, Netscape recently released version 6.1 of its Mozilla-based browser suite, and with the release of Windows XP will come the new Internet Explorer 6, which promises to consolidate many of your Internet needs into one tool.

What's New in IE 6?

When you first look at Internet Explorer 6, you might expect to see big, snappy changes from browsers of days gone by. What I found was something that looked a lot like the IE I was used to. In fact, until I started pushing buttons and prodding the browser the way I usually torture new software when I get it, I would not have immediately found the differences.

Microsoft is clearly trying to keep consistency in its interface, and this is not such a bad thing. Seeing how IE 6 will look in the environment it is supposed to be showcased in—Windows XP—will be interesting.

So, what is different in IE 6? Quite a bit, actually. On the interface side, clearly the addition of the Explorer Bar stands out. The Explorer Bar enables users to search the Web; play music, video. and mixed media files without launching a separate application; and even search the contents of their own system without leaving the application.

IE 6 is also tightly integrated with the default Mail and News clients for your system, enabling you to directly send messages via email or newsgroups from the application.

Image management includes the set of management tools that appear when you right-click an image. These handy tools include the Auto Image Resize function, which automatically resizes an image to fit inside the browser window. Privacy and security management are improved as well, with security configuration using the effective "zone" paradigm. The privacy manager is a new and effective way of keeping cookies under control. Content management has been improved in this release of IE, making it even easier to control which types of Web sites your family can and cannot visit.

IE 6 does not represent a quantum leap in interface and design changes, but instead offers users a cleaner and more efficient way to access the Internet with subtle, behind-the-scenes changes.

13. Internet Explorer 6: One-Stop Browsing

Immediate Solutions

Browsing with IE 6

Browsers have really been around for a long time, but we never called them browsers. Instead, we called them text readers or read-only applications because all these programs did was open simple files of text and let someone read them—like a book. These programs were on what computers called dumb terminals.

It seems odd to call a computer dumb, but compared to the computers used today, these computers weren't really smart. All they did was show information from big, monster servers the size of an average living room. These servers weren't all that smart, either, but they were good enough to take a lot of information and help businesspeople and scientists make sense of it.

The problem was that these dumb terminals could talk only to the servers they were connected to. There was an Internet back then, but there was no World Wide Web. Internet traffic was mainly limited to messaging and file transfers.

Then, in 1990, a scientist in Switzerland, Tim Berners-Lee, got a brilliant idea. What if you could read files on any computer connected to the Internet any time you wanted? You could put those files on a special server that had one job—showing anyone those files. Berners-Lee knew this idea would only work if all those files were made readable by any computer. File compatibility was (and still is) a huge obstacle for users to overcome. Therefore, Berners-Lee suggested that people use HTML files. Because they are essentially just ASCII text files, HTML files could be read by any computer, would let people make the text any way they wanted, and would have hyperlinks—something that would revolutionize the way people absorbed material.

Browsers came about as instruments to read all these new HTML files. As with the dumb terminals, Berners-Lee just wanted people to quickly read information in files—not change the files. So, he and his colleagues figured out a way to make a program that did nothing but read HTML. Other people got involved and made the application read more complicated HTML.

People began calling the information on the World Wide Web *pages*, and calling the act of reading those pages *browsing*—and that's where the name *browser* came from. Later, when the general public started using the World Wide Web, browsing was called *surfing the Web*. The name *browser* stuck, though, because it tells you what this program does—it lets you browse through all the wonderful information on the Web. You can call any program like this a browser, of course. A program that does nothing but show pictures could be a picture browser. Nowadays, though, we keep the name with the Web browsers—for example, Internet Explorer.

Browsing is more than just clicking through a collection of hyperlinks. What really makes the whole thing work is the Uniform Resource Locator (URL). URLs are pseudo-English labels that are applied to nearly every Web server on the planet. Every Web server has its own IP address, but URLs make it easy for regular people to type an address into the Address field of IE and bring up a page.

Of course, after you look at URLs such as **http://llanfairpwllgwyngyl-lgogerychwyrndrobwllllantysiliogogogoch.co.uk**, using the IP address might actually be a blessing, but for the most part, the URLs are easier.

13. Internet Explorer 6: One-Stop Browsing

NOTE: *Llanfairpwllgwyngyllgogerychwyrndrobwllllantysiliogogogoch is a village on the Isle of Anglesey in North Wales that currently holds the Guinness record for the longest English place name.*

You begin browsing with Internet Explorer as soon as you start the application. At this point, the home page for the browser is opened, as you can see in the following steps:

1. Click Start|Internet Explorer to open the browser application to the home page (see Figure 13.1).

2. Click the Address field so that the URL in the field is highlighted.

3. Type the URL for the Web site you want to visit in the Address field.

NOTE: *You do not have to type the URL identifier **http://** before the Web site address. Internet Explorer will fill it in for you.*

---

4. Press Enter or click the Go button in the Address bar to go to the new page.

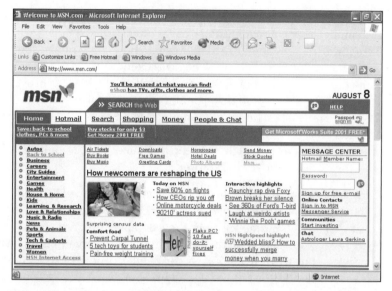

Figure 13.1   The Internet Explorer interface.

5. Place your mouse pointer over an underlined hyperlink. The link will change color, and the full URL for the link will appear in the status bar at the bottom of the screen.

6. Click the hyperlink to go to the new page.

You won't have to type in the full address every time you revisit a Web site, thanks to the AutoComplete feature in the Address field. Just start typing the URL, and Internet Explorer will display a list of similar URLs for you to choose from, as you can see here:

1. Click the Address field so that the cursor will appear in the field.

2. Type the URL for the Web site you want to visit in the Address field. A list of similarly named URLs will appear (see Figure 13.2).

3. If the correct URL appears, click the option to go to the new page.

Human beings are creatures of habit, and often we find ourselves clinging to the familiar as we move through our busy lives. IE's developers recognize this characteristic, which is why they have given us links and favorites to use as shortcuts to frequently visited Web pages.

Using a favorite is as simple as following these short steps:

1. Click the Favorites menu option to open the Favorites menu.

2. Click the favorite site you want to view to go to the new page.

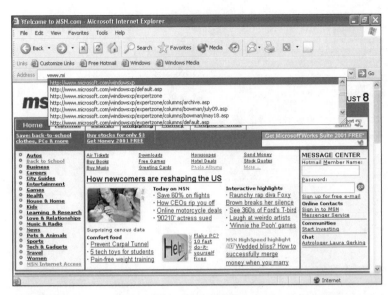

Figure 13.2 The AutoComplete feature will save you a lot of typing.

Links are even simpler. Just click the appropriate Link button in the Links bar, and the new page will appear.

After you have been browsing for a while, you may need to go back to a Web page you visited earlier in the current browsing session. Two controls in the Standard toolbar, the Back and Forward buttons, will enable you to navigate through the pages you have visited.

Note, however, that navigation through Web pages is not tracked for every Web page you visit during a session. Internet Explorer, like many other browsers, uses a sequential navigation method that tracks only the Web pages along a particular path. For instance, assume you were browsing on Page A, then Pages B, C, and D. On Page D, you found a link back to Page B and clicked the link to revisit that page. Now, assume that from Page B, you went off and visited Pages E and F. If you were then to use the Back button to cycle back through the pages you visited during this session, the order of pages you would see would be F to E to B to A. Pages C and D, because they were on another "track" of browsing, would no longer be a part of the browser's navigation—even if you were to cycle forward through the pages again using the Forward button.

Of course, you can do more with the Back and Forward buttons than just cycle through Web pages one at a time, as you can see in these steps:

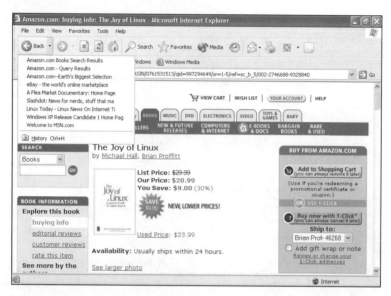

Figure 13.3   You can step through your session's pages quickly.

1. After navigating to a few Web pages, click the drop-down list control for the Back button to see a list of recently navigated pages (see Figure 13.3).

2. Click one of the options listed to go to that page.

3. Click the drop-down list control for the Forward button to see a list of recently navigated pages.

4. Click one of the options listed to go to that page.

One of the nicer features of Windows is the capability to call up the default Web browser whenever any hyperlink or Web page shortcut is clicked—in any application. This capability is particularly handy in email clients such as Outlook Express or Outlook, where you often receive URLs from friends and colleagues.

To open a URL in another source document, simply click the URL. Internet Explorer will open to that page immediately.

Managing Web Images

A new feature in Internet Explorer 6 is the inline image control toolset. These tools allow you to directly manipulate images within a Web page without having to call them up in a separate graphics tool. The tools are straightforward and easy to use. With them, you can save, print, and resize the picture on the Web page. You can even email the image to someone directly from the Web page.

To save an image file, follow these steps:

1. In Internet Explorer, navigate to a Web page that contains a graphics file.

2. Hold the mouse pointer over the image. The image tools will appear within the image (see Figure 13.4).

3. Click the Save This Image button. The Save Picture window will open to the My Pictures folder (see Figure 13.5).

4. Navigate to a folder to save the file.

5. Click Save. The image will be saved, and the Save Picture window will close.

Printing an image is just as easy, as you will see here:

1. In Internet Explorer, navigate to a Web page that contains a graphics file.

2. Hold the mouse pointer over the image. The image tools will appear within the image.

3. Click the Print This Image button to open the Print dialog box (see Figure 13.6).

Figure 13.4   IE's image control tools.

Figure 13.5   Saving a Web page image.

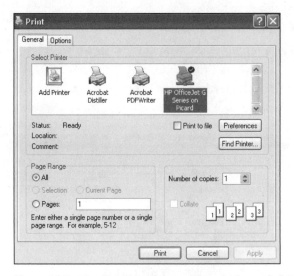

Figure 13.6   Confirm the printer settings before printing.

4. Click Print. The image will be printed, and the Print dialog box will close.

Because IE 6 is so interconnected with Outlook Express and Outlook, you can quickly send someone an image from a Web page by following these steps:

1. In Internet Explorer, navigate to a Web page that contains a graphics file.

2. Hold the mouse pointer over the image. The image tools will appear within the image.

3. Click the Send This Image In An E-Mail button. The Send Mail dialog box will open, followed by the Send Pictures Via E-Mail dialog box (see Figure 13.7).

4. Click the Show More Options link. The Send Pictures Via E-Mail dialog box will expand to show more sizing options.

5. Click the Small radio button to select it.

6. Click OK. The Send Pictures Via E-Mail and Send Mail dialog boxes will close, to be replaced by an email message window from your default email client.

As you can see in Figure 13.8, the picture is pre-attached to the message. You just need to follow your email client's procedures to address the message and send it, and the image will be on its way.

When images are displayed within Internet Explorer, they are automatically resized to fit completely within the window. Usually, this resizing is not very noticeable because many Web page designers size their images with users' screen resolutions in mind. If you want to see more detail and a clearer image, you can expand the image to its original size, as demonstrated in these steps:

1. In Internet Explorer, navigate to a Web page that contains a graphics file.

2. Hold the mouse pointer over the image. The image tools will appear within the image.

3. Click the Expand To Regular Size button to increase the image size to its original dimensions.

4. Click the Fit Image To Window button to decrease the image size to fit completely within the browser window.

Figure 13.7   You can resize the photo to make it more compact to send to someone.

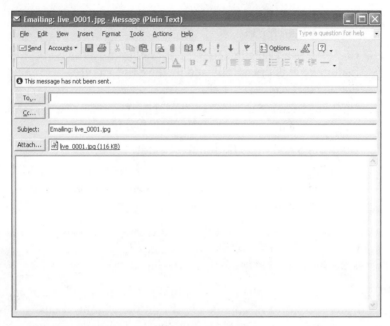

Figure 13.8   The image is ready to send.

Securing IE 6

The Internet, ever the microcosm of the human race, has its share of darkness just like the real world in which it exists. Somewhere out there in the murky ether known as the Internet may lurk a Web site just waiting for you to come along so it can download something malicious to your system. Granted, these sites are few and far between, but they're out there nonetheless. Sites such as this don't exactly advertise themselves, of course, so you often need to keep a modicum of protection activated while you surf the Web.

Internet Explorer handles security with a "zone" concept. Every Web site should fit into one of these four zones:

- Internet
- Local Intranet
- Trusted Sites
- Restricted Sites

Each zone maintains one of four different levels of security, from Low to High, as follows:

- *Low*—Few safety measures. All scripts found will run without hindrance.

- *Medium-Low*—No unsigned scripts will be downloaded without user permission. Most content will be displayed.

- *Medium*—Similar to Medium-Low, except that the user will be prompted more often when potentially dangerous content is discovered.

- *High*—No scripts will be run, and very little content will be viewed without user confirmation.

As you might expect, each zone has its own default setting for security, as shown in Table 13.1.

These security settings can be adjusted for each zone. If you are not entirely comfortable with a Medium-Low setting for your intranet site, you can change this setting by following these steps.

1. In Internet Explorer, click Tools|Internet Options to open the Internet Options dialog box.

2. Click the Security tab to open the Security page (see Figure 13.9).

3. Click the Local Intranet icon so that the settings for the zone will be displayed.

4. Click the slider control and drag it one notch up to the Medium setting.

5. Click Apply to apply the new setting.

6. Click OK to close the Internet Options dialog box.

You can also add certain sites to a particular zone. This capability is especially useful when you have a frequently visited site that you want IE to display without any prompts for you. You can add a site to a zone in these few short steps:

1. In Internet Explorer, click Tools|Internet Options to open the Internet Options dialog box.

Table 13.1   Zone security settings.

Zone	Security
Internet	Medium
Local Intranet	Medium-Low
Trusted Sites	Low
Restricted Sites	High

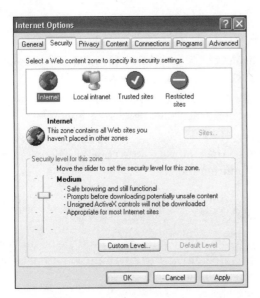

Figure 13.9   Changing the security settings for a zone.

2. Click the Security tab to open the Security page.

3. Click the Trusted Sites icon so that the settings for the zone will be displayed.

4. Click the Sites button to open the Trusted Sites dialog box (see Figure 13.10).

5. Type the URL of the Web site into the Add This Web Site To The Zone field.

Figure 13.10   Adding a site to a zone.

NOTE: *The AutoComplete feature will assist you in entering the URL for the site.*

6. Click the Add button to add the site to the list of trusted sites.

TIP: *If you are adding a nonsecure server to the list of trusted sites, you need to clear the Require Server Verification checkbox.*

7. Click OK to close the Trusted Sites dialog box.
8. Click Apply to apply the new setting.
9. Click OK to close the Internet Options dialog box.

Using the Explorer Bar

The Explorer Bar is perhaps one of the most misnamed components in the Internet Explorer browser. Not really a toolbar as much as it is a separate pane in the IE browser window, the Explorer Bar allows immediate access to some of the most basic functions you will need during your travels on the Web.

These functions include the following:

- Search
- Favorites
- Media
- History
- Windows Explorer

Activating any of these functions will open a new pane on the left side of the IE window that will contain all the tools you need to perform desired tasks.

NOTE: *The Search functions will be discussed in more detail in the "Searching with MSN" section later in this chapter.*

In the "Browsing with IE 6" section, you learned how to call up a favorite Web site using the Favorites menu. Now, you can perform the same task with the Explorer Bar like this:

1. In Internet Explorer, click the Favorites button to open the Favorites Explorer Bar (see Figure 13.11).
2. Click a favorite link to go to the Web page immediately.

13. Internet Explorer 6: One-Stop Browsing

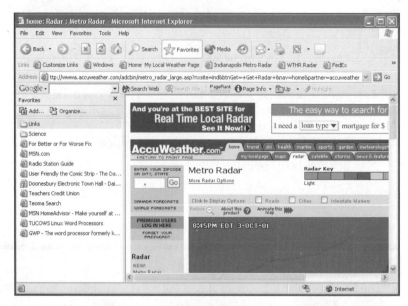

Figure 13.11   The Favorites Explorer Bar.

If you are interested in multimedia content while you're surfing, the Media Explorer Bar will definitely be a useful tool. With it, you can view video content or listen to audio while surfing around the Net. To use the Media Explorer Bar, follow these steps:

1. In Internet Explorer, click the Media button. The Media Explorer Bar will open to the **WindowsMedia.com** page (see Figure 13.12).

2. Click a desired link. The docked Media Player applet at the bottom of the Explorer Bar will immediately begin to play the content.

Another useful feature for hard-core Internet surfers is the History feature. Unlike the Back and Forward navigation controls, the History function tracks every page you visit. Like the Favorites Explorer Bar, the History Explorer Bar is a cinch to use. Just follow these steps:

1. In Internet Explorer, click the History button to open the History Explorer Bar (see Figure 13.13).

2. Navigate to the date when you last visited the desired Web site.

3. Click the desired link to go to the Web page immediately.

Related solution:	Found on page:
Playing Multimedia Files	304

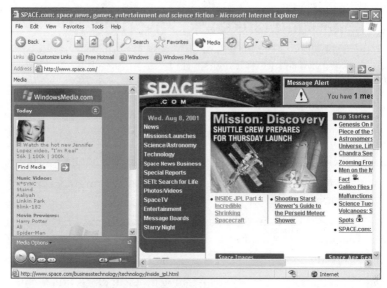

Figure 13.12   The Media Explorer Bar.

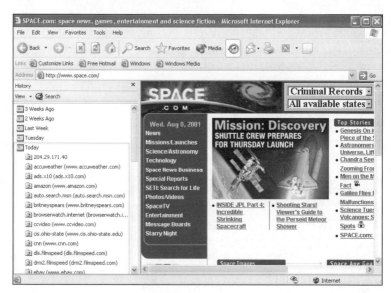

Figure 13.13   The History Explorer Bar.

Personalizing Links and Favorites

One of the first tasks you will likely perform with IE is creating favorites to get you to the Web pages you frequently visit much faster. Favorites and links are analogous to bookmarks in other browsers, and the two are really no different functionally, except that favorites are accessed from the Favorites menu or the Favorites Explorer Bar and links are accessed from the Links toolbar.

You can add a favorite to your browser with this quick procedure:

1. In Internet Explorer, navigate to the page you want to make a favorite.

2. Click Favorites|Add To Favorites to open the Add Favorite dialog box (see Figure 13.14).

3. Edit the title of the Web page in the Name field as needed.

4. Click OK. The Add Favorite dialog box will close, and the new favorite will appear in the Favorites menu and Favorites Explorer Bar.

If you go around adding favorites to your browser willy-nilly, you will probably end up with a rather messy favorites list. Fortunately, you can quickly organize the favorites in these few steps:

1. Click Favorites|Organize Favorites to open the Organize Favorites dialog box (see Figure 13.15).

2. Click the Create Folder button to create a new folder icon.

3. Type the name for the new folder and press Enter to rename it.

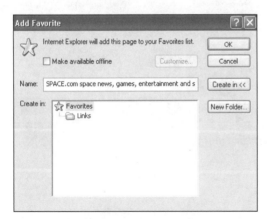

Figure 13.14   Adding a favorite.

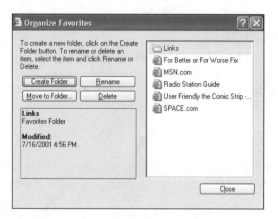

Figure 13.15   Getting favorites in order.

4. Click a favorites item to select it.

5. Click the Move To Folder button to open the Browse For Folder dialog box.

6. Click the destination folder to select it.

7. Click OK. The Browse For Folder dialog box will close, and the favorite will be moved to the folder.

8. Click Close to close the Organize Favorites dialog box.

As convenient as favorites are, links are even easier to deal with. You can add a link to the Link bar as follows:

1. In Internet Explorer, navigate to the page you want to make a link.

2. Click the Web page icon immediately to the left of the URL in the Address field.

3. Drag the icon to the Link toolbar and drop it in a preferred place to create the new link.

You can easily remove a link, too, by following these steps:

1. Right-click a link. The context menu will appear.

2. Click Delete to open the Confirm File Delete dialog box.

3. Click Yes. The Confirm File Delete dialog box will close, and the link will be removed from the Link bar.

Reading Newsgroups

The Internet, contrary to popular belief, is not made up of just the Web and email alone. Before the Web, there was the Gopher interface, a folder-driven file repository system. And, before Web message-posting sites, there were the news servers.

Both server types are still around, though you would be hard-pressed to locate a Gopher server. News servers, however, are still going like gangbusters. News servers manage newsgroups, which are electronic messaging bulletin boards that can be accessed by anyone with a newsgroup reader.

Although Internet Explorer cannot read newsgroups alone, it can quickly access a Windows XP application that can: the Outlook Newsreader. When you first begin to use the Outlook Newsreader in conjunction with IE, you will need to set up a newsgroup account. Many public and private newsgroup services on the Internet will allow you newsgroup access. One of the best places to check is your own Internet provider.

Follow these steps to start Outlook Newsreader for the first time and set up an account:

1. In Internet Explorer, click Tools|Mail And News|Read News to start the Outlook Newsreader application (see Figure 13.16).

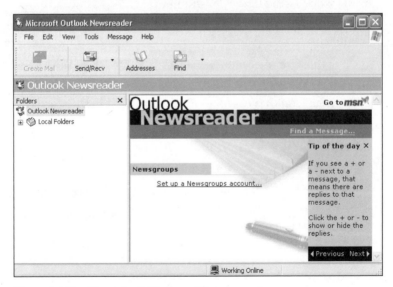

Figure 13.16   The default Windows XP newsreader.

2. Click the Set Up A Newsgroups Account link. The Internet Connection Wizard will open to the Setting Up Internet News page.

3. Click the Create A New Internet News Account radio button to select it.

4. Click Next to move to the Your Name page.

5. Type your name in the Display Name field.

6. Click Next to move to the Internet News E-Mail Address page.

7. Enter an email address in the E-Mail Address field.

8. Click Next to move to the Internet News Server Name page.

9. Enter the name of the news server to which you will connect in the News (NNTP) Server field.

10. Click the My News Server Requires Me To Log On checkbox, if necessary, to select it.

11. Click Next to move to the Internet News Server Logon page.

12. Enter your username in the Account Name field.

13. Enter the password for the account in the Password field.

14. Click Next to move to the Congratulations page.

15. Click Finish. The Internet Connection Wizard will close, and the new account will appear in the newsreader.

After the account is created, you will need to see what newsgroups are available for you to peruse. Follow these steps to view the list of available newsgroups and subscribe to the ones you want to have regularly updated:

1. Double-click the account icon. The Outlook Express message box will appear, asking whether you would care to download the available newsgroups at this time.

2. Click Yes. The Newsgroup Subscriptions and Download Newsgroups dialog boxes will appear. When all the available newsgroups are available, the Download Newsgroups dialog box will close.

3. In the Newsgroup Subscriptions dialog box, select the newsgroups you wish to subscribe to (see Figure 13.17).

4. Click the Subscribe button to subscribe to the newsgroups.

5. Click OK. The Newsgroup Subscriptions dialog box will close, and the selected newsgroups will appear in the account pane.

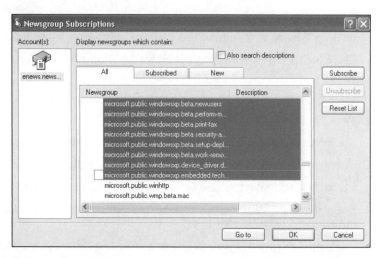

Figure 13.17   Subscribing to newsgroups.

When you have some newsgroups to look at, you will need to look at the messages they contain. Like bulletin boards, newsgroups contain variable numbers of messages, which are updated continually. After a while, older messages are no longer carried by a news server and are cycled out.

To view a newsgroup's message set, just click a newsgroup in the account pane. The message headers in that newsgroup will be downloaded into the message header pane (see Figure 13.18).

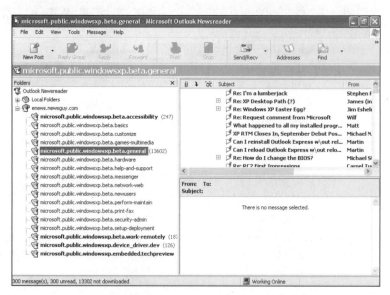

Figure 13.18   Looking at the message headers of a newsgroup.

Viewing the messages themselves is also simple. Click a message header in the message header pane, and the content of the message will be downloaded into the message pane.

The controls in the Outlook Newsreader are similar to that of many email clients. Table 13.2 lists the controls used for basic newsgroup operations.

Table 13.2   Basic newsgroup operations.

Control	Action
New Post	Posts a brand-new message with an original topic to the selected newsgroup.
Reply Group	Posts a reply to a selected message to the newsgroup.
Reply	Sends an email message as a reply to a selected message; this reply will not be shown in the newsgroup.

Using FTP Sites

Another useful set of servers on the Internet are the File Transfer Protocol (FTP) servers. These servers, which also predate the Web, have only one job: to transfer files back and forth between a client and the FTP server.

Because FTP is based on the Unix commands that originally comprised much of the Internet commands, using FTP can be a bit of a cryptic experience. Windows XP, however, makes using it so simple that you will be able to use an FTP server like any other folder on your computer.

To browse an FTP site, just type a URL for an FTP server into the Address field. The contents of the FTP server will appear, and the application will change to the Windows Explorer interface. When the FTP site is visible, you can browse, move, or copy files just as you would any folder on your system. The only limitations will be the security setup on the FTP server itself and the time delay involved in downloads and uploads to the Internet.

Related solutions:	Found on page:
Copying Files	77
Moving Files	79
Deleting Files	80
Creating New Folders	83

13. Internet Explorer 6: One-Stop Browsing

Searching the Internet

At one time in the not-too-distant past, the entire list of Web sites could fit within one Web page. Hard as it may be to believe, this situation lasted for quite a while on the Web because the Web's early growth was not quite the exponential explosion it is today. Today, no Internet directory site can keep track of the entire Web. Yahoo comes close, but the simple truth is that the Web is growing too fast for any directory service to keep up.

The next best solution is the active Web search sites. These sites use sophisticated Web bots and crawlers to continuously traverse the Internet, looking for new material. Internet Explorer has it own built-in direct access to one of these search tools. And, an add-on to IE may be the best search tool ever made for this browser.

Searching with MSN

When you run a search through IE, the search is routed to the MSN search engine and the results reported on an MSN-generated page. The neat thing about these searches is that you don't have to use keyword-only searches; you can type in a plain-language question as well.

Searches can be run formally or informally, depending on your needs. To run a formal search, use these steps as a guideline:

1. In Internet Explorer, click the Search button to open the Search Explorer Bar (see Figure 13.19).

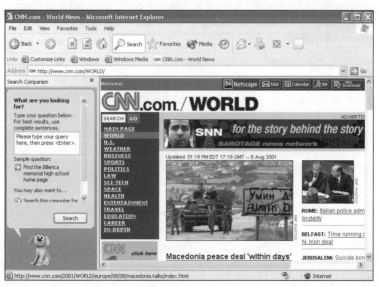

Figure 13.19   Scanning the globe...

2. Enter a query in the Query field.

3. Press Enter or click the Search button to begin the search and display the results in the browser window.

4. If the search does not generate good results, click the Automatically Send Your Search To Other Search Engines link. The results from other search engines will be displayed in the browser window.

You can also initiate an informal search in the Address field by typing a question mark followed by the search term(s). This search will also use MSN's Web Search engine, but it must use keywords, not plain-language queries. Press Enter and the search will begin.

Searching with Google

I would be remiss if I failed to mention one of the most powerful search tools available for IE. This third-party add-on is distributed by the Google search engine, which, despite its odd name, is one of the best search engines on the Web today.

To use this add-on, you must obtain it and install it on your system. These steps will show you how:

1. In Internet Explorer, navigate to **http://toolbar.google.com**.

2. Click the Get The Google Toolbar button near the bottom of the page to open the Install The Google Toolbar page.

3. Read the license agreement, close all active IE windows but this one, and click the Install The Google Toolbar button. The Choose Your Google Toolbar Configuration window will open.

4. Read the information about PageRank and click the configuration option you prefer. The Installing The Google Toolbar page will appear, followed by a Security Warning dialog box (see Figure 13.20).

5. Click Yes. The download will proceed, closing and reopening the Internet Explorer window.

When the toolbar is installed, you can activate or close it like any other IE toolbar (see Figure 13.21). To use the Google Toolbar, enter a search term in the Search field and press Enter. The results will be displayed on a Google-generated results page.

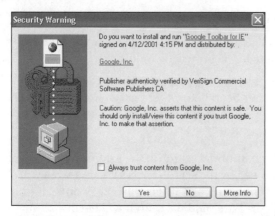

Figure 13.20   Authorizing a download.

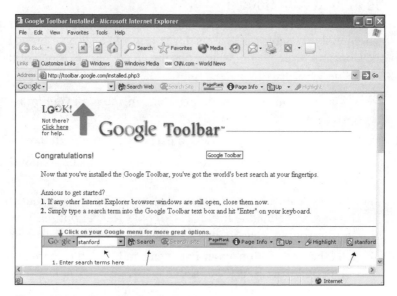

Figure 13.21   The nifty Google Toolbar.

Chapter 14

Communicate with XP

In Brief

Remember Citizen's Band radios? For a brief, odd time in the 1970s, the United States was fascinated by CB radios. Truckers, who had been using them for years, wondered what all the fuss was about. A device that had been used to communicate on the open road suddenly had its own lexicon and culture surrounding it.

The only thing like it at the time was amateur radio. CBs, however, had a much lower entrance requirement because there were far fewer regulations governed CBs, and the cost of using them was much less than ham radios.

CBs grew to almost mythic status, as songs and movies were created about the lore of the truckers and highwaymen who had built their own language using these simple radios. But, CBs had their limitations. Mobile units could typically reach only 5 to 7 miles, and you had to talk to whoever was out there at the time. If no one was there, you had to do something else to keep yourself awake.

CB radios are still in use, of course, but the hype and hysteria have died down considerably. They are no longer a fad. Today, they have been replaced by cellular and satellite phones that can let you reach anyone in the world from anywhere on the planet. Because the phones are private (for the most part), people no longer needed to make up a colorful set of code words to disguise a message's meaning. In other words, the cell phone has no sense of romanticism.

The role of computers in communications has typically been quiet, too. Computers have, until very recently, played a secondary role in communications by routing telephone calls and microwave transmissions.

The popular use of email messaging is an exception. As with the CB radios of old, a small cultural phenomenon has grown around the simple act of sending and receiving messages with :) in them to convey happiness. Pop media have picked up on this wave, culminating in a movie or two about the whole thing.

Like the CB, email is easy to use. All you need is a computer and a connection to the Internet. Because many offices, schools, and libraries have these tools available, you don't even have to own a computer to take advantage of email. CBs and email fulfill a basic human need: the desire to reach out and connect with others. We are not complete, it seems, without relationships.

Technology improved upon the CB radio with the cell phone. So, too, will technology improve the computer to move messaging beyond email.

This chapter will examine two directions that technology is taking communications on the computer. The first direction is online conferencing, where participants can meet online and collaborate on issues as if they were in the same room—even if they are thousands of miles away.

The second direction is less dramatic and more personal. Instead of sequential messaging, you can use a communications system to converse with someone live in real time. This is, of course, instant messaging. Recently, it has grown in popularity as much as email messaging.

Instant messaging is fast, easy to use, and even has its own special lexicon of terms and vocabulary. With all these advantages, can a movie be far behind?

10-4, good buddy!

Online Conferencing Features

Online conferencing and instant messaging are fundamentally different, even though on the surface they seem much the same. Although both methods of communication seem the same, instant messaging really begins and ends with the Internet chat function. Online conferencing moves beyond instant messaging by adding more features than just chatting. These features include audio, video, file transfer, application sharing, and collaboration.

The primary tool for online conferencing in Windows XP is NetMeeting, which has had an interesting history at Microsoft. When it was initially developed, NetMeeting was to be *the* Microsoft tool of all instant communications. For a while, it seemed to fulfill this role very well. But, some shifts in philosophy in Redmond have convinced Microsoft to put its support behind the MSN Messenger (now Windows Messenger) tool for instant messaging and focus NetMeeting on online conferencing.

14. Communicate with XP

To understand the reason for the change, you need to understand the way NetMeeting communicates. When a user connects to the Internet, his or her computer is always assigned a unique IP address. This address is important because it is the only thing that will let requested data find its way back to your system. Because there are many users and not quite as many IP addresses to be had, many Internet service providers assign IP addresses dynamically. Thus, when you connect to an ISP on one day, you may have a different IP address than you had the day before. This is especially the case for home dial-up users.

DSL and cable connections to the Internet have started using static IP addresses for all their users, but these providers are expected to shift to dynamic IP assignments in the near future, a result of their own success.

With all this shifting of IP addresses from one day to the next, it is a wonder that any computer can find another, particularly with a service such as NetMeeting. To work around this problem, NetMeeting uses a centralized server configuration to keep track of who's who. These servers are the Internet Location Servers (ILS). Also called directory servers, they serve the function of knowing who is online and what each user's current IP address is. When other NetMeeting users log on to the same ILS, their information will also be displayed, and they will see that you are available to be contacted with NetMeeting.

Users can use any ILS on the planet to hold a meeting; they only need to prearrange the same ILS to connect. For privacy's sake, users can log on to an ILS without appearing in the public directory. Only associates who know you are going to be in that ILS will be able to connect to you. ILS serves only as a connecting point for NetMeeting users. After a call is started, the ILS is no longer engaged.

When Microsoft began to see the success of the America Online instant messaging system, it decided to throw its support to a similar system on its content-provided network, MSN. Thus was born the MSN Messenger—an online chat tool with (at the time) far fewer features than NetMeeting.

But, Microsoft had a problem. Even though Messenger was a much simpler tool than NetMeeting, it still needed a way to connect to other Messenger users. Microsoft's own ILS machines fit the bill nicely, but to use them would create far too much traffic for the servers to handle, what with NetMeeting *and* Messaging clients constantly hitting the servers. So, in late 1999, Microsoft pulled its support for ILS usage in

NetMeeting. Instead, NetMeeting users would have to use third-party ILS machines or use Messenger itself to initiate NetMeeting calls.

NOTE: *To find a list of available ILS devices, you can visit the NetMeeting Zone at* **www.netmeeting-zone.com/bestservers.asp**.

The requirements for NetMeeting are not too hard to manage. Net-Meeting requires Internet Explorer and a sound card with microphone and speaker jacks. You don't need a video camera, but if you have one, you can make video calls.

The Windows Messenger

In the beginning, Messenger (then called MSN Messenger) was a rudimentary online chat tool. It located your friends online and let you type chat messages to them. No muss, no fuss.

Over time, MSN Messenger became a much more robust tool, rivaling the capabilities of even NetMeeting. File sharing, voice and video conversations, even long-distance telephone calls with Net2Phone technology were possible. And, what Messenger could not do—such as application sharing and collaboration—it would co-opt NetMeeting to accomplish.

Interestingly, the new Windows Messenger 4 has scaled back on some of the features offered with MSN Messenger 3.6. Net2Phone is no longer available, though direct calls can be made from PC to PC. NetMeeting integration has been removed as well, once again separating the use of these two applications.

Windows Messenger now has these features:

- Email notification (with Hotmail accounts)
- File sending
- Financial stock monitoring
- Instant messaging between two or more people
- Invitations for remote assistance
- Invitations to play online games
- PC-to-PC voice and video calls
- Protection for minors with the Kids Passport System
- User online/offline status
- Whiteboard use

14. Communicate with XP

This list clearly indicates a reduction from the number of earlier features, possibly as a way to avoid yet more legal issues for Microsoft from its competitor AOL. The name change alone seems to suggest this reasoning.

Regardless, all Windows XP users can try out this tool, whether or not they have an MSN account. Windows Messenger is activated upon the initial installation of Windows XP, so it is all ready to be used.

You should be aware of one drawback to using Windows Messenger: Some of the features in the application, particularly audio and video transmission, cannot be used unless the other users you are connected to have Windows Messenger and Windows XP. MSN Messenger, unfortunately, will not work. You can, however, still chat and share files with earlier versions of Messenger.

14. Communicate with XP

Immediate Solutions

Installing NetMeeting

NetMeeting is oddly presented within Windows XP. On the one hand, it's available for immediate use. On the other hand, you have to run through the installation procedures first—installation procedures that are well hidden.

TIP: Before you start this procedure, close all applications that play or record sound.

This method of presentation may be part of Microsoft's plan to emphasize the Windows Messenger tool. Whatever the reason, installing NetMeeting can be a rather cryptic process, so here are the steps to follow:

1. Click Start|Run to open the Run window.
2. Type "conf.exe" in the Open field.
3. Click OK. The Run window will close, and the NetMeeting window will open (see Figure 14.1).
4. Click Next to move to the Information page (see Figure 14.2).
5. Enter your information in the appropriate fields.
6. Click Next to move to the Directory Server page.

Figure 14.1   Starting the NetMeeting installation.

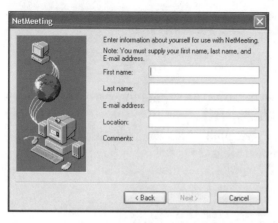

Figure 14.2   Enter your personal information.

7. If you plan to use the Windows Messenger to initiate
    NetMeeting calls, check the Log On To A Directory Server
    When NetMeeting Starts checkbox to clear the option.

8. If you want to keep your status on the ILS private, click the
    Do Not List My Name In The Directory checkbox to select it.

9. Click Next to move to the Connection Speed page (see
    Figure 14.3).

10. Click the radio button matching your connection speed to
    select it.

11. Click Next to move to the Shortcut page.

12. Leave the options checked and click Next. The Audio Tuning
    Wizard will appear.

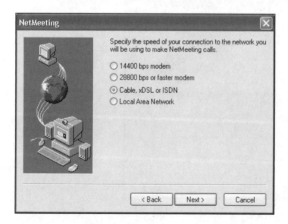

Figure 14.3   Choose your connection speed.

At this point, you will be asked to configure the audio settings for NetMeeting. To continue, follow these steps:

1. Click Next to move to the Device page, which will appear if you have more than one audio device (see Figure 14.4).

2. Using the drop-down lists, select the proper devices for recording and playback.

3. Click Next to move to the Playback Testing page.

4. Click Test to play a test sound.

5. Click the Volume slider control to adjust the sound to a comfortable level.

6. Click Stop to stop the test sound.

7. Click Next to move to the Record Testing page (see Figure 14.5).

Figure 14.4   Select the device to handle your audio input.

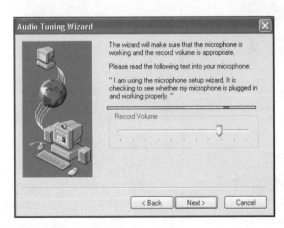

Figure 14.5   Test your vocal volume.

14. Communicate with XP

281

8. With a normal tone of voice, speak the phrase displayed in the wizard into your microphone.

9. If any red areas appear, adjust the Record Volume slider control down until your voice is no longer in the red and yellow zones.

10. Click Next to move to the Finished page.

11. Click Finish. The Audio Tuning Wizard will close and NetMeeting will open.

Configuring an Online Conference

The best part of NetMeeting is how simple it is to use. After you establish your own account, getting connected to your fellow NetMeeting users is a simple matter. You can place a call to an online colleague by using NetMeeting or Windows Messenger. In this section, we'll focus on the tasks that Windows Messenger cannot do: host an online conference.

Hosting an Online Conference

To begin an online conference, you first need to invite others to the meeting. Your invitation is easily handled with the Host A Meeting dialog box, as shown in the next steps:

1. In NetMeeting, click Call|Host Meeting to open the Host A Meeting dialog box (see Figure 14.6).

Figure 14.6   You can set up a meeting from here.

2. Type a name for the conference in the Meeting Name field.

3. If you want to limit the participants in this meeting, click the Only You Can Accept Incoming Calls and Only You Can Place Outgoing Calls checkboxes to select them.

4. If you want to limit the type of traffic in the meeting, click any of the Meeting Tools checkboxes to select them. The options that are selected can only be started by you.

5. Click OK. The Host A Meeting dialog box will close, and you will be listed as a meeting participant in the NetMeeting window (see Figure 14.7).

6. Click the Find Someone In A Directory button to open the Find Someone dialog box (see Figure 14.8).

7. Click the name of the person in your contacts list you wish to invite. The person's status will change to Waiting For Answer.

8. When the person on the other end accepts the invitation to the meeting, the connection will be made, and that person will be listed as a meeting participant.

Related solutions:	Found on page:
Setting Up a Dial-Up Internet Account	184
Setting Up a Broadband PPPoE Internet Account	189

Figure 14.7   The NetMeeting window.

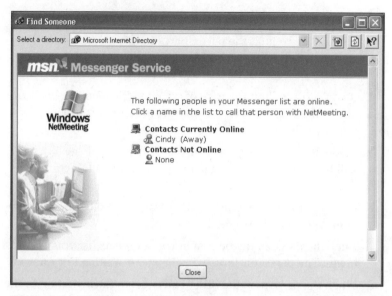

Figure 14.8   Sending out invitations.

Joining an Online Conference

If you are not the one hosting a conference, you will still find it easy to join a meeting—should you be invited. When an invitation arrives, you will immediately be prompted by two windows: a small pop-up window near the notification area of the taskbar and a larger Conversation window that will actually pose the invitation question (see Figure 14.9).

To join the conference, follow these steps:

1. In the Conversation window, click the Accept link. A message indicating you have accepted the invitation will appear in the Conversation window, the NetMeeting window will open, and a NetMeeting Incoming Call dialog will appear (see Figure 14.10).

2. While the sound of a telephone ringing is still being played, click the Accept button. The NetMeeting Incoming Call dialog box will close, and your name will be added to the meeting participants' list in NetMeeting.

TIP: When the NetMeeting Incoming Call dialog box appears, you must click Accept before the ringing stops; otherwise, the invitation will automatically be declined.

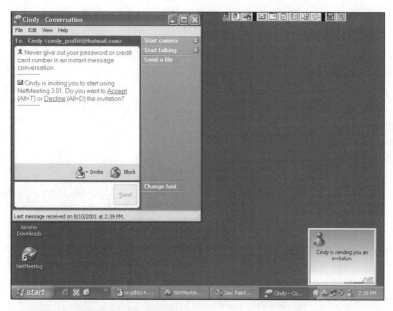

Figure 14.9 Getting an invitation.

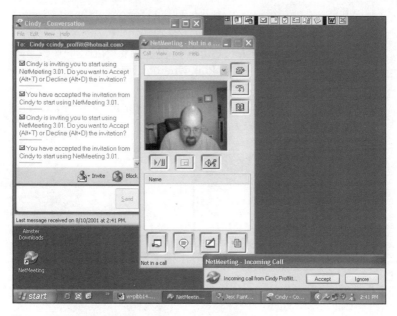

Figure 14.10 Pick up the phone!

Running an Online Conference

You can run an online conference in many ways. If you have video and audio capabilities, you may just choose to run it as a conference call. Even without A/V, you can still use chat to communicate your ideas to the other people in the conference. Some wonderful tools also are available to help enhance your conference—tools that let you share more than just words.

Using Chat

If you do not have a microphone or video hooked up on your system, you can still get a lot of information across with the chat function. After the meeting starts, follow these steps to begin a chat session:

1. In NetMeeting, click Chat to open the Chat window for all meeting participants (see Figure 14.11).

2. Type your text in the Message field.

3. Press Enter or click the Send Message button. Your text will appear in the Chat field of all participants' Chat windows.

4. When another person in the meeting responds, that message will appear in your Chat field (see Figure 14.12).

5. To end the chat session, click File|Exit. The NetMeeting Chat dialog box will appear, asking whether you want to save the chat session.

6. Click the option you desire and follow the steps to the end of the program.

Figure 14.11   Starting a chat.

14. Communicate with XP

Figure 14.12   Chat away to your heart's content.

If you want to send a chat message to only one of the conference members in private, you merely have to readdress the chat message by using these steps:

1. Type your text in the Message field.

2. Click the drop-down list control for the Send To field. A list of the meeting participants will appear.

3. Click the participant to whom you want to send the message to select him or her.

4. Press Enter or click the Send Message button. Your text will appear in the Chat field of only the selected participant.

5. If the person responds privately, his or her message will appear in your Chat field with gray text and a [private] notation.

Using the Whiteboard

Some people can't seem to get their point across without using pictures to explain their ideas. For these people, something like a whiteboard used in a meeting can come in handy. NetMeeting recognizes this valuable tool with an electronic version of a whiteboard that all participants can use. Modeled after the Microsoft Paint application, the whiteboard component is easy and fun to use, as you will see in the following steps:

1. In NetMeeting, click Whiteboard to open the Whiteboard window for all meeting participants (see Figure 14.13).

2. Click the Text tool so that the text cursor will appear.

3. Click a portion of the screen and type in some text. The text will appear in all the participants' Whiteboard windows.

14. Communicate with XP

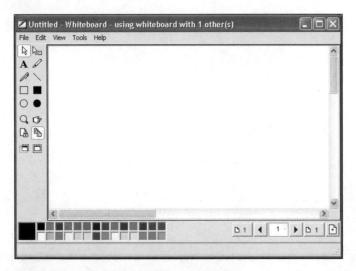

Figure 14.13   Starting a whiteboard session.

4. Click a graphics tool so that it will appear.

5. Create some simple graphics on the screen. The graphics will appear in all the participants' Whiteboard windows.

TIP: Use thicker lines when drawing on the whiteboard. Thinner lines may get lost in the transmission and not appear on the other Whiteboard windows.

---

6. Click the Remote Pointer tool. A purple pointer icon will appear in all the participants' Whiteboard windows.

7. Click and drag the pointer icon. The actions will be mirrored on all the participants' Whiteboard windows.

8. To end the Whiteboard session, click File|Exit. Another Whiteboard dialog box will appear, asking whether you want to save the session.

9. Click the option you desire and follow the steps to the end of the program.

Sharing Applications

One of the coolest features of NetMeeting is the capability to share applications that are running on any participant's system. This feature makes it possible to let others view and even use applications from wherever they are! To share applications, follow these steps:

1. In NetMeeting, click Share Program to open the Sharing dialog box (see Figure 14.14).

Figure 14.14   Sharing applications is easy.

2. In the Share Programs field, click the application you want to share to select it.

3. Click the Share button. The application will be displayed on all participants' systems.

TIP: *The application will be visible only if it is on top of the host system's desktop.*

---

4. If you want to let others work with the application, click the Allow Control button. A Controllable caption will appear on all participants' shared windows.

5. If a user needs to control the application, he or she will use the Control|Request Control menu option in his or her shared window. Choosing this option will display the Request Control dialog box on your system for a brief time.

6. Click Accept to give the other user control of your application.

TIP: *To avoid the back and forth of a control request, click the Automatically Accept Request For Control checkbox in the Sharing dialog box.*

WARNING! *End-User's License Agreements may have problems with multiple users accessing a single-license application. Microsoft's EULA does allow application sharing of any of its applications, but third-party developers may take issue. Check your application's EULA for more details.*

7. Click Unshare. The application will be unshared, and the shared program windows will close on the other participants' systems.

Transferring Files

Often, during a meeting, you will inevitably get a comment along the lines of "Oh, you don't have that file? I'll email it to you when we're done here." If this situation ever happens in a NetMeeting conference, you don't have to wait. Just follow this procedure to get the file out immediately:

1. In NetMeeting, click Transfer Files to open the File Transfer window.

2. Click the Add Files button to open the Select Files To Send dialog box.

3. Navigate to the file or files you wish to send and click to select them.

4. Click Add. The file or files will be added to the File Transfer list (see Figure 14.15).

5. Click the Participant drop-down list control to display the list of participants.

6. Click the person to whom you want to send the file to select him or her.

7. Click the Send All button. A copy of the file will be sent to the participant's Received Files folder.

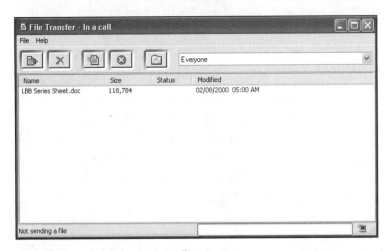

Figure 14.15   You can send one file or many.

Configuring Windows Messenger

When Windows XP is first installed, it will ask you to set up a .NET Passport account. Even if you are not inclined to use the communications tools within Windows XP, it is still a good idea to get one for potential later use because .NET's distributed applications framework promises to provide an interesting set of tools in the future.

Getting a .NET Passport is easy and free of charge. All you need is a little time and an Internet connection, as you will see here:

1. Click the Apply For Passport icon that appears the first several times you log on to Windows XP. The .NET Passport Wizard will open.
2. Click Next to move to the Do You Have An E-Mail Account page.
3. Click the Yes, Use An Existing Account radio button to select it.
4. Click Next to move to the What Is Your E-Mail Account page.
5. Type your email address in the E-Mail Address Or Passport field.
6. Click Next to move to the Type And Confirm A Password For Your New Passport page.
7. Enter your password in both Password fields.
8. Click Next to move to the Please Answer A Secret Question page.
9. Select a secret question and type the answer in the Answer field.
10. Click Next to move to the What Is Your Location? page.
11. Enter the correct information in the appropriate fields.
12. Click Next to move to the You're Done page.
13. Click Finish to close the .NET Passport Wizard.

After the Passport is established, you will need to verify the email account that you submitted in the Passport application. You can do so in three easy steps:

1. Open your email client and find a message from the Passport Member Services.
2. Open the message.
3. Click the first hyperlink in the message. Internet Explorer will open to the Email Validated screen.

When the email address is confirmed, you can log on to Windows Messenger freely. If you ever change your email account, you can enter the change in your Passport settings and have the new address reconfirmed.

Using Windows Messenger

After you create an account for Windows Messenger, you can sign on to the service and begin to use it as follows:

1. Double-click the Windows Messenger icon in the Notification Area of the taskbar to open the Windows Messenger window.

2. Click the Click Here To Sign In link to open the .NET Messenger Service dialog box.

3. Confirm the correct email address is displayed and type the password for that account in the Password field.

4. Click the Sign Me In Automatically checkbox to select it.

5. Click OK. The .NET Messenger Service dialog box will close, and the Contacts page will appear in the Windows Messenger window (see Figure 14.16).

Before you begin to use any function within Windows Messenger, you will have to configure any audio or video devices connected to your system by using the Audio And Video Tuning Wizard. This one-time-only function occurs after you first sign in and before you can do anything else in Messenger. It will pop up immediately after you start any tool in Messenger the first time you run the application. To use it, do the following:

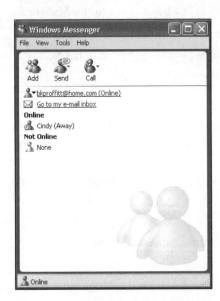

Figure 14.16   The Contacts page in Windows Messenger.

1. In the Audio And Video Tuning Wizard, click Next to move to the Camera page.

2. Select the camera you wish to use in the Camera field.

3. Click Next to move to the Adjust Your Camera page (see Figure 14.17).

4. Move your camera until it is at the correct angle.

5. Click Next to move to the Audio Performance Tips page.

6. Click Next to move to the Audio Devices page. Using the drop-down lists, select the proper devices for recording and playback.

7. Click Next to move to the Speaker Volume Testing page.

8. Click Click To Test Speakers to play a test sound.

9. Click the Speaker Volume slider control to adjust the sound to a comfortable level.

10. Click Stop to stop the test sound.

11. Click Next to move to the Microphone Testing page.

12. With a normal tone of voice, speak the phrase displayed in the wizard into your microphone.

13. If any red areas appear, adjust the Microphone Volume slider control down until your voice is no longer in the red and yellow zones.

14. Click Next to move to the end page of the wizard.

15. Click Finish to close the Audio And Video Tuning Wizard.

14. Communicate with XP

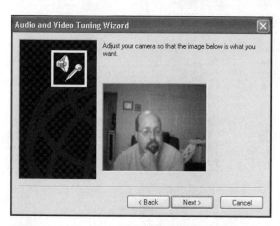

Figure 14.17 Whoa! Who is this handsome devil?

Whenever you add new audio or video hardware to your system, just run the Audio And Video Tuning Wizard again to adjust the new device's settings.

Sending a Message in Windows Messenger

The most commonly used function in Windows Messenger is surely the online chat function. In Messenger, however, this function has been upgraded from "chat" to conversation. Given the richness of the tool, you can easily see why. You can begin a conversation in Windows Messenger by following these few short steps:

1. Click the Send button to open the Contacts menu.

2. Select the person with whom you wish to start the conversation. The Conversation window will appear (see Figure 14.18).

3. Type a message to the person in the Message field at the bottom of the Conversation window.

4. Press Enter or click the Send button to send the message.

Placing a Call in Windows Messenger

If you want to initiate a voice conversation with someone in Windows Messenger, you place a call rather than send a message. Placing a call is as simple as sending a message, though there is one extra step. When calls are placed, people are invited to accept or decline the call first, as you can see in the following steps:

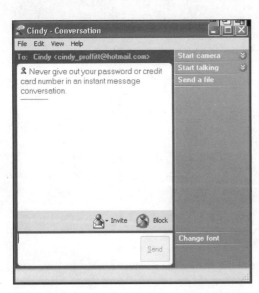

Figure 14.18   The primary chat window for Windows Messenger.

1. Click the Call button to open the Contacts menu.

2. Select the person with whom you wish to start the call. The Conversation window will appear and indicate the person has been invited.

3. If the person accepts, a notice will appear informing you of this fact, and the volume controls will appear for the call.

4. If the person has a camera on his or her end, click the Start Camera control to expand the video screen.

NOTE: Remember, audio and video transmissions are currently not possible between earlier versions of Messenger and Windows Messenger.

NOTE: Though it was not available as this book went to press, Microsoft has announced a new partnership with Dialpad Communications, Inc. that will provide a new version of Windows Messenger that includes PC-to-phone capabilities for as little as 2.9 cents per minute for domestic U.S. calls. This new version is expected to be released on or near the October 25 release date for Windows XP.

Sending a File in Windows Messenger

If you need to send someone a file as you are making a call or having a conversation, you will need the recipient's permission before the files will be transferred. This added security measure will help prevent unwanted files from sneaking onto someone's computer.

To send a file, follow these steps:

1. In the Conversation window, click the Send A File control to open the Send A File window.

2. Navigate to the file or files you wish to send and click to select them.

3. Click Open. The Send A File window will close, and the file or files will be sent.

4. If the person accepts the file, the transfer will begin.

14. Communicate with XP

Chapter 15

Multimedia and XP

In Brief

One definition of multimedia is straightforward: the use of computers to present text, graphics, video, animation, and sound in an integrated way. This is a bit of a conceit, because long before computers, multimedia was being produced by other machines.

Perhaps the earliest form of complex machine-created art was text art. In the early days of computers, this art was constructed by using combinations of ASCII text to create simple to complex pictures. You may remember seeing them when you first learned about computers. The first form of this art was not created with a computer—nor was it done in the twentieth century. The first form of text art was created with an old Bar Lock typewriter in 1898 by a secretary named Flora Stacey (see Figure 15.1).

When the radio teletype was invented in the early twentieth century, the tradition of text art quickly showed up on that medium as well. Radio teletype operators began to use their new form of communication to send wonderfully complex forms of artwork using the overstrike capabilities of the teleprinters. Given the slow transmission rate, which was around 50 baud, printing a single picture could take hours, but the operator thought the effort was worthwhile.

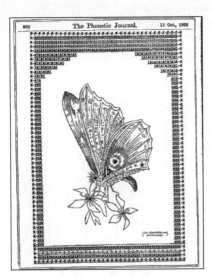

Figure 15.1   Everything in this picture was created using a typewriter—including the butterfly.

The first computers did not use video monitors to display their output. Instead, punch tape, punch cards, and printers were used. Creative programmers used this brand-new technology to create Christmas trees on punch cards and more complex works on their printers. Other programmers tried to compose simple little tunes using the tones and clicks made by their machines.

Computers were never really designed to handle pictures, animation, audio, and video. This capability was more of an afterthought that occurred when computer processors got really fast and video monitors came into existence. At this point, more users began noticing the similarities between computers and televisions.

If a computer has a screen and a television has a screen, folks wondered, why couldn't they both display pictures? Never mind the fact that computers and televisions were about as technologically alike as an elephant and a rhododendron. The new monitors represented a challenge to programmers: how to bring animation and video to these new devices.

Was all this multimedia? In the strictest sense, yes. Machines designed to create one form of media were being used to create another form. More than one medium on one device certainly qualifies as multimedia. Of course, what we think of multimedia is full-motion video with stereo sound blasting out of our speakers. The notion of text art as multimedia merely seems quaint. It will be interesting to see what happens next. What new technology will make *our* multimedia seem quaint?

What Windows Media Player 8 Has to Offer

Media Player has come a long way since its early days as CD Player. In those times, the application was used solely to provide playback for audio CDs. Microsoft had additional applications to play some sounds and eventually the tiny little AVI video clips you could download off the Internet. Eventually, CD Player and all the rest of these applications were combined into the single Media Player application. This was done in part for convenience's sake and also in part to react to the success of yet another Microsoft competitor: Real Media, whose RealPlayer technology comprises a significant portion of the audio and video files on the Internet today.

15. Multimedia and XP

Media Player is made up of several components. It can play back audio from CDs, several audio file formats (including AIFF, AU, MIDI, and WAV), the AVI and MPG video formats, and, of course, its own native Windows Media format.

The Windows Media format is now at version 8, like the player itself, and offers a new compression technology that allows superior playback of audio and video files. Microsoft and third-party vendors using the new format claim that it will deliver near-VHS quality at 250Kbps bandwidth and near-DVD picture and sound at 500Kbps. Granted, these bandwidth speeds are pretty high, but you no longer need to endure jerky, low-quality film clips at any speed.

Windows Media 8 can be viewed with Windows Media Players 7.1 and 8. This is a good thing, too, because Media Player 8 is available only for Windows XP users. Media Player 8 also features a customizable new interface, DVD playback (with a DVD encoder), and easy-to-use CD recording tools. It can also assist you in organizing your media collections and finding quality streaming multimedia from the Internet. Not bad for something that just used to play CDs.

NOTE: *Though it was not available as this book went to press, Microsoft will be releasing a Plus for Windows XP product at the same time Windows XP is released. This add-on will feature a number of new add-ons for Windows XP, including voice command enhancements for Media Player 8. The Media Player will also feature improvements to boost the clarity of sound on PC speakers.*

Why CD Burning Used to Be So Tricky

When writable CDs became available, many people were heartened by the release of this new medium. Here was a storage medium that could hold up to 640MB, or 74 minutes of high-quality music! Storage problems would become a thing of the past, and people could concentrate on other, more important issues, such as world peace.

Such was not to be, unfortunately, as the promise of writable CDs quickly was deflated by cold, harsh realities. Burning a CD was no simple matter, and often the writing process failed completely, leaving the user with a piece of plastic that could possibly be used only as a coaster for drinks.

You can buy two types of discs for CD burners: CD Read-Only (CDR) and CD ReWritable (CDRW). CDRs typically cost less than a dollar but can be burned only one time. CDRWs can be recorded over and over. Although CDRWs may sound like the optimal solution, keep in mind that the life expectancy of a CDRW is often lower than a CDR. All that writing and rewriting tends to corrupt the CDRW that much faster.

Most CDRs can store 640MB of data or 74 minutes of music, though some CDRs on the market today can store 700MB or 80 minutes. Keep in mind that 640MB is roughly equivalent to 12 hours of MP3 files and 30 minutes of good-quality MPEG video.

The CDs you burn are different from the CDs you buy because retail CDs are pressed in a factory, not burned with a laser. People often have a mistaken impression that when CDs are burned, the files are stored on the CD in the exact same way they are stored on a hard drive. In fact, the methods are quite different. Before any file is burned to a CD, it is first converted to an image file. The image file is the collection of 1s and 0s that will actually be zapped onto the material of the CD. When read by a qualified CD player, these 1s and 0s (which are physically denoted by microscopic pits and peaks on the CD) can be translated into a file system that the computer can read or audio files that the rest of the CD player can make use of.

The most common CD burning problem is the "buffer underrun" error. When an image is created for the CDR, it is then sent to the laser component at a constant stream. This data is sent in a memory buffer first and then fed to the laser. If the computer gets interrupted or slowed to the point that no data is in the memory buffer, the process fails and a buffer underrun occurs. This means you just made yourself another coaster.

This entire process is counter-intuitive if you are used to just telling a file manager "Please put my files here" and the task is done. Most CD-burning applications must step you through a tedious procedure in which files to be burned onto the CD are marked, an image is created from the marked files, and finally the image is burned onto the CD. And, all the while, you hope that nothing interrupts the process.

Windows XP has not really changed this procedure, but it has made parts of the procedure so transparent that it does not really matter. Instead of using a separate application, you can now burn CDs directly from Windows XP or from the Media Player application. You don't have to directly deal with complicated image files, either. You simply indicate the files you need to put on the CD, move them to a temporary holding folder, and then initiate the burning process.

Windows XP has also simplified the process of creating audio CDs as well, making this process little more than choosing the music tracks and setting them to the disc in the order you want.

15. Multimedia and XP

NOTE: *You should be aware that there are some tasks Windows XP cannot do with burning CDs. For instance, it cannot create a CD from a pre-made image file copied from another CD. These files, which are usually found in the CIF or ISO formats, must be burned onto a CD using third-party CD burning software.*

Lights, Camera, Action!

The DVD is a product that was almost dead before it even hit the shelves. When it first arrived on the scene in 1997, the DVD was not snatched up by the Hollywood movie studios. In fact, three of the major studios (Disney, Fox, and Paramount) made a concerted effort to kill the promotion by Warner Brothers' Warren Lieberfarb and the rest of the WB studio.

Some of this reluctance to promote DVDs was fear of the new technology because many studio executives were reluctant to give pirates the ultimate prize: digitally perfect versions of their movies, just begging to be copied and sold as bootlegs all over the world. And, some of this was simple pride: Though Sony and Philips were the developers of the DVD technologies, Warner Brothers owned some of the patents for converting film to DVD. The other studio executives were a bit miffed to have to use someone else's technology for their films.

By the end of 1998, a feasible copy protection scheme was made available, and the rest of the Hollywood studios began to come around. They also discovered something very interesting: People who already owned a VHS copy of a movie would be more than willing to buy a DVD version of the same film. Usually, consumers made this decision on the basis of the clarity of digital audio and video alone. Ever the marketers, studios began to sweeten the pot, taking advantage of all the additional storage space the DVDs have to offer.

Instead of just showing a crisp, visually superior version of the film, DVDs began to include goodies, such as multiple language tracks, outtakes, and the director's cuts of the film. This last feature has become popular within Hollywood as well; directors are more than willing to show all the work they've done for a movie and are even using the existence of the director's cut to sooth actors whose scenes were cut by promising to make sure these scenes get on the DVD.

Is Hollywood's promotion of DVDs successful? In 2000, American consumers spent $4.2 billion buying and renting DVDs.

Because a DVD can store up to 14 times more data than a CD-ROM, its use as a PC storage medium is obvious. Because a DVD drive can also play CDs, its presence on a computer is becoming more and more common. And, in yet another convergence of technology, users figure that if they have a DVD drive and this fancy-schmancy monitor, there ought to be a way to play those movies on a PC.

So, developers and manufacturers quickly came up with a solution to just that problem. Only one additional piece of technology was needed: a DVD encoder. DVD output, after all, is made to be displayed on a television. And, similar as they are superficially, televisions and monitors use vastly different kinds of video signals. To compensate, you just have a DVD encoder translate the output of the DVD to something your monitor can use. This encoder can take the form of hardware or software, though hardware is recommended, because a dedicated device will deliver more consistent quality.

Playing a DVD movie within Windows XP is now as simple as playing an audio CD, provided you have the correct equipment. If you do, you too can play Hollywood movies on your PC.

Now, if only it were as easy to get the buttered popcorn stains off the keyboard...

Immediate Solutions

Playing Multimedia Files

Many different kinds of multimedia files are available, but they really break down into four basic types: audio, video, streaming audio, and streaming video.

"Streaming" multimedia files are designed to be parceled out on a requested basis in a continuous stream of information that lets you view the multimedia file as it's being sent to your computer. This is opposed to the more traditional method of pulling an entire file down from the Internet and then playing it when it's stored on your hard drive.

NOTE: *For more information on streaming multimedia files, refer to the "Listening to the Radio" and "Watching an Online Movie" sections later in this chapter.*

Traditional files are usually rather large simply because so much information is contained within them. After they are downloaded to your computer, however, they are yours to keep.

Before I show you how to play and record multimedia files, let me be clear on one point: Many music and video files are usually under some sort of copyright that prohibits their being distributed without the permission of the copyright owner. For instance, it is no secret that thousands of copyrighted music files are out there on the Internet, free for the taking. Regardless of your personal stance on the issue of copyrights, you are encouraged to respect existing copyrights in any medium. Legal lecture over; now on to the Media Player.

If you have a file on your computer that falls into the category of multimedia, viewing or listening to it requires just a few steps:

1. In Windows Explorer, navigate to the folder containing the file you wish to play.

2. Double-click the file's icon. The Media Player will open and begin playing your file.

3. To stop the file's playback, click the Pause button. The file will stop at that point in its playback (see Figure 15.2).

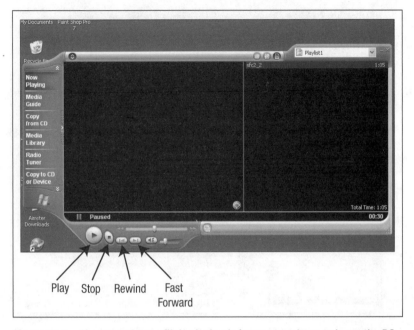

Figure 15.2   You can pause a file's playback, in case you have to leave the PC.

4. To restart the playback, click the Play button to resume the playback at the paused point.

5. To stop the playback altogether, click the Stop button to stop the playback and return to the beginning of the file.

6. Click the Play button once more to begin the playback.

7. Click and hold the Seek slider control.

8. Move the slider control to the left or right. The file will advance or revert to another point in the playback.

9. Release the Seek control to resume playback at the new point.

This methodology will work whether the file is audio or visual in nature.

Music files that are contained within the My Music folder are even simpler to start, as you can see in the following steps:

1. Click Start|My Music to open the My Music folder (see Figure 15.3).

2. Click the song you want to begin playing to select the song file.

3. Click the Play All link. The Media Player will open and start the song's playback.

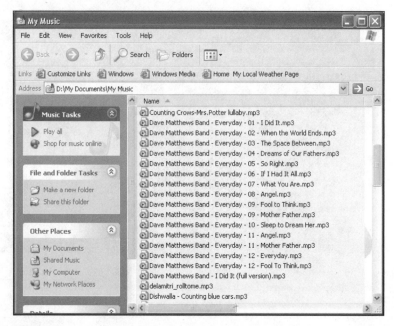

Figure 15.3   It's nice to have all your music in one place.

4. To move to the next song in the folder, click the Fast Forward button to begin playing the next song.

5. To move to the previous song in the folder, click the Rewind button to begin playing the previous song.

NOTE: *All the songs in the My Music folder will be played and then cycle back to the first song in the folder. This continuous loop will keep going until you halt the Media Player by clicking the Stop button or exiting the application.*

Finally, you can play tracks off a music CD. Normally, this operation is simple: Insert the CD and it will begin to play. But, Windows XP has a default setting to ask you what kind of action you want to take every time it sees a new type of CD. This means that the first time you insert a music CD, Windows XP will ask you what to do. XP is not being stupid by asking this question; it's being careful. So, to start a simple playback with no recording, you will need to follow these steps:

1. Insert the music CD into the CD-ROM drive. The Audio CD dialog box will appear (see Figure 15.4).

2. Click the Play Audio CD option to select it.

Figure 15.4   You can decide what to do with all music CDs from now on.

3. Click the Always Do The Selected Action checkbox to select it.

TIP: If you don't click the Always Do The Selected Action checkbox, this dialog box will appear every time you insert an audio CD into the drive.

---

4. Click OK. The Audio CD dialog box will close, and the Media Player will open to play the CD (see Figure 15.5).

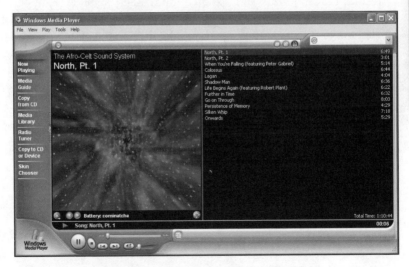

Figure 15.5   A playing CD with full playlist and visualization.

Every music CD in the world has a unique identifier that can be queried against a common database with the nondescriptive name Compact Disk Digital Audio (CDDA). If your CD's information is on the CDDA, it will immediately be downloaded and displayed. Using this feature could save you a lot of time typing in titles of tracks and artist information.

Recording Music CDs

One of the more common tasks most users want to do with Media Player is record music off their CDs. I find this feature very useful because I can store most of my music on my hard drive without having to deal with several dozen CD cases in and around my already cluttered work area.

There is nothing wrong with copying music for your own purposes. The problems come about when you start sharing those files with other people who haven't paid for them. Even with this restriction, copying your own music files onto your hard drive is still useful.

Media Player will record *(rip)* files from a music CD in one of two formats: Windows Media and MP3. MP3 is perhaps the most popular format for audio files in existence today because it offers superior sound quality with the smallest possible file size. Although Microsoft encourages the use of the Windows Media format, you might want to consider using MP3s for their nearly universal compatibility. Many personal devices can play digitally stored MP3 files, and some home and car stereos can even play MP3 files directly rather than standard CDA music track files.

By default, Media Player will rip music files in the Windows Media format. If you want to use MP3 format instead, you will need to follow this procedure:

1. In Media Player, click Tools|Options to open the Options dialog box.

TIP: If the menu is hidden in Media Player, click the Show Menu Bar icon in the top-right corner of the Media Player window.

2. Click the Copy Music tab to open the Copy Music page (see Figure 15.6).

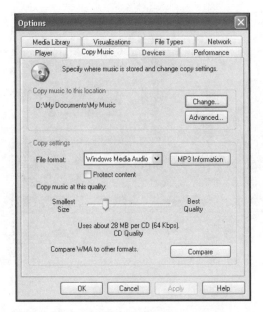

Figure 15.6 Setting your ripping options.

3. Click the drop-down list control for the File Format field to see the list of formats.

4. Click the MP3 option to select it.

5. Click Apply to apply the new settings.

6. Click OK to close the Options dialog box.

Now that you have established the format with which you want to record, actually ripping the CD involves just these few steps:

1. Insert the music CD into the CD-ROM drive. The Media Player will open to play the CD.

2. Click the Copy From CD link to open the Copy From CD page (see Figure 15.7).

3. Click the checkboxes for the tracks you do *not* want to record to clear the options.

4. Click the Copy Music button to begin copying the first selected track.

5. When you're finished, you can close the Media Player or continue to listen to other tracks.

Figure 15.7   Copying music tracks is easy.

Organizing Multimedia Files

If you have an extensive music collection, you will definitely want to keep your music files as organized as your CDs. And, if your CDs are not organized, you really have no excuse not to do so with your online collection.

The Media Player uses a Media Library metaphor to organize all your multimedia files. Note, however, that the contents of the Media Library will not always reflect the entirety of your music collection stored on your computer because the Media Player puts only music and video files that you have actively recorded or opened with the Media Player in the Media Library. If this sounds confusing, you're right. Here's an example to help explain this situation.

User Musicman loves collecting music. Thousands of tracks are stored on his computer's hard drive—mostly MP3s copied from his huge CD collection. Before he migrated to Windows XP, he had been using a third-party application to manage his music files. After he began using XP, he decided to try out the new Media Player 8 that came with the operating system.

To Musicman's dismay, when he opened the Media Library section of the Media Player, just a few sample music files were listed! Where were all his music files? Still where they always were, within the same folders on his hard drive. But, because Musicman had not created the files within Media Player, nor formally opened them, the Media Library did not know they were there.

The easiest solution to this predicament is to actually add the files within Media Player one time. After you do so, the Media Library will list the files and automatically organize them into album, artist, and genre categories, too!

To bring multimedia files into Media Player, follow these steps:

1. Click File|Add To Media Library|Add Files to open the Open dialog box.

2. Navigate to the folder containing your music. If you use more than one folder, you will need to repeat these steps.

3. Select all the files within the folder you want to bring to the Media Library.

4. Click Open. The selected files will be brought into the Media Library and automatically organized.

When your files are in the Media Library, you can view them all at once or in categories. For music files, those categories are Artist, Album, and Genre. Viewing the Media Library is simple: Just click the Media Library link in the Media Player.

Every music file has additional track and album information attached. This information includes the artist, genre, album, composer, media type, and song length, to name a few. Sometimes, you may need to edit this track information. For instance, the CDDA insists on using the genre name Sound Track, whereas I prefer the Soundtrack label. Toe-may-toe, toe-mah-toe, sure, but if you're picky like me, here's how to edit track information:

1. Click the track you want to edit to select it.

2. Right-click the field you want to change. The context menu will appear.

3. Click the Edit menu option to select the field for editing.

4. Type your changes and press Enter to make the changes.

If your music is fairly new, there is a good chance that a lot of information about the album can be made available to you. To access the Media Details, follow these steps:

15. Multimedia and XP

1. Within the Media Library, click the album you wish to learn about to select it.

2. Click Media Details. The details about the album will be displayed, if available (see Figure 15.8).

3. Click the Artist Profile button to display information about the artist.

4. To return to the Media Library, click the Back button.

Another way to organize your media files is to create a playlist. A playlist is a set of files that you like to see or hear in a particular order. To create a playlist, follow these steps:

1. Click the New Playlist button to open the New Playlist dialog box.

2. Enter a name for the playlist.

3. Click OK. The New Playlist dialog box will close, and the new playlist will appear in the list of playlists.

4. Click a song you want to add to the playlist to select it.

5. Click Add To Playlist to see a menu with all the playlists.

6. Select the playlist you want. The file will now appear in that playlist.

Figure 15.8   Everything you always wanted to know about your music.

Listening to the Radio

Streaming media is a fancy term for online multimedia content that is downloaded to the client computer but not stored there. This method offers two big advantages. The first advantage is for the end user. As streaming media is sent to the client machine, it is processed immediately by the streaming media application, which gives the end user instant playback without having to wait for the entire file to download. After the file is played, the data is deleted, thus saving on precious hard drive space.

The second advantage to this approach is to the producer of the content. Because streaming media cannot be saved by the client, live events such as concerts can be broadcast without the fear of an unscrupulous end user bootlegging the material. Streaming media can also be sent out to many users simultaneously, which makes the broadcast of on-demand events and music possible.

One of the most popular applications of streaming audio is the live broadcast of radio station content on the Internet. Both standard and Internet-only radio stations are widely available on the Internet, many of which are suitable to listen to even on 28.8 dial-up connections. The sound quality of these radio broadcasts is not exceptionally sharp, but it's no worse than listening to a local station on a small radio. And, if you're listening to a station in Kenya from Wausau, you're doing pretty well already.

The component that handles listening to radio broadcasts is the Radio Tuner. It keeps track of popular radio stations and lets you search for stations based on genre or any keyword.

To play content from a radio station, follow these steps:

1. In Media Player, click the Radio Tuner link to open the Radio Tuner page (see Figure 15.9).

2. If an interesting station appears in the Featured Stations section, click its link to expand the listing to show more information about the station (see Figure 15.10).

3. Click Play. The Media Player will connect to the station, and the content will be played.

4. To pause the transmission, click Pause.

5. To stop the transmission, click Stop.

15. Multimedia and XP

Figure 15.9   Radio stations from around the world.

Figure 15.10   Every station has information about itself.

If you want to look for another radio station that is not on the Featured Stations list, you can search through all the stations available by using this procedure:

1. On the Radio Tuner page, click the Find More Stations link to open the Find Stations page (see Figure 15.11).

2. Click the drop-down list control for the Browse By Genre field to see the list of options.

Figure 15.11   Looking for radio stations.

3. Click a genre. The option is selected, and the search results will be displayed.

4. If an interesting station appears in the Search Results, click its link to expand the listing to show more information about the station.

5. Click Play. The Media Player will connect to the station, and the content will be played.

If you find a radio station that appeals to you, you can add it to your My Stations list so that you don't have to hunt for it all the time. To do so, click the Add To My Stations link in an expanded station listing. The link will change to an Added To My Stations caption.

Watching an Online Movie

Music is not the only thing you can find for entertainment on the Internet. You can find movie files in many places as well.

Many of these files may be clips or previews of other, longer events. But, a surprising number of video files are short or full-length movies—many of which are created and distributed by independent filmmakers who might otherwise not be able to let the public see their work.

The best place to find online videos is in the Media Guide section of Media Player. This is actually a Web page that shows the latest in featured video content. To view an online movie, use these steps:

1. In Media Player, click Media Guide to open the current Media Guide (see Figure 15.12).

2. Click a link to a video, using a connection speed most appropriate for your bandwidth. The video will appear in the Now Playing section.

If that process seemed a bit anticlimactic, Table 15.1 lists Web sites that will allow you to run full-length motion pictures—some of which are free of charge.

Related Solutions:	On Page:
Setting Up a Dial-Up Internet Account	184
Setting Up a Broadband PPPoE Internet Account	189

Figure 15.12   The online Media Guide features many short videos.

Table 15.1   Full-length movie Web sites for Media Player.

Site	URL
ALWAYSi	www.alwaysi.com
CinemaNow	www.cinemanow.com
CinemaPop	www.cinemapop.com
FilmSpeed	www.filmspeed.com
SightSound	www.sightsound.com

Playing DVDs

If you are fortunate enough to have a DVD drive and DVD encoding device, you can play DVD movies on your PC. How you will get any work done is beyond me, but to each his own.

Playing a DVD is pretty much the same procedure as playing a music CD:

1. Insert the DVD into the DVD drive. The DVD dialog box will appear.
2. Click the Play DVD option to select it.
3. Click the Always Do The Selected Action checkbox to select it.
4. Click OK. The DVD dialog box will close, and the Media Player will open to play the DVD.

If you are a parent, you know it's important to keep an eye on what your children watch. DVDs are no exception. If you want to make sure your little ones will watch only appropriately rated movies, you can set up Media Player to control this by taking these steps:

1. In Media Player, click Tools|Options to open the Options dialog box.
2. Click the DVD tab to open the DVD page.
3. Click the Parental Control checkbox to select it.
4. Select the ratings you want to be the highest each user can view.
5. Click Apply to apply the settings to each user.
6. Click OK to close the Options dialog box.

15. Multimedia and XP

Burning Music CDs

If you are a real music aficionado, it is likely you have a CD writer drive on your PC for the purposes of creating your own music CDs. Making your own music CDs is this generation's answer to dubbing cassette tapes with favorite hits. With Windows XP, the process is just as simple, too:

1. Insert a blank CDR into the CD Writer drive.

2. Click the Copy To CD Or Device link to open the Copy To CD Or Device page (see Figure 15.13).

3. Click the checkboxes for the music files you want to record. A total time will appear as you add files.

4. When the time nears the total capacity for the blank CD, click the Copy Music button. A conversion and copying process will begin. When this process is complete, the CD will be ejected from the drive.

TIP: *Because of buffer underrun, it is always a good idea to avoid running a lot of applications or starting a new application when you're burning a CD.*

Figure 15.13   Recording a CD is no longer a mystery.

Configuring Media Player

Media Player is a unique application in that not only does it play multimedia files, but it also can change its own look and appearance like a chameleon. Media Player uses a technological trick known as skins to change its appearance. *Skins* are different interfaces for the same application. These interfaces can give any application a whole new look, and Media Player is no exception. The interface designers pulled out all the stops to make each Media Player skin look as different as possible.

You can choose skins based on your own personal preference, as shown in these steps:

1. In Media Player, click the Skin Chooser link to open the Skin Chooser page (see Figure 15.14).
2. Click a skin option to preview it.
3. When you find a skin you like, click the Apply Skin button to apply the new skin (see Figure 15.15).
4. To switch to the Full Mode, click the Return To Full Mode control.

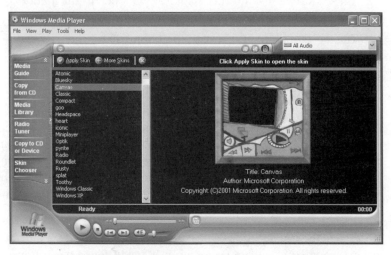

Figure 15.14   You can choose a skin to meet your aesthetic desires.

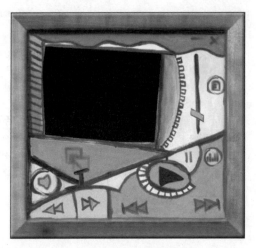

Figure 15.15   Picasso's Media Player.

If none of the skins available in Media Player appeal to you, you can quickly obtain a new skin online as follows:

1. In Media Player, click the Skin Chooser link to open the Skin Chooser page.

2. Click More Skins. Internet Explorer will open to the Media Player Skins Web page.

3. Click a skin graphic. The skins will immediately be downloaded and installed on the list of skins.

4. Click the new skin to preview it.

5. Click the Apply Skin button to apply the new skin.

As you have been working with Media Player, you have certainly noticed the visualizations that appear as music plays. *Visualizations* are abstract visual animations that roughly follow the beat and tone of the music. When violins are being played, the visual effect may be rather soothing. If drums are being heard, the effect may be significantly more jarring.

To change the visualizations, you can first choose a category and then cycle through the available screens, as you will see in these steps:

1. In Media Player, click Now Playing and start a music file or CD.

2. Click the Visualization Or Album Art control under the left corner of the visualization. A context menu will appear.

3. Click the Particle category to see the first visualization (see Figure 15.16).

Figure 15.16   Particles in motion.

4. Click the Next Visualization button to see the next visualization.

When you locate a pleasing visualization, simply leave it visible on the screen.

Chapter 16

Remote Windows XP

In Brief

At last count, I have a total of five computers in my home. This is an excessive number (something that my wife is constantly reminding me of) but necessary because of the work I do. Three of the computers run Windows XP Professional; the fourth, Windows 2000 Server; and the fifth, SuSE Linux. One of the machines is a laptop with a wireless connection, so I can use it anywhere in the house, and the rest are stationed throughout my home.

My house is by no means large, but the sedentary nature of my occupation means that I tend to be a bit lazy from time to time. Rather than get off my lazy behind to move from one computer to the next, I often find myself wishing I could just log on to the machine I need and do my work from where I'm sitting. Then, I remember what my doctor said about my weight at the last physical exam, and I get up and move.

Lazy authors notwithstanding, this capability is called working remotely. Today, more and more businesses are tapping into this technology (for more important reasons than user laziness). Working remotely allows employees to use their primary desktop from wherever in the world they might be, whether it's Timbuktu or the next cubicle in the office.

Remote Access vs. Remote Control

When local area network (LAN) technology was perfected in the 1980s, it became an integral part of corporate operations. LANs enable users to share information instantaneously and effortlessly, access common resources such as printers or CD-ROM drives, and communicate quickly and easily.

The most pressing limitation of LANs is the fact that no matter what type of LAN you have, signal strength forces the network to be physically rather small. LANs very rarely stretch beyond the confines of a corporate office. At most, they may be installed through a corporation's campus.

The problem is, the employees of a corporation are not confined within the office buildings in which they work (though some days it may feel like this is the case). Workers go home. Workers travel to other sites. Workers visit customers. Even if the entire workforce is endowed with mobile laptop workstations that can be docked and synchronized upon the employees' return to the office, invariably somebody is going to discover that a critical set of data was left in the workplace.

As I mentioned earlier in this book, remote access—either by dial-up or Virtual Private Network (VPN) connection—can enable users who are away from the office to access the LAN via phone or Internet. By doing so, the remote users can see the resources of the LAN as if their computers were directly attached to it.

NOTE: *For information on remote access using a dial-up connection, refer to "Setting Up a Dial-Up Networking Account" in Chapter 10. To learn more details about VPN remote access, refer to "Using a VPN Connection" in Chapter 12.*

This type of remote access is called *remote node* because the remote computer essentially acts as another node on the corporate LAN. But, another type of remote access enables even more direct control. Referred to as *remote control*, this form of remote access does not have the remote computer act as a node on the LAN. Instead, the remote computer controls a computer that *is* directly attached to the LAN.

This form of remote control is far more robust than remote-node access. One of the biggest advantages of remote-control access is the remote user's ability to run applications on the remote computer that may not even be installed on the remote computer. For instance, if a remote user needs to look at some information in QuickBooks on her base computer, she can use remote-control access to connect to her base computer to start QuickBooks remotely and find the data she needs—even if QuickBooks is not installed on her remote PC.

The most common method of remote control uses a screen painting method. The desktop of the base computer is literally transposed into a window on the remote PC. If the mouse pointer is moved in the remote desktop's view of the base PC, that action is mirrored on the base PC itself. The same holds true for keyboard input.

Many good remote control tools are out on the market, PCAnywhere and Citrix being two excellent offerings. Windows XP comes with its own native remote control tool for you to use. Called Remote Desktop, it will connect to any other authorized Windows XP machine or any Windows machine running Terminal Server.

16. Remote Windows XP

As you might expect, running Remote Desktop is a bit slow, even on the fastest of connections. A lot of work is involved in processing the signals and screen paints from the remote desktop, so a lag is usually noticeable in control inputs. This lag time means Remote Desktop is not a tool that you will use constantly. At best, you should use it to perform short, necessary tasks with your base computer and then log off. After a while, the lag time would become counterproductive to whatever task you were trying to accomplish. One exception would be if you had to start a long-term computational operation. In that case, you could connect remotely, start the computation, and let the remote application run merrily away.

Other tools within Windows XP enable you to enhance remote access. Windows XP has the capability to preemptively store network files and folders so that you can access them offline later. Some synchronization tools also will let you synchronize the data between your base and remote PCs—very useful if you find you will be away from your base computer for a long period of time.

Immediate Solutions

Configuring Remote Desktop on the Base Machine

To run Remote Desktop, you will need at least one Windows XP machine running—preferably two. The machine running Windows XP can be either the base machine or the remote machine; it doesn't matter. If one machine is not a Windows XP machine, it is important that the other machine has the Terminal Services (TS) client running on it.

In this section, you will learn how to set up the base machine whether it is running Windows XP or some other flavor of Windows. For base PCs that are not running Windows XP, the Terminal Services client must be running. For Windows 2000 Server users, this is usually not a big deal because the TS client is often running anyway. For Windows 95, Windows 98, Windows NT 4, and Windows 2000 Professional, however, you will need to install this client or provide an equivalent.

Fortunately, such an equivalent is already at hand on the Windows XP Professional CD-ROM. This application is called the Remote Desktop Connection, and even if you're not running Windows XP on your base machine, you can still set it up so that your remote XP machine can connect to it. Just use this procedure to set it up for any 32-bit version of Windows:

1. On the base machine, insert the Windows XP Professional CD-ROM. The Setup window will open to the Welcome page (see Figure 16.1).
2. Click the Perform Additional Tasks link to move to the Additional Tasks page (see Figure 16.2).
3. Click the Set Up Remote Desktop Connection link. The files will be extracted, and the Remote Desktop Connection Wizard will open.
4. Click Next to move to the License Agreement page.
5. Click the I Accept radio button to select it.
6. Click Next to move to the Customer Information page (see Figure 16.3).

16. Remote Windows XP

327

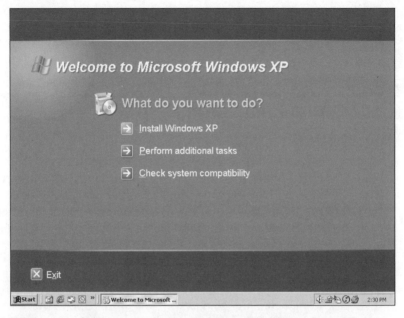

Figure 16.1   Setting up the Remote Desktop connection on a non-XP
machine.

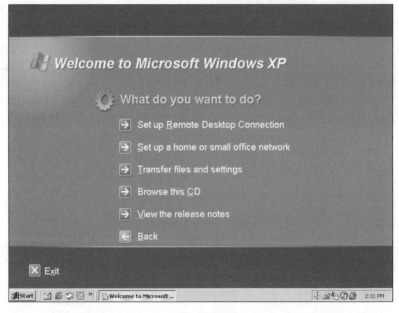

Figure 16.2   Handy tools for dealing with non-XP machines in your network.

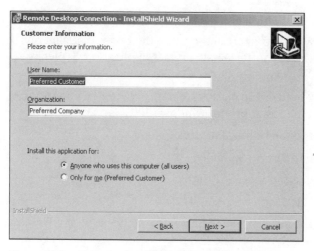

Figure 16.3 Enter your pertinent information here.

7. Type your logon name in the User Name field.

8. Type your company's name in the Organization field.

9. Click Next to move to the Ready To Install The Program page.

10. Click Install. The application will be installed, and the InstallShield Wizard Completed page will appear.

11. Click Finish to close the Remote Desktop Connection Wizard.

12. Click the Exit button to close the Setup window.

If you have older machines, you haven't been left out of the loop. Remote Desktop will also connect to Windows for Workgroups 3.11 and Windows NT 3.51 machines. Unfortunately, neither Windows XP nor its CD-ROM contains the highly specialized tools to implement this solution. If you have a Windows 2000 Server on the network with one of these older operating systems, however, you can use this solution:

1. On the Windows 2000 Server, share the folder that contains the client files for the Terminal Services application. Typically, this is the C:\Windows\System32\Clients\Tsclient folder.

2. On the Windows for Workgroups 3.11 computer, connect to the network that contains the Windows 2000 Server machine.

3. Connect to the shared Tsclients folder.

4. Navigate to the Win16 folder.

5. Double-click the setup.exe file. Follow the instructions to install the TS client on the Windows for Workgroups machine.

16. Remote Windows XP

For Windows NT 3.51 users, the solution is similar, as you will see:

1. On the Windows 2000 Server, share the folder that contains the client files for the Terminal Services application. Typically, this is the C:\Windows\System32\Clients\Tsclient folder.

2. On the Windows for Workgroups 3.11 computer, connect to the network that contains the Windows 2000 Server machine.

3. Connect to the shared Tsclients folder.

4. Navigate to the Win32 folder.

5. Navigate to the Acme351 folder.

6. Double-click the setup.exe file.

7. Follow the instructions to install the TS client on the Windows NT 3.51 machine.

If your base machine is going to be running Windows XP, the setup procedure is much easier. All you really have to do is flip a setting on your XP PC to allow remote users to connect to your system, as shown in these steps:

1. Click Start|Control Panel to open the Control Panel window.

2. Click the Performance And Maintenance link to open the Performance And Maintenance page.

3. Click the System link to open the System Properties dialog box.

4. Click the Remote tab to open the Remote page (see Figure 16.4).

5. Click the Allow Users To Connect Remotely To This Computer checkbox to select it.

6. Click Select Remote Users to open the Remote Desktop Users dialog box (see Figure 16.5).

7. Click Add to open the Select Users dialog box.

8. Type the display names for the users you want to connect to your machine in the Enter The Object Names To Select field.

9. Click OK to close the Select Users dialog box.

10. Click OK to close the Remote Desktop Users dialog box.

11. Click Apply to apply the settings.

12. Click OK to close the System Properties dialog box.

Related solution:	Found on page:
Managing Peripherals with the Control Panel	136

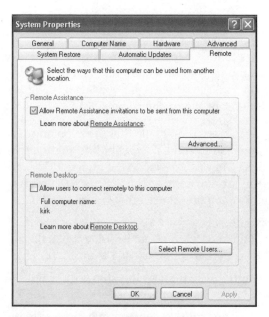

Figure 16.4   The settings for a remote control session.

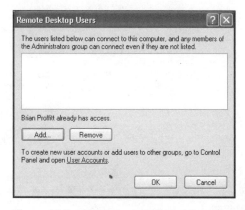

Figure 16.5   If you are not the only user on your system, you may need to give the others permission to connect remotely.

Running Remote Desktop on the Remote Machine

When you need to use Remote Desktop, you should be very pleased with how easy the application is to operate. Across a local network, the lag time is negligible, and even across the Internet, the responsiveness is not terrible.

Again, note that the Remote Desktop probably should not be used for long-term connections, particularly over the Internet. The most efficient approach would be to log on, perform your tasks, and log off. Using the Remote Desktop to grab files and pull them to your location is also another good use. The whole point of using this feature is to try to maximize your efforts and minimize your time.

Remote Desktop is easy to start, though the first time you do so, you will need to give the application some necessary information to log on to the base PC, which is now referred to as the remote PC because it is presumably far away from wherever you are. Using these steps, log on to the now-remote computer for the first time:

1. In the remote computer, click Start|All Programs|Accessories| Communications|Remote Desktop Connection to open the Remote Desktop Connection window (see Figure 16.6).

2. Click the Options button. The Remote Desktop Connection window will expand to show more options (see Figure 16.7).

3. Type the IP address or network computer name for the remote computer in the Computer field.

4. Type the user ID you want to use to log on to the remote computer in the User Name field.

5. Type the password for that user ID in the Password field.

6. If you are connecting to another computer in your Windows domain, type the domain name in the Domain field.

7. Click the Display tab to open the Display page (see Figure 16.8).

8. Click the Remote Desktop Size slider control to adjust the display size of the base desktop.

TIP: *If you prefer to work in a picture-in-picture mode, set the resolution smaller than your current desktop resolution.*

Figure 16.6   The basic Remote Desktop Connection window.

9. Click the drop-down list control for the Colors field and select a color option.

TIP: To improve the speed of the connection, choose a lower color setting.

Figure 16.7   The advanced Remote Desktop Connection window.

Figure 16.8   Select your remote display settings.

16. Remote
Windows XP

333

10. Click the Local Resources tab to open the Local Resources page (see Figure 16.9).

11. Click the drop-down list control for the Remote Computer Sound field and select a sound option. Table 16.1 lists the options and what they mean to you and perhaps others you work with.

TIP: If you're using applications that make a lot of noise (and goodness knows some applications are pretty annoying with their sound effects), you might want to be considerate to your office mates if you are connecting to your remote PC from afar. Use the Do Not Play option to mute your base PC.

---

12. Click the drop-down list control for the Keyboard field and select a keyboard option.

Table 16.1   Remote Desktop sound options.

Option	Function
Bring To This Computer	Sounds on the remote PC will play both on the remote PC and the one you are working from.
Do Not Play	All sounds on the remote computer will be muted.
Leave At Remote Computer	Sounds on the remote PC will play only on the base PC.

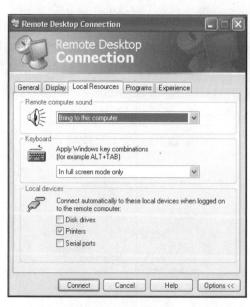

Figure 16.9   Choose the resources to use on the remote PC.

16. Remote Windows XP

13. Click the appropriate checkboxes to access devices connected to the remote PC to select them.

14. Click the Experience tab to open the Experience page (see Figure 16.10).

15. Click the drop-down list control for the Connection Speed field and select the appropriate option. The appropriate graphics options will be automatically selected.

16. Click the graphics option checkboxes to select or clear them.

TIP: *The more graphics options you select to view, the greater the lag time. Remember, you're logging on to work, not to admire aesthetics.*

---

17. Click the General tab to return to the General page.

18. Click the Save As button to open the Save As dialog box.

19. Save the connection settings under an appropriate name.

20. Click Save to close the Save As dialog box.

21. Click Connect. The Remote Desktop Connection window will close, and the remote PC's desktop will be displayed in the Remote Desktop window.

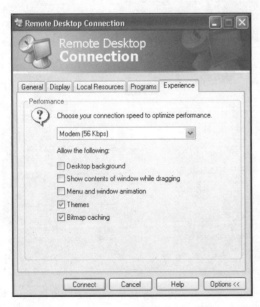

Figure 16.10   You can control how rich the remote connection will be.

If you're worried that you will have to perform all these steps every time you connect to a remote computer, don't be. These preliminary setup steps are just that—preliminary. After you save them, you can use them to connect in just a few short steps:

1. In the remote computer, click Start|All Programs|Accessories| Communications|Remote Desktop Connection to open the Remote Desktop Connection window.

2. Click the drop-down list control for the Computer field and select the name of the computer to connect to.

3. Click Connect. The Remote Desktop Connection window will close, and the remote PC's desktop will be displayed in the Remote Desktop window (see Figure 16.11).

Using a remote connection is no different than using the computer as if you were really there. In this case, all the options available to a Windows 2000 Server user are available. Files can be opened and edited just as you normally would. Applications can be run as before. In other words, now you have to get some work done.

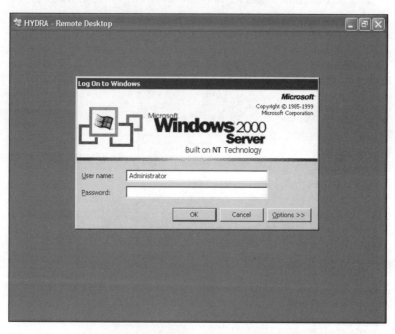

Figure 16.11   A remote connection will behave as if you're sitting in front of that machine.

When you're finished with the remote session, simply follow these steps:

1. Click the Remote Desktop window's close button. The Disconnect Window Session dialog box will appear.

2. Click OK to close the Disconnect Window Session dialog box and Remote Desktop window.

Accessing Files and Folders Offline

Here are the three words every cubicle jockey loathes to hear: "The network's down." This statement—which ranks right up there with "The CEO's heading this way" or "There are no more donuts in the break room" as the worst things to say in the workplace—is usually followed by much moaning and gnashing of teeth. For without the network, how can any work be done?

Having the network go down is a real problem for many companies because network downtime, coupled with many corporations' policy to keep company-related data stored on the network and not locally on a client PC, can lead to serious losses of productivity.

Corporate users have found themselves between a rock and a hard place as they must contend with a store-everything-on-the-network policy and the realities of network downtime. Windows XP, however, has a new set of tools that can circumvent this tight spot quite neatly.

The process is called using folders and files offline, and it makes use of the synchronization technology employed in Internet Explorer to keep track of specific Web pages for later offline use. In this case, however, a network folder is selected for synchronization, which will essentially store the data in this folder in two places: on the network and on the client PC. Storing data this way does not violate most network storage policies because the automatic synchronization features will keep the data in all copies of the folder's files (local and network) perfectly the same whenever the user logs on and off the network.

16. Remote Windows XP

WARNING! *When more than one network user is synchronizing the same folder or files, care must be taken that someone's work is not lost. Establish synchronization procedures in your workplace to address this issue, such as not allowing edits to a file when someone else has opened it.*

Because of the way synchronization occurs when a user logs on and off the network, you cannot use offline folder functionality if you are using Fast User Switching. If you want to make this change, you will need to deactivate Fast User Switching by using this procedure:

1. Click Start|Control Panel to open the Control Panel window.

2. Click the User Accounts link to open the User Accounts window.

3. Click the Change The Way Users Log On Or Off link to open the Select Logon And Logoff Options page (see Figure 16.12).

4. Click the Use Fast User Switching checkbox to clear the option.

5. Click Apply Options. The new settings are applied, and the User Accounts home page will reappear.

6. Click the User Accounts window close icon to close the User Accounts window.

7. Click the Control Panel window close icon to close the Control Panel window.

After turning off Fast User Switching, you will need to activate the offline function on your computer by following these simple steps:

1. Click Start|My Computer to open the My Computer window.

2. Click Tools|Folder Options to open the Folder Options dialog box.

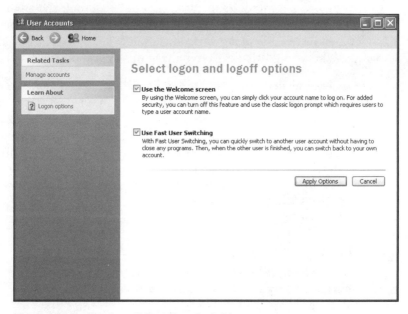

Figure 16.12   Turning off Fast User Switching.

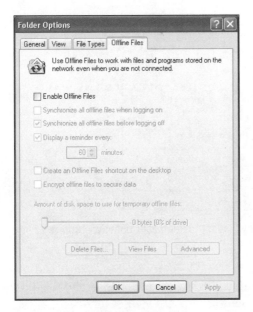

Figure 16.13   Offline file settings.

3. Click the Offline Files tab to open the Offline Files page (see Figure 16.13).

4. Click the Enable Offline Files checkbox to select it.

5. Leave the options in the Offline Files page as is, except to click the Create An Offline Files Shortcut On the Desktop checkbox to select it.

6. Click Apply to apply the settings.

7. Click OK to close the Folder Options dialog box.

You've done all the setup work. Now, you just have to select which files and folders on the network you will want to access offline. You will find that this procedure is easy:

1. In My Computer, click the My Network Places link to open the My Network Places page.

2. Navigate to the folder you want to make available offline.

3. Right-click the target folder. The context menu will appear.

4. Click the Make Available Offline menu option to open the Offline Files Wizard.

5. Click Next to move to the Synchronization page (see Figure 16.14).

6. Click the Automatically Synchronize the Offline Files When I Log On And Log Off My Computer checkbox to select it.

Figure 16.14   Decide how you want to keep your data synchronized.

7. Click Next to move to the final page.

8. Click Finish. The Offline Files Wizard will close, and the files in the folder will be synchronized onto your system.

From now on, every network logon and logoff this user performs will be preceded by a quick synchronization check. This check will slow these two events, but the delay may be worthwhile. If the network goes down, you will be in very good shape, as the next steps illustrate.

When the network is down, the Offline Files icon will appear in the Notification Area of the taskbar (see Figure 16.15). Proceed as follows:

1. Click the Offline Files icon to open the Offline Files Status dialog box (see Figure 16.16).

Offline Files Icon

Figure 16.15   This icon may indicate that the network is down.

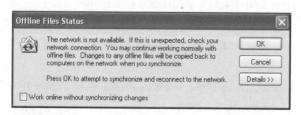

Figure 16.16   You should try to reconnect to the network at least once.

2. Click OK. Your computer will try to reconnect to the network and to the designated offline files folder. If it cannot reconnect, you can now use the offline versions of your files.

3. Click Start|My Computer to open the My Computer window.

4. Click Tools|Folder Options to open the Folder Options dialog box.

5. Click the Offline Files tab to open the Offline Files page.

6. Click View Files to open the Offline Files Folder.

7. When the network is back online, click the Offline Files icon to open the Offline Files Status dialog box.

8. Click OK. Your computer will synchronize any edits you made with the network folder's files.

Related solutions:	Found on page:
Implementing Fast User Switching	173
Sharing Files with Other Users	174
Synchronizing Internet Pages and Data	359

16. Remote
Windows XP

Chapter 17

Mobile Windows XP

In Brief

On *Star Trek*, the crew of the good ship Enterprise used tricorders whenever they beamed down to a harsh alien world. These nifty little devices seemed to do it all: scan for life-forms, process data, and record vital clues in the environment around their users (though never detecting alien threats quite in time to save the crew wearing the red shirts, it seemed).

Despite this bug, tricorders seemed to be the in thing for computing in the twenty-third century. Later in the history of Starfleet, they were still being used, though they were supplemented by small, palmtop-sized devices called PADDs. PADDs, it seems, were also computers, though without all the fancy sensors.

Although you may think I'm just another geek prattling on about some silly television show, note that the creators behind all this fictional equipment are no different from the inventors who make the real technology we use today. Both groups tap into their imaginations to find a vision of what they think technology should be. The only difference is in how that vision is made real.

If you're not sure about this premise, you are invited to watch an old episode of *Star Trek* and look at the ubiquitous communicator. In a classic example of life imitating art, today's cellular flip-phones bear a striking resemblance to those fictional devices. Lucky guess or predictive vision? You can be the judge of that. But, what has been art and story in the past may well become the reality of the future. Getting to that future is not always a smooth journey, as the early inventors of mobile computers quickly discovered.

The Special Needs of the Laptop

Arguably, the first technical designer to put forth the idea of a portable computer was Alan Kay. Kay introduced the idea while he worked at the Xerox Palo Alto Research Center (PARC), though he actually came up with the idea while he was a post-graduate student at Utah State University in the 1970s.

Kay called his idea the Dynabook. He described the Dynabook as "a portable interactive personal computer, as accessible as a book." This device would be notebook sized and affordable for all, would handle wireless communication, and would have a flat panel display—concepts that were decades ahead of their time.

While he worked at Xerox PARC, Kay did not work on a hardware implementation of his idea, but a lot of the interface ideas he envisioned for the Dynabook ended up in the GUIs being developed at PARC. In fact, Kay is credited for developing the concept of using application "windows" and double-clicking icons—both ideas he wanted to use in the Dynabook.

Kay left Xerox PARC in 1981 and landed at Apple Computers. There, his Dynabook idea was developed. Along the way, the concept of the device changed into something quite different: a hand-held information device that would become the ill-fated Apple Newton.

The first true laptop computer, the GRiD Compass, was built in 1979 by William Moggridge of GRiD Systems Corp. It featured a black magnesium alloy case, a gas plasma display, and a 1200-baud internal modem. Memory for the Compass was not handled with a hard or removable disk. Instead, nonvolatile magnetic bubble memory was utilized. A whopping 256KB of memory, to be exact. And, although it was a portable computer, it was extremely heavy and required a power outlet because it did not have batteries.

The price tag for this pioneering equipment was $8,000, which made it a perfect purchase item for the U.S. government. In fact, the laptop was originally created on NASA specifications, and several models of GRiD laptops (including the Compass) were used on shuttle missions. Because of their highly specialized nature, the GRiD computers would eventually fade into obscurity. A similar problem would affect the next advance in laptop computers produced by Gavilan Computer in 1983.

Gavilan Computer was a company founded by Manny Hernandez, who promoted the portable computer to the fullest, calling it the world's first laptop (conveniently forgetting the GRiD systems from four years before). However, Hernandez is credited with coining the term *laptop computer*, and certainly Gavilan machines had the makings to become the world's first commercially successful laptop.

The Gavilan laptop featured 64KB of RAM, an 8088 processor and a touchpad mouse, and it weighed just nine pounds. It was even sold with a portable companion printer (which upped the weight of the combined package to 14 pounds).

Gavilan was poised to become the Next Big Thing. The product was cool, and trade show crowds loved the idea of a laptop computer. The problem lay in features of the Gavilan systems. It had its own operating system, which had little application support, and it used an odd-sized floppy drive. This meant that any work done on the Gavilan laptops was going to stay there because Internet access was scarce in the early 1980s.

The next big offering came just a year later, in 1984. Flush with success, Apple Computer introduced the Apple IIc—a computer model that might be very familiar to older GenXers because this computer was prolific in public schools throughout the United States in the mid-1980s.

The IIc was a true hybrid computer. In one configuration, it sat under a monitor and acted as a desktop station. The actual computer case itself was notebook-sized and featured a handle, which meant it could be used as a portable unit. The Apple IIc featured a 65C02 microprocessor, 128KB of memory, an internal 5.25-inch floppy drive, two serial ports, a mouse port, a modem card, and an external power supply. The unit weighed about 11 pounds and could be bought with an optional liquid crystal display (LCD) panel. When in the unit/LCD panel configuration, the IIc was a portable unit—though you had to connect the two units whenever you sat down to work.

Perhaps the first successful laptop computer came from Big Blue itself—IBM. In 1986, IBM released the PC Convertible. Like the Gavilan laptops, the PC Convertible used an 8088 microprocessor. There the similarities end, as the PC Convertible used 256KB of memory, two 3.5-inch floppy drives, and an LCD display. The PC Convertible also came with its own basic office suite software. The unit weighed 12 pounds and sold for $3,500. It is regarded as the first commercially successful laptop computer and began a new wave of laptops on the open market.

Over the years, laptops have gotten lighter, faster, and (at least in screen size) bigger. They have also (thankfully) gotten cheaper, though laptops are still more expensive than equivalent desktop machines. But, although their speed and processing power rivals that of desktop equipment, laptops are still not widely adopted as users' primary machines.

In the effort to make the laptop machine more portable, some compromises have had to be made. Keyboard size, pointing devices, peripheral devices—all have had to take a backseat to the second goal of making laptops: making them light.

And what's the first goal? That would be the Holy Grail of laptop design: making them run longer with less energy.

Everything in the world uses energy. You are using some right now to read this book just as I am using energy to write it. Computers use energy, too, though surprisingly not as much as you might think. The average desktop computer and monitor combination consumes just 270 watts of power—far less than the 725 watts your refrigerator is using and the 1800 watts used by the clothes dryer. In fact, computers use less energy than most household appliances.

Laptop computers use even less energy than desktop configurations. The average laptop pulls in 50 watts when plugged into the wall. This is a good thing, too, because your laptop's battery will need to feed the beast when you are not supplying it with AC power.

Laptop batteries come in three forms: Nickel Cadmium (NiCad), Nickel Metal Hydride (NiMH), and Lithium Ion (Li-Ion). Of the three, Li-Ion batteries are the longest lasting (they have twice the capacity of NiCad batteries), and if you are looking to buy a new laptop, you should make sure this is the type of battery you are getting. The other nice thing about Li-Ions is the fact that they don't need to be burned-in—a conditioning technique used to charge older laptop batteries to their fullest.

Power is perhaps the biggest problem laptop designers and users face. Fortunately, while designers are working to build a better battery, Windows XP has provided tools to manage your laptop's power.

Another concern of laptop users is how to shuffle the data on the laptop around to other computers. Rarely, it seems, is a laptop computer someone's primary device. Laptops are often relegated to secondary computer status—something to be used when away from the primary desktop. Because of this "second-string" status, the work done on a laptop often needs to get moved to desktop PCs as quickly as possible. You can go about this task in several ways, which range from the cumbersome (emailing files back and forth from one machine to another) to the useful (shuffling files via a network connection) to the hyper-efficient (hot-docking the laptop to a network-enabled docking station and using auto-synchronization on the selected work files).

In Chapter 16, you learned a bit about using Windows XP's Synchronization tool when working with remote computers. The tool also comes in handy when you're working with laptops that have to constantly share data with desktop machines, as you will see in this chapter.

17. Mobile Windows XP

Another bugaboo that plagues laptop owners is the flat-screen LCD display. Too often, these displays lack the clarity of a cathode ray tube (CRT) monitor on a desktop machine. In the past, Windows included some helpful tools to make the mouse pointer more visible on the fuzzy LCD displays. Those tools are still part of Windows XP's repertoire, but now Windows XP has a brand-new technology called ClearType to make displayed fonts very clear on LCD screens.

Seeing Is Believing: ClearType

I need to deliver a little science lesson to explain the benefits of Windows XP's new ClearType technology.

A CRT monitor (like its cousin the television) uses fired-electron technology to paint pixels on the phosphorescent screen of the monitor. The charged particles strike the screen in some combination of three frequencies on the visible light spectrum—red, green, and blue. By adjusting the amplitude of these three colors, a CRT device can create one of 16,777,216 colors on a single pixel of the screen.

A liquid crystal display (LCD) uses a completely different method of generating a color on a screen. On LCD screens, there is no such thing as a full pixel. Instead, each pixel unit is divided into three parts: one-third for red, one-third for green, and one-third for blue. To generate a color on an LCD pixel, the three parts of the pixel work in concert to generate their separate colors in varying intensities. Because the pixels are so small to begin with, the human eye is tricked into combining the colors into a single color.

The problem is, the human eye can be tricked only so far. The eye can notice errors cumulatively and begin working to auto-correct for those errors without any conscious effort (or notice) from the brain. This constant micro-correction can lead to eye fatigue more rapidly than if the eye were looking at a natural object.

In the case of the LCD screen, the eye is very sensitive to detail errors between black and white contrast—the two colors 99 percent of users use to display their fonts on screen. So, the fonts on an LCD screen are more likely to appear fuzzy to the eye than on a CRT screen.

Fonts have always been a problem on any screen, of course, because all screens use pixels to display objects. When you use square building blocks like pixels to create curved objects like fonts, eventually you will see jagged edges on the letters. This jagged-edge effect is fought by making screen resolutions (and therefore pixels) smaller and using anti-aliasing technology. Anti-aliasing uses a mathematical algorithm and nine color filters to visually "smooth" out the edges of fonts and ease the contrast errors between black fonts and white backgrounds.

When used on LCD screens, standard anti-aliasing does not work as well because of the different nature of the pixel display. What ClearType does, essentially, is make a new anti-aliasing scheme specifically for LCD monitors. This new scheme does a better job of taking into account the neighboring pixels' separate color intensities and using just three color filters (red, green, and blue).

The technology behind ClearType is a maze of mathematical algorithms that only a scientist could love, but the result is nothing short of amazing: Fonts, and indeed all objects on an LCD display, are far more crisp than ever before.

Power, connectivity, and display: three areas in which laptop users have had to make compromises. The new tools in Windows XP will mean fewer compromises and more control over these properties of laptop use.

17. Mobile
Windows XP

Immediate Solutions

Configuring Power Options

Power management comes in more forms than changing a few settings on your computer and hoping for the best. Power management is an ongoing set of practices you should use every time you turn on your laptop computer.

You can apply these general tips to your own laptop's power management:

- *Avoid system shutdown.* If you have to leave your work on the laptop but know you're coming back to it in a half hour or so (perhaps while the airliner you're flying in is climbing to 10,000 feet), you should not shut down the system completely. A laptop uses up far more energy during a system startup than you would ever save during a complete shutdown period. Instead, place the system in Hibernate or Standby mode. Either low-power mode is much less energy-intensive to start from.

TIP: *Using Standby or Hibernate is also great for those times at the airport security gate when the agents ask you to turn on the system so they can see whether it's a real computer. Restarting is much faster from these two modes and will save you a lot of time.*

- *Don't be bright.* The brighter the LCD display, the more energy gets used. Tone it down when you're using the laptop on battery power.

- *Plug the power leaks.* Many laptops lose a lot of energy supplying power to peripherals, including internal modems, speakers, PCMCIA cards, and floppy and CD-ROM drives. If any of these devices are removable and unneeded, remove them. For devices that are fixed in your machine, use the system BIOS setup function to shut off power to any device that is not in use.

TIP: *Place any CD-ROM within the CD-ROM drive to prevent Windows from checking the drive every so often to see whether you've placed a CD in it.*

- *Use a spare battery.* And, I mean *use* it. Don't just buy a spare and leave it sitting around. Eventually, that spare will drain on its own and leave you with nothing. Alternate the use of your two batteries on a regular schedule to extend the life of both batteries.

- *Keep the hard drive still.* When an application has to rev the hard drive, that's energy getting consumed. Lengthen the period of time between AutoSave functions. Use applications that are less hard-drive intensive yet still get a bulk of the work done, such as entering text in WordPad rather than Word XP. Also, be sure to increase the RAM of the laptop as high as it will go or you can afford. The more virtual memory a system has, the less it will use the physical hard drive as a swap disk.

- *Use Windows XP Power Options.* You knew this tip was coming, right? But, it's no less important. By configuring the Power Options within Windows XP, you will greatly reduce the amount of energy consumed on the laptop.

Using those Power Options is a simple process, as you will see in the next sections.

Managing Power Schemes

You should not be surprised that various power settings are available within Windows XP. Also available is the capability to save the entire collection of power settings within unified schemes.

The benefits of using power schemes are especially pertinent to laptop users because these machines will often find themselves using different power supplies. One day, the laptop will be running on battery power. The next day, it might be plugged in with an AC adapter, and the next, it may be docked to a workstation. Each situation requires different styles of power management, and it would be a pain to have to reset each power configuration setting every time a new power supply was used.

The nature of these configuration settings is simple. You set the amount of time that is to pass on an inactive computer before certain system events occur: hard disk shutdown, monitor shutdown, system standby, and system hibernation.

Before you can create a power scheme, however, you will have to make those configuration changes at least once, as indicated in the following steps:

1. Click Start|Control Panel to open the Control Panel window.

2. Click Performance And Maintenance to open the Performance And Maintenance page.

3. Click Power Options to open the Power Schemes tab of the Power Options Properties dialog box (see Figure 17.1). Note

17. Mobile Windows XP

Figure 17.1   Managing power schemes.

the two scheme columns that appear: Plugged In and Running
On Batteries.

4. Click the drop-down list control for the Turn Off Monitor field
   in the Plugged In column to display the list of options.

5. Click a duration to use to select the option.

6. Repeat Steps 4 and 5 for the other duration settings on the
   Power Schemes page.

7. Click the Save As button to open the Save Scheme dialog box
   (see Figure 17.2).

8. Type a power scheme name in the Save This Power Scheme As
   field.

9. Click OK to close the Save Scheme dialog box.

10. Click Apply to apply the new settings.

11. Click OK to close the Power Options Properties dialog box.

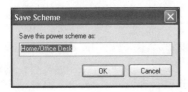

Figure 17.2   Saving a power scheme.

After the power scheme is saved, implementing it involves this quick set of steps:

1. Click Start|Control Panel to open the Control Panel window.
2. Click Performance And Maintenance to open the Performance And Maintenance page.
3. Click Power Options to open the Power Options Properties dialog box.
4. Click the drop-down list control for the Power Schemes field to display the list of options.
5. Click a power scheme option to select it.
6. Click Apply to apply the new setting.
7. Click OK to close the Power Options Properties dialog box.

Related solution:	Found on page:
Managing Peripherals with the Control Panel	136

Hibernating Your Laptop Safely

Sometimes, people get a bit confused as to what constitutes system standby versus hibernation. In Windows XP, the differences between these two low-power modes are quite clear.

In system standby, the laptop shifts to a low-power mode in which the monitor and hard disks are turned off. The first time you touch a key or the mouse, the computer reawakens and you can start right back where you left off. Standby does not save where you were in your work, so if a power failure occurs, you will lose any unsaved work.

Not so with hibernation. Hibernation goes a bit further than standby by first saving your data and the system state to disk before turning off the monitor, hard disk, *and* computer itself. When you wake the system, the computer returns all the applications and files to the state they were in when you implemented the hibernation.

Hibernation is one of the states controlled in the power schemes, so its implementation should be automatic. Sometimes, you may want to deactivate hibernation, particularly if you're going to be connected to a power source for a long time. Use this procedure to turn off (and, later, turn on) hibernation:

1. Click Start|Control Panel to open the Control Panel window.
2. Click Performance And Maintenance to open the Performance And Maintenance page.

17. Mobile Windows XP

3. Click Power Options to open the Power Options Properties dialog box.

4. Click the Hibernate tab to open the Hibernate page (see Figure 17.3).

5. Click the Enable Hibernation checkbox to clear the option.

6. Click Apply to apply the new setting.

7. Click OK to close the Power Options Properties dialog box.

If you want to start system hibernation manually, you can assign a certain action, such as closing the laptop's lid, to activate the hibernation state. If you have not already disabled hibernation as shown in the steps above, just follow these steps to make these assignments:

1. Click Start|Control Panel to open the Control Panel window.

2. Click Performance And Maintenance to open the Performance And Maintenance page.

3. Click Power Options to open the Power Options Properties dialog box.

4. Click the Advanced tab to open the Advanced page (see Figure 17.4).

5. Click the drop-down list control for the When I Close The Lid Of My Portable Computer field to see the list of options.

6. Click Hibernate to select it.

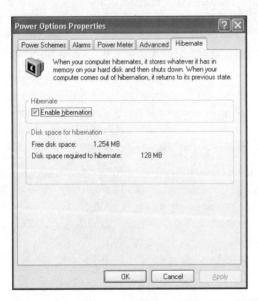

Figure 17.3   You can turn hibernation on and off here.

Figure 17.4   Assign power options to laptop controls.

7. Click Apply to apply the new setting.

8. Click OK to close the Power Options Properties dialog box.

Putting Your Computer on Standby

System standby is not as drastic a measure as hibernation and is therefore more useful in situations in which you don't think you will be away from your work very long.

The fastest way to manually set the system on standby is illustrated here:

1. Click Start|Turn Off Computer to open the Turn Off Computer window.

2. Click Stand By to place the system in Standby mode.

With a little extra effort, you can assign a system control to start Standby mode for you, just as with hibernation:

1. Click Start|Control Panel to open the Control Panel window.

2. Click Performance And Maintenance to open the Performance And Maintenance page.

3. Click Power Options to open the Power Options Properties dialog box.

4. Click the Advanced tab to open the Advanced page.

5. Click the drop-down list control for the When I Press The Sleep Button My Portable Computer field to see the list of options.

6. Click Stand By to select it.

7. Click Apply to apply the new setting.

8. Click OK to close the Power Options Properties dialog box.

Setting Your Battery Alarms

No matter how much battery conservation you practice, there will inevitably come a day when you will start to run low on energy. Murphy's Law demands that this will happen while you are working on the most important paper in your professional career.

It would be nice, then, to be forewarned of imminent power loss, to at least give you a chance to save your work and shut down everything. You can have such a warning by using the power alarms. Two alarms are available in XP's power toolset: Low Battery and Critical Battery. Each will go off when the battery reaches a certain percentage of its total capacity.

By setting these alarms at different values, you can give yourself a good amount of warning time:

1. Click Start|Control Panel to open the Control Panel window.

2. Click Performance And Maintenance to open the Performance And Maintenance page.

3. Click Power Options to open the Power Options Properties dialog box.

4. Click the Alarms tab to open the Alarms page (see Figure 17.5).

5. Click the slider control for the Low Battery Alarm and move it to a new position.

6. Click the slider control for the Critical Battery Alarm and move it to a new position.

7. Click the Alarm Action button to open the Alarm Actions dialog box.

8. Click the drop-down list control in the When The Alarm Goes Off The Computer Will field to display the list of options.

9. Click an option to select it.

10. Click OK to close the Alarm Actions dialog box.

11. Click Apply to apply the new setting.

12. Click OK to close the Power Options Properties dialog box.

17. Mobile
Windows XP

356

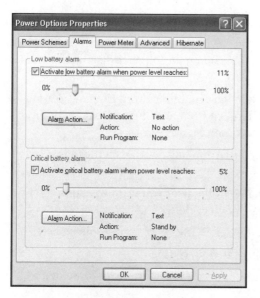

Figure 17.5   Setting alarm levels.

Implementing Hot Docking

One of the latest features in laptop hardware is the capability to dock to a desktop station while the laptop is still running. All the peripherals connected to the docking station—the keyboard, monitor, and mouse—are immediately activated. This function is known as *hot docking*.

Windows XP supports hot docking, so you need to do very little but follow the hardware manufacturer's instructions to hot-dock your computer.

When it comes to *hot undocking*, however, you may have to perform some work. For Windows XP systems that were installed "clean," all users can undock a laptop computer hot, with no need to change any settings. If the laptop system is using an upgraded installation of Windows XP, though, each system user must be explicitly given permission to hot-undock the computer. Follow this procedure to make these assignments:

1. Click Start|Administrative Tools|Local Security Policy to open the Local Security Policy window.

2. Click the Local Polices expansion icon to see the list of settings groups.

3. Click the User Rights Assignment folder to see the list of user rights (see Figure 17.6).

4. Double-click the Remove Computer From Docking Station value to open the Remove Computer From Docking Station Properties dialog box (see Figure 17.7).

5. Click the Add User Or Group button to open the Select Users Or Groups dialog box.

6. Type the display name of the user you want to add in the Enter The Object Names To Select field.

7. Click OK to close the Select Users Or Groups dialog box.

8. Click Apply to apply the new setting.

9. Click OK to close the Remove Computer From Docking Station Properties dialog box.

10. Click the close icon to close the Local Security Policy window.

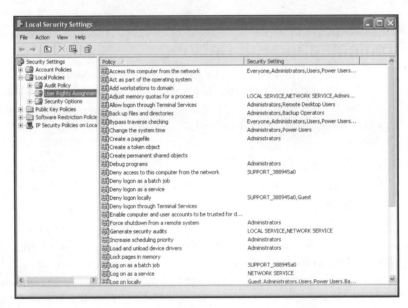

Figure 17.6   User rights are set here.

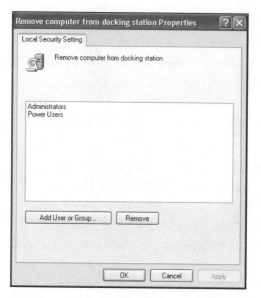

Figure 17.7   You can choose who can perform a hot undock.

Synchronizing Internet Pages and Data

In Chapter 16, you learned how to use Windows XP's synchronization tools using the Offline Files function. Synchronization can also be used for other purposes, including two functions that are a real advantage for laptop users.

Laptops by their very nature are often unconnected to the rest of the world, acting as solitary, standalone computers. This is especially true when you're traveling, when connecting to the Internet may not always be possible. If you would like to examine some Web pages, you can preload their contents on the laptop while it *is* connected to the Internet—allowing you to surf part of the Web while not being connected later.

To use this feature, you will need to make a Web page part of your favorites list and then specify you want to make it available offline, as shown in these steps:

1. In Internet Explorer, navigate to the page you want to make a favorite.

2. Click Favorites|Add To Favorites to open the Add Favorite dialog box.

3. Edit the title of the Web page in the Name field as needed.

4. Click the Make Available Offline checkbox to select it.

5. Click the Customize button to open the Offline Favorite Wizard.

6. Click the In The Future, Do Not Show This Introduction Screen checkbox to select it.

7. Click Next to move to the Setup page (see Figure 17.8).

8. Click the Yes radio button to select it.

9. Enter a value in the Download Pages field. This field specifies the number of *levels* away from this page you want to keep offline.

10. Click Next to move to the Schedule page.

11. Click the I Would Like To Create A New Schedule radio button to select it.

12. Click Next to move to the Schedule Creation page (see Figure 17.9).

13. Set the frequency and time for synchronization.

14. Enter a name for the new schedule in the Name field.

15. Click Next to move to the Password page.

16. Enter the information as needed and click Finish to close the Offline Favorite Wizard.

17. Click OK. The Add Favorite dialog box will close, the new favorite will appear in the Favorites menu and Favorites Explorer Bar, and the Synchronizing operation for this page will begin.

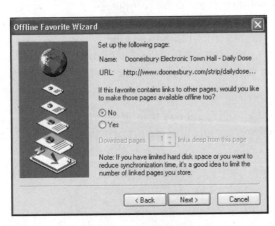

Figure 17.8   Setting up offline Web pages.

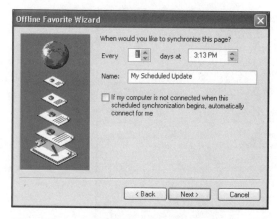

Figure 17.9   Scheduling synchronization.

When the pages are set for offline use, they will be synchronized into a special cache file on your system. When the system is disconnected from the Internet, it will use the cached file to display as much of the Web site as was gathered.

Synchronization can take place as frequently as every day. You can also manually synchronize, as demonstrated here:

1. In Internet Explorer, click Tools|Synchronize to open the Items To Synchronize dialog box (see Figure 17.10).

2. Click the checkboxes for the pages you wish to synchronize to select them.

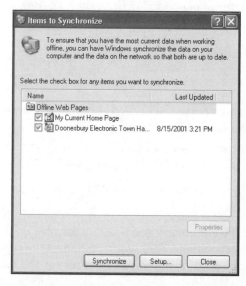

Figure 17.10   Select which pages to synchronize.

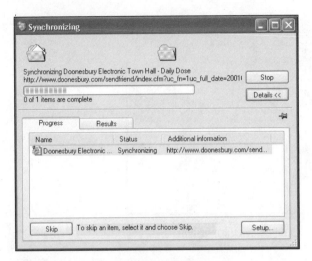

Figure 17.11   Synchronization in action.

3. Click Synchronize. The Synchronizing dialog box will appear to mark the progress of the operation (see Figure 17.11).

The other useful feature that's perfect for laptop users is the Briefcase synchronization tool. Whether you connect your laptop to the desktop computer directly or through the network, the Briefcase makes it simple to keep all your files current on both machines.

First, you need to create a new Briefcase on the laptop computer by using these steps.

1. Click Start|My Computer to open the My Computer window.

2. Navigate to the folder in which you want to create the new Briefcase.

3. Click File|New|Briefcase. The Briefcase will appear in the open folder.

When the two computers are connected (directly or through the network), follow these steps to use the Briefcase:

1. Double-click the Briefcase icon in the laptop computer. The My Computer window will open to the Briefcase folder.

2. Copy the files from the desktop computer to the open Briefcase folder on the laptop.

You can now disconnect the computers and work on the files on the laptop at your leisure. After you finish your work, reconnect the computers and follow these steps to synchronize the files on the two systems.

17. Mobile
Windows XP

362

1. Double-click the Briefcase icon in the laptop computer. The My Computer window will open to the Briefcase folder.

2. Click the Update All Items link to synchronize all the files in the Briefcase.

Related solutions:	Found on page:
Personalizing Links and Favorites	264
Accessing Files and Folders Offline	337

Viewing with ClearType

If you're using a laptop machine, you can use ClearType to get a much clearer picture on the LCD screen.

NOTE: *You can use ClearType on a standard desktop monitor, but the effect on a CRT screen is rather fuzzy and not desirable.*

The ClearType setting is simple to activate, as shown in these steps:

1. Right-click the Windows XP desktop. The context menu will appear.

2. Click Properties to open the Display Properties dialog box.

3. Click the Appearance tab to open the Appearance page.

4. Click the Effects button to open the Effects dialog box (see Figure 17.12).

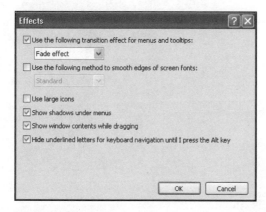

Figure 17.12   Selecting visual effects.

5. Click the Use The Following Method To Smooth Edges Of Screen Fonts checkbox to select it.

6. Click the drop-down list control of the Use The Following Method To Smooth Edges Of Screen Fonts field to display the options.

7. Click ClearType to select it.

8. Click OK to close the Effects dialog box.

9. Click Apply to apply the setting.

10. Click OK to close the Display Properties dialog box.

Related solutions:	Found on page:
Customizing the XP Desktop	56
Customizing with Visual Themes	59
Setting Up a Screen Saver	60
Changing the Resolution of Your Screen	62

Chapter 18

Update Windows XP

In Brief

Here is how the computer used to work: You use the software until someone comes out with an upgrade. You go to the store. You buy the software you want. You take the software home. You install the software on your computer. You use the software until someone comes out with an upgrade, and the whole cycle starts all over again.

Here is how the computer will work in the very near future: You use the software until someone comes out with an upgrade. A message flashes on your screen that the upgrade is available and asks whether you would be so kind as to log off for a moment while the system is upgraded. You log off the Internet. You log on to the Internet. You use the software until someone comes out with an upgrade, and the whole cycle starts all over again. You don't have to pay for the upgrade because you are already paying a monthly subscription fee to use the application. Nothing significant is changed on your computer because the application was never installed on your computer—it exists in a central server somewhere in your part of the country, shared by thousands of other users. Only your data is on your personal computer.

If this description seems farfetched, you may not have heard about .NET, Microsoft's new venture in distributed computing. This is the future that .NET is going to provide for any user willing to use it. This system will work through a relatively new form of markup language that will deliver content over the Internet in much the same way HTML delivers Web pages. This language is called Extensible Markup Language, or XML, and like its cousin HTML, it is a text-based markup language—only much more sophisticated.

In HTML, all content is held within tags. Tags tell the Web browser how to format the text contained within the tags. All the tags are based on an HTML standard, and all Web browsers have that standard (called a Document Type Definition, or DTD) built in. Thus, on every Web browser, the **<p>** tag will always make a paragraph block out of the text the tag contains.

In XML, the same principle applies. All content is contained within tags. Now, however, the DTD is no longer a standard. In HTML, the DTD is fixed, which gives you a set number of HTML tags that all behave in a certain way. In XML, the DTD can be modified to contain any tag you want. Furthermore, those tags can be modified to display the content in any way.

An XML client will be able to modify itself to this changing situation because, instead of having a permanent DTD built in like a Web browser, the XML client will get the DTD for the document *first*. Then, as the rest of the document is loading, it will learn what the DTD wants to do with this document and display the tagged content accordingly.

Now, here's the really cool part. Because XML is so malleable, designers can create documents that look and behave exactly like the interface of an application. Menus, dialog boxes, toolbars—all the things you see and work with in an application can be created with XML. These documents can also be created with far less code, which means far less memory.

Having a pretty look is not the only thing an application needs. It needs code to activate functions based on user input. When I click the File menu in Word XP, I'd better see the File menu. Such actions can be provided by the same scripting found within ActiveX controls and Java applets today. By plugging scripts into the XML interface, you will create a fully functional application.

In the very near future, applications will not be hundreds of megabytes of code sitting on your computer and generating all the functions and interface from that code. Applications will essentially be documents downloaded from the Internet—documents with so many robust features that they look and feel exactly like the old-style applications. Users will not be able to tell the difference.

.NET technology has a long way to go before it is fully implemented in this fashion. But, Windows XP is one of the platforms getting ready for it. You can already see glimmerings of .NET in Windows XP; it's in the .NET Passport you must acquire to use Windows Messenger. This connection is more than superficial, however. For example, one of the Web sites beginning to use .NET technology is MSN (**www.msn.com**). If you're using Windows Messenger, surf to this site some time. In the upper-right corner of the MSN home page is the Message Center, where all your online contacts from Messenger are displayed, if the Windows Messenger client is running. .NET technology detects that you have Messenger running and adjusts the display of the Web page accordingly. This is just one small example. If you want more, try the gaming zone in MSN, where you can play online games using XML and .NET interfaces.

.NET has influenced Windows XP in other ways as well, particularly with the new Automatic Updates tool.

18. Update Windows XP

How Windows XP Keeps Itself Fresh

Here is how the computer with Windows XP Professional works today: You use the software until someone comes out with an upgrade. A message flashes on your screen that the upgrade is available and asks whether you would care to download and install the upgrade. You respond yes to both these questions. The code for the upgrade is downloaded. The code for the upgrade is installed. You use the software until someone comes out with an upgrade, and the whole cycle starts all over again. You don't have to pay for the upgrade because you have already paid for the application, and this update service is part of the package.

That is the service provided for Windows XP with the Automatic Updates feature. This autonomous little tool keeps track of all the software and hardware on your system. It then scopes out the Windows Update Web site to see whether there are any pertinent upgrades for the applications and equipment you have. When the Automatic Updates application detects an upgrade it thinks you should have, it lets you know and you can decide to download and install it at that time.

If this description sounds familiar, it should. This functionality is similar to the Windows Update tool used in earlier versions of Windows. You'll notice some key differences, though. The Windows Update tool monitored the Windows Update site for critical updates that applied to *all* Windows users and promptly invited users to visit the Windows Update Web site to download and install the upgrades themselves. The new Automatic Updates tool is tailored to your system's needs and will keep you abreast of more than just the critical updates. You also will not have to actively visit a Web site to obtain the updates; in fact, you can set Automatic Updates to download and install upgrades with little to no intervention on your part.

Note that Windows Update has not gone away completely. The Web site is still in existence, ready to assist you in pulling down updates you need. The Windows Update Web site has not faded away from existence because it still provides a vital service that the Automatic Updates can't: Windows Update can let you see all the updates that you may want, not just the ones you need.

For example, both Windows and Automatic Updates can tell you that the new security patch for Internet Explorer 6 is out and ready to use. But, only Windows Update will let you see that the new public beta of that hot new client software you've been curious about is also available. The distinction between the two tools is simply a difference between what you need and what you want.

Contrary to popular belief (or suspicion), Microsoft does not own all the software on your PC. So, how will you handle upgrading the latest version of Quicken? Or getting the new drivers for your sound card? Your ability to upgrade is just a matter of knowing where to look.

Device and Third-Party Updates

Every fourth month or so, I like to perform a task I call the "Great Driver Hunt." The Great Driver Hunt is really very simple: I have a list of devices installed on my computer that I use to try to locate updated drivers for those devices. First, I look on the manufacturers' Web sites for the drivers, and then I swing by the Windows Update site to see whether I missed any there.

For the most part, I usually catch a new version of a device driver during every other hunt, give or take. And, usually I discover little to no discernable difference in how the device works after I install the new driver. But, I sleep better at night knowing that my computer has been made more efficient.

I find that comprehensive sweeps like this are necessary as operating systems and the hardware they use become increasingly complicated. Unfortunately, many users don't regularly check their device drivers. This is a real concern, because in some instances an update could make the difference between running an application well or not at all.

The Automatic Updates application does a good job of keeping your system's drivers up to date, which will cut down on the need to manually update the drivers. You still may find a need to update the drivers, however, and Windows XP has a nice tool to help you perform this task.

As for third-party applications, right now it's a catch-as-catch-can situation. Many software vendors are including updating functions within their applications, but at the present time, these updating tools depend solely on the whims of the applications' developers.

Note that many third-party software developers are moving toward some sort of online upgrade system. The increasing installation of broadband connectivity to homes is one reason for this move. Because download times are becoming shorter, software publishers do not think much of asking their customers to download a patch from time to time. Installing patches, it seems, makes the customers feel better about the software. (Never mind the fact they may have bought buggy software to begin with.)

As for full upgrades, the notion of going to the store and buying a box of software may soon become a thing of the past. Online software sales and distribution are steadily increasing, as more and more broadband customers want to save time and gas to just download the latest and greatest version of their favorite software.

The Internet has not only changed the way we communicate, it is also well on the way to changing the way we operate our computers.

18. Update
Windows XP

Immediate Solutions

Running Windows Update

Ever since Windows Update made its debut as a tool in Windows 98, users have always had some doubts about using it. Just how does the Windows Update site know what's on your computer? Is Microsoft really spying on what's inside your machine?

Of course, many of us have kept these doubts to ourselves, for fear of being associated with the same people who think the United Nations has black helicopters poised to take over the free world. But, concerns about online privacy have reached a fever-pitch, and it's not at all paranoid to be concerned about who knows what about you and your loved ones. Besides, like the old saying goes, just because you are paranoid doesn't mean someone's not out to get you.

In the case of Windows Update, you have little to be concerned about because the Web site and the servers that host it never find out what's on your PC. That information is held safely on your computer.

Windows Update works like this: When a PC queries the Update Web site, the Web site immediately sends the *entire* list of available updates to your computer. There, the local Windows Update Identifier ActiveX control goes into action, quickly comparing the update list to what's on your machine. The ActiveX control also takes into account what you've already installed from previous Update sessions in this calculation. When it's finished, the *local* Windows Update ActiveX control (not the Web site server) will generate the content of the Windows Update Web page, having cut out all the update listings you don't need and displaying the ones you should look at.

Because of this technique, Microsoft and its employees haven't a clue what's on your machine. If you're still suspicious, try this reason on for size: Microsoft Windows is installed on millions of computers around the world. Do you think the company has the time or server capacity to figure out customized update requests from each and every computer? Not a chance. It's far easier for the traffic on the Web site to just send a single file with all the updates and let the local clients handle it.

Running Windows Update is fast, simple, and relatively safe from the privacy point of view. So, here's how to run an Update session:

1. Click Start|All Programs|Windows Update. Internet Explorer will open to the Windows Update Web page (see Figure 18.1).

2. Click Scan For Updates. The list of updates will be downloaded and compared to the configuration of your machine. If updates are found, they will be listed in the category list within the Windows Update pane on the left pane of the screen. You will also see links to Review and Install the updates in the right pane.

3. Click a Category link to view the list of updates in that category.

4. If you decide to select an update to download and install, click the Add button next to the update to select it.

5. After you select all the updates you want, click the Install Now button. The Install page will appear, and the updates will be downloaded and installed on your computer.

6. Click the close icon to close the Internet Explorer window.

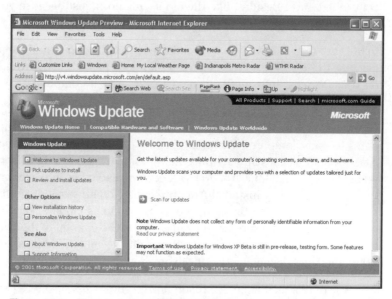

Figure 18.1   The start of an Update session.

Configuring Windows Update

If you get one thing from using Windows XP, you should understand this: *Everything* is configurable. Very little within Windows XP cannot be changed and made the way you want it. This philosophy permeates much of Microsoft's interfaces, including its Web sites. The

Windows Update Web site, which is positioned as an online extension of Windows XP, is certainly no exception.

You can modify the look of the Windows Update site to fit your needs by using these steps:

1. Click Start|All Programs|Windows Update. Internet Explorer will open to the Windows Update Web page.

2. Click the Personalize Windows Update link to open the Personalize Your Windows Update Experience page (see Figure 18.2).

3. Click the checkboxes for the options you wish to change to clear or select them.

4. Click the Save Settings button to make the changes immediately.

5. Click the close icon to close the Internet Explorer window.

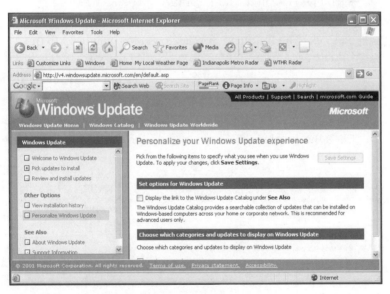

Figure 18.2   Customizing Windows Update.

Running Automatic Updates

The title of this section is actually a bit misleading. When you "run" an application, the implication is that you have some measure of control over when the application gets started. In truth, the Automatic Updates feature is running all the time, constantly on the lookout for new updates from Microsoft. When an update is found, the program will no longer run completely in the background and will start notifying you as it is supposed to do. But, you, as the user, really have no control over when Automatic Updates is actually going to pop up. It could happen any time, day or night, seven days a week.

When Automatic Updates does finally come up, working with it is frighteningly easy. Depending on the configuration you have set for the application, you may just have to click one button and let Windows XP handle the rest.

Automatic Updates basically has three settings, which you will learn how to set in the next section: off, which means you will have to manually go to the Windows Update site and get your updates there; download updates first and ask to install; and ask to download and ask to install. Presuming you have set Automatic Updates to ask before downloading and installing, follow these steps when the Automatic Updates icon pops up in the notification area of the taskbar:

1. Click the Automatic Updates icon or the balloon notification message. The Automatic Updates window will open to the Updates For Your Computer page (see Figure 18.3).

2. Click a Read This First link for one of the upgrade packages. The information window for the update will open (see Figure 18.4).

3. Click the Close link to close the update information window.

4. Click the checkbox for any link you don't want to download to clear it.

Figure 18.3   Automatic Updates lets you know that packages are ready to download.

18. Update
Windows XP

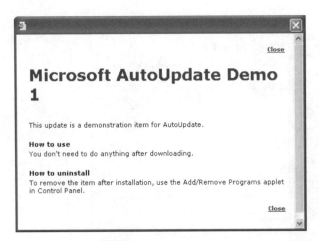

Figure 18.4   Learn all you want about a potential update to your computer.

TIP: If you don't want to download a large update right now, you can choose to download only some of the packages. If you don't want to download anything now, click the Remind Me Later button and choose a time to be reminded by the Automatic Updates notification icon later.

    5. Click the Start Download button. The Automatic Updates window will close, and the application will begin to acquire the selected packages from the Windows Update site.

When the downloads are complete, the Automatic Updates icon will appear in the notification area of the taskbar, and a message will let you know that downloads are ready to be installed. If you have set Automatic Updates to download first and ask to install, this will be your first notification from Automatic Updates. Proceed as follows:

    1. Click the Automatic Updates icon or the balloon notification message. The Automatic Updates window will open to the Ready To Install page (see Figure 18.5).

    2. Click Install. A new Ready To Install page will appear, listing the updates that were downloaded (see Figure 18.6).

    3. Click Install. The Installation In Progress page will appear, and the updates will be installed. When the installation is finished, the Installation Complete page will appear.

    4. Click OK to close the Automatic Updates window.

18. Update Windows XP

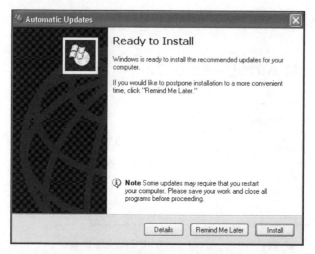

Figure 18.5 Getting prepared to install new updates.

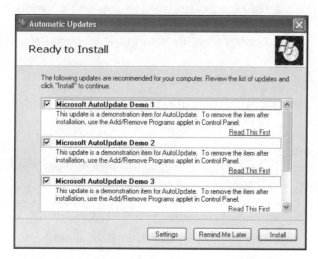

Figure 18.6 One more chance to examine the update packages.

Configuring Automatic Updates

Given the three choices for using Automatic Updates, which should you choose?

The first choice, leaving the tool off altogether, may not seem like a bad idea at first. Users who have slow dial-up connections or have high usage fees for telephone or Internet connectivity may want to be in total control of what traffic gets sent over their connections, no matter how benevolent that traffic might be. Corporate users may like the feature, but their IT managers might be less than thrilled with unauthorized updates tying up the network at any given moment. Thus, turning it off might not be such a crazy notion after all.

The next option, letting the updates download and then letting you know they're there to be installed, is the maximum of efficiency. Because the downloads take place in the background, they are effectively invisible and instantaneous—at least as far as user perception.

The final option is to let Automatic Updates notify you when the packages are ready to be downloaded and let you decide when and if they are downloaded. This option is my personal favorite because the notion of anything (again, no matter how benevolent) downloading to my computer without my permission or awareness is rather bloodcurdling, to say the least.

Part of maintaining good security on your system is being aware of everything that comes onto your computer. Granted, even the most secure-looking transmissions can be faked, but at least you will know what caused the problem in the first place. Although it is very unlikely that someone will use the Update delivery system as a tool of destruction, it is possible. Remember, people used to say email messages could never carry a virus.

By letting yourself control the download process, you can also fit the download into your schedule. This option is particularly useful if you are on a dial-up connection and don't want to clog up the pipe to the Internet while you're trying to accomplish other work on the Internet.

Whatever decision you end up making, you change the Automatic Updates options like this:

1. Click Start|Control Panel to open the Control Panel window.
2. Click the Performance And Maintenance link to open the Performance And Maintenance window.
3. Click the System link to open the System Properties dialog box.
4. Click the Automatic Updates tab to open the Automatic Updates page (see Figure 18.7).
5. Click the radio button for the Notification Settings option you want to select.
6. Click Apply to apply the settings.

18. Update Windows XP

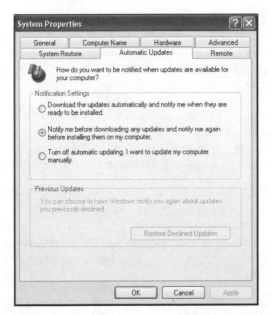

Figure 18.7   Decide how Automatic Updates will work for you.

7. Click OK to close the System Properties dialog box.

8. Click the close icon to close the Performance And Maintenance window.

Related solution:	Found on page:
Exploring Local Security Settings	394

Viewing Update History

It's a good bet that you will perform many upgrades on your system as you maintain it. But, will you remember all the upgrades you did? This knowledge may come in handy if you can't recall whether you installed the security upgrade to block that virus you're hearing about on the news every day. For peace of mind at least, you can check the history of all your system updates and make sure you've installed what you were supposed to.

You check the update history for both Automatic Updates and Windows Update on the Windows Update site, as you can see in these next steps:

1. Click Start|All Programs|Windows Update. Internet Explorer will open to the Windows Update Web page.

2. Click the View Installation History link to open the Installation History page (see Figure 18.8).

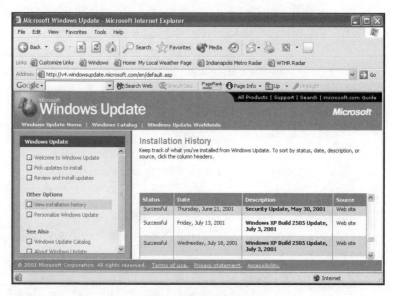

Figure 18.8   Checking out your update history.

Implementing a Device Driver Update

Both Windows Update and Automatic Updates do a good job keeping your hardware device drivers up to date. Some third-party vendors, however, may not be a part of the Microsoft update program, and you will need to get a driver update from another source. If this is the case, you should start the process from within the Device Manager, which is the safest way of getting the new driver installed. After you obtain the new driver and save it onto a floppy disk, follow these steps to install the driver:

1. Click Start|Control Panel to open the Control Panel.

2. Click the Performance And Maintenance link to open the Performance And Maintenance window.

3. Click the System link to open the System Properties dialog box.

4. Click the Hardware tab to open the Hardware page.

5. Click the Device Manager button to open the Device Manager.

6. Double-click the device to open the device's Properties dialog box.

7. Click the Driver tab to open the Driver page.

8. Click the Update Driver button to open the New Hardware Wizard.

9. Insert the floppy disk with the new driver into the floppy drive.

10. Click the Install Software Automatically (Recommended) option.

11. Click Next. The New Hardware Wizard will begin to look for the hardware drivers on the software supplied by the manufacturer.

12. When the driver is found, click Finish. The New Hardware Wizard will close, and the new driver will be installed.

13. Click OK to close the device's Properties dialog box.

14. Click the close icon to close the Device Manager window.

15. Click Apply to apply the settings.

16. Click OK to close the System Properties dialog box.

17. Click the close icon to close the Performance And Maintenance window.

Related solutions:	Found on page:
Performing an Inventory with Device Manager	8
Implementing Device Driver Rollback	132

Updating Microsoft Applications

Although getting third-party software to update itself online is still hit or miss, Microsoft has (naturally) done a pretty good job with giving its own software the capability to be updated online. Granted, this is a good marketing ploy to keep customers coming back to Microsoft. But, why knock a good thing?

One of the most popular Microsoft applications is undoubtedly Microsoft Office. It's suite of applications, sold together or separately, is one of the highest-selling pieces of consumer software in the world. Despite this huge popularity (or perhaps because of it), Office is also one of the most complex applications on the market. This complexity has led to enhanced user functionality. But, there's no denying this complexity has also led to some real headaches as new additions to the code may conflict with other parts of the code in new and creative ways.

Because of these problems, Microsoft launched its own update service for the Office suite beginning in Office 2000. This service has become very popular, particularly because one component of Office, Outlook, has been found to have numerous security problems that need repairing.

Running the Microsoft Office Update service is simple; it can be started from any of the Office applications, as you can see in this procedure:

TIP: *Before beginning this task, make sure you have your Office CD-ROM available. You may need it to confirm your identity as an activated Office user.*

1. In any Office application, click Help|Office On The Web. Internet Explorer will open to the Microsoft Office Assistance Center (see Figure 18.9).

2. Click the Product Updates link. The Office Update Identifier ActiveX control will begin to scan your system to determine what updates are needed. When it is finished, the Office Product Updates page will appear (see Figure 18.10).

3. Click the checkbox for the update you want to install to select it.

Figure 18.9   Office has an extensive online help center.

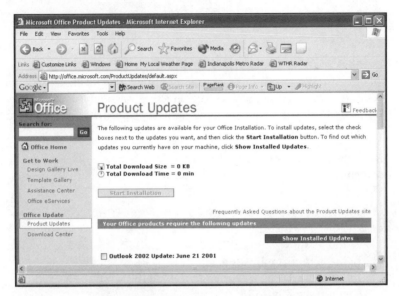

Figure 18.10   Updating Microsoft Office.

4. Click Start Installation to open the Office Product Updates
   Installation Wizard Web Page dialog box (see Figure 18.11).

Figure 18.11   Implement the installation of the update.

5. Click Install Now to open the End User License Agreement page.

6. Read the license and click Accept. If you have any Office programs open, the Please Close Programs page will appear.

7. Close your Office applications.

8. Click Continue. The update package will be downloaded and installed. The Windows Installer will be activated and will reconfigure Office based on the new code. When it is finished, the Installation Status page will appear (see Figure 18.12).

9. Click OK. The Office Product Updates Installation Wizard Web Page dialog box will close, and the Office Update Identifier ActiveX control will begin to scan your system again.

10. When the next scan is complete, click the close icon to close Internet Explorer.

11. Restart the system. The changes will take effect in the appropriate Office application.

Figure 18.12   The update is completed.

Chapter 19

Secure Windows XP

In Brief

Windows XP has the looks and the power. But, can it withstand assaults from the forces of evil? The answer to this question is a qualified yes. Yes, Windows XP can act as an effective deterrent to all sorts of malicious attacks—provided the users can keep the system protected with good, solid security practices.

The fact of the matter is, people are the weakest security layer for any computer system.

Cracker Kevin Mitnick coined the phrase *social engineering*, which was what he called the business of bluffing his way to getting information about a computer. Mitnick and other crackers can social-engineer users by identifying themselves as system administrators and asking for their passwords. Users, not realizing that there is never a reason the sysadmin would need their passwords, will give out the information almost immediately. Anything to help the IT guys, right?

This con applies to the IT staffers, too. Anyone can get conned, and IT employees are often the targets for social engineering because they have the most knowledge to reveal.

If we are the weakest link, then it's time to upgrade our attitudes about computer security. Without proper practices, the best security software in the world is no more useful than a coaster to put drinks on. If you are not diligent, someone can get onto your computer in many ways without your knowing about it. Let's start with a review of some of the most frequently used break-in methods and what Windows XP can do to help stop them.

Break-Ins 101

Listen up and pay attention, class: You're about to learn the three most popular ways someone can access your PC. They are:

- Direct physical access
- Virus and worm attacks
- Network attacks

Physical access is the most straightforward way someone can get to your machine and its data. Contrary to the notions that Hollywood promotes, crackers don't gain access by using rappel lines from the ceiling. Usually, someone, maybe even someone you know, casually saunters up to your PC and just reads what's there.

Obtaining access is often not very difficult, particularly in an office environment where one hand does not know what the other hand is doing. If you work for a medium-sized or large company, do you know everyone personally? Likely not. So, what would you do if you came back to find someone had been typing away at your computer while you were away from your desk, with the reason "I just needed to check one of your documents." This kind of thing happens quite a bit in an office environment, filled with people who are often not patient enough to wait until you get back from a break to get the data they need. And, although using your computer without your permission is a bit rude, 99 percent of the time it's just impatience.

Crackers also can easily bluff their way onto your machine, using that social engineering mojo. A cracker may say he's a new consultant for the IT department, coming to check on a problem with the network, and could you please log him in. Because most of us tend to defer to people we perceive as authorities on a given topic (in this case, our PC), we would likely fuss a bit about being interrupted and then slide out of our chairs and let the newcomer do his work on our PC. The question is, is that work genuine or of malicious intent?

Every once in a while someone is going to come along with some clearly bad thoughts in mind for you, your company, or the world in general. At this point, limiting physical access is a paramount issue. Limiting access is important for the general users' PCs and critical for all your server appliances.

Companies tend to regard security issues for their servers as a sort of necessary evil, not fully realizing the danger of letting unauthorized personnel near these machines. The level of damage someone can do to a company by messing around with a PC is phenomenal.

Two ways that Windows XP can limit the dangers of physical access are advanced passport control and support for smart cards. Smart cards are credit-card–sized devices that contain integrated circuits and a PIN number. The PIN number is used in place of or in conjunction with the regular password. Because PINs are never sent over the network, they form a tight barrier for anyone trying to casually use someone else's computer.

Not all threats to a computer come from a person sitting in front of the machine. Many threats come from remote sources, delivered in the form of viruses. At the risk of being repetitive, because the topic of viruses is examined *ad nauseum* in popular media, here's the quick definition of a computer virus: A *virus* is a computer program, sometimes embedded within another file or application, that will run on an infected computer against the user's wishes. The three basic kinds of viruses are the straightforward virus, the Trojan horse, and the worm.

The plain-old "ordinary" virus always reproduces a copy of itself at some point in its life span. Sometimes, it is the very act of replication that does the harm to the PC, because an endless replication cycle of even the slightest bit of code would eventually fill up the memory and ultimately stall the system. Other viruses will simply create a nuisance effect, such as displaying some stupid message on the top of your screen or causing your computer to forget what printers are connected to it. And, some will act as doomsday weapons and destroy any files they can sink their electronic claws into.

Viruses are classified by how they are spread. Regular viruses can cling to executable files, or even the boot sector of a floppy disk, ready to infect the next PC they come to. Viruses with special propagation methods are given special classifications.

The Trojan horse virus type is so-named because of the similarity to the ploy used by Odysseus and his fellow Greeks when they took on the city of Troy with the big wooden horse. A Trojan horse virus outwardly looks like a completely different file, sometimes not even an executable. A Trojan horse can hide in files that appear to be documents or even images. If the Trojan horse is hidden within an executable file, often the executable does what it is expected to do—while at the same time it's doing something sneaky to your PC.

Worms are special forms of viruses that spread themselves over some kind of network connection to infect other computers. Worms typically exploit some kind of network security flaw to get into other PCs. The infamous Code Red virus is a good example of a worm because it used network connections to spread itself.

Viruses are perhaps the best-known form of attack to PCs, but usually they do little damage, other than replicate themselves. However, the sheer number of viruses out there (50,000 at last count) tends to scare the living daylights out of even the least cautious PC user.

Windows XP has no built-in antivirus features. Given the weight of the preceding few paragraphs, the lack of such features may seem like suicide for the Microsoft developers. But, in reality, tracking and building defenses for all these different viruses is a massive proposition, the kind that a company must devote nearly all its efforts to. Microsoft has wisely left this task to other third-party developers who make it their business to crack down on virus epidemics.

Still, some safety tools in Windows XP will slow down virus infection. One of the best is the driver-signing feature. If you implement a strict digital signature policy for new drivers, you can prevent potentially harmful programs from running on your PC. Many Trojan horse applications can be stopped cold if you implement the hot start login, in which users must press Ctrl+Alt+Delete before they can see the login screen. This barrier is insurmountable to Trojan horses trying to break into your system.

Viruses are not very smart. They are just remote extensions of a person's distorted imagination. The real threat is when the intellect of a true cracker is pitted against you and your security resources. This kind of attack can make a virus seem like a breeze in a thunderstorm.

Crackers make up the third level of security breaches: completely remote attacks on your system. To get at your system, they just need to see your box on a network, even if that network is on the Internet. Having a dial-up connection is no guarantee of protection, either. To crackers, a door is a door. The question is, have you locked the door well enough to keep them out?

Crackers use various tools to break down the defenses of your system, the most dangerous being their brains. Besides this rather scary and obsessed bit of equipment, they can use a full rack of ammunition to pick the locks, including Trojan horses and scripts designed to ferret out the secrets of your PC before you even realize what happened.

Some crackers borrow their techniques from the FBI and DEA, who typically announce their presence in full body armor and brandishing semi-automatic weapons when they invade a suspect's home. Between the sight of this and all the screaming to get down on the floor, no one has a chance to react. A smash-and-grab attack from a cracker has a similar disorienting effect for PC users.

The truly dangerous cracker attacks are the quiet ones—the ones you don't see for hours, perhaps days, after the fact. These attacks are masterful in their stealth and patience, leaving few clues behind that someone was even there.

Script kiddies are a new breed of cracker who probe for vulnerable systems at random on the Internet. The script kiddies aren't looking for specific information or targeting a specific computer. They want to get administrator access on any computer they can. They usually do so by focusing on a small number of known security holes in Windows. By searching the Internet for machines with just these holes, they will eventually find a machine they can get into.

What do these crackers usually want? The answer to this question is a tough one to pin down as well because many times their goals are as diverse as their methods. Many attacks are aimed at Web sites, where crackers and script kiddies take inordinate pleasure in replacing the contents of a Web page with their own versions. On the surface, changing Web content doesn't sound like a big deal, unless the Web site in question is something like CNN or Amazon, where revenue is involved in the faultless running of the site.

Other crackers don't want to deface Web sites so much as take them down. Using a technique known as Distributed Denial of Service (DDoS) attacks, they will actually break into someone's computer and tell that computer to do nothing but send requests to the target Web site. When a cracker has broken into a significant number of PCs, which are now called zombies, the zombies will aim a massive number of requests at the Web site. Web sites operate on the principle of sending out pages to any PC requesting them, so when a bunch of zombied PCs launch a hundred million requests for pages in less than a few minutes, the effect is akin to putting a pea into a microwave and turning it on high for 10 minutes: The pea implodes into a shriveled black piece of carbon.

Others crackers will get access into a system and then sit back and monitor the activity on the PC to see what they can learn about the person or company who owns the machine. There may be no method of profit here, just the rush of finding out someone's dirty little secrets.

Some crackers operate in a more capitalistic frame of mind. These people jump into a PC to see what kind of data they can get to sell for their own profit. Like the pirates of the seven seas, they pillage and plunder computers from the relative safety of their own havens. Not too many crackers fall into this particular mindset, which is a very good thing.

You can protect yourself from crackers hitting your Windows PC in quite a few ways, not the least of which is setting up the Internet Connection Firewall, as you learned in Chapter 10. Other methods include limiting network access to your computer either by blocking out everyone completely or by forcing all users who log in remotely (including yourself) to have guest-level access so that they can do little harm.

Keep an eye on your security logs, too. You should make sure no one has tried to make unauthorized attempts onto your system. If someone has, you can make some changes to your system to keep the intruder guessing.

The latest method of protection from crackers is the new Encrypting File System (EFS). With EFS in place, you can lock up the most critical files on your system and prevent anyone but you from seeing their contents.

No matter what decisions you end up making, try to be more cautious than you normally would. Don't think that just because you're Joe Average out in Bippus, Indiana, that no one would ever want to get into your little ol' PC. If you have a disk drive and a solid connection, that alone makes you a good target to be a zombie for a DDoS attack on someone else's Web site.

Ever vigilant. That's the key to successful computing.

Immediate Solutions

Converting Drive to NTFS

Imagine a bee buzzing around your garden. If you were to follow this bee back to its home, you would find a seemingly chaotic mass of buzzing insects, each looking as if it were aimlessly wandering about with nothing better to do than hang out and buzz. As we all know, however, bees all have a specific purpose, working together for the collective benefit of the hive. One group of bees has the job of taking care of all the cute little baby bees after the queen lays her eggs. Now, think back to your science classes: Where are the baby bees raised? If you said the honeycomb, you're right. If you're wondering what the heck this has to do with the NT File System (NTFS) and Windows XP, just bee patient.

The honeycomb is an ingenious device composed of hexagonal cells made of beeswax, where honey and bee larvae are stored for safe-keeping. Now, ponder this: How would the bees get by if they did not have honeycombs? The answer is they wouldn't.

Keeping the honeycombs in mind, consider how data is stored on a disk drive. Data, you see, cannot be stored on a drive without some sort of structure already in place for the data to be organized. When data is placed on a drive, it is written into this structure, called a *file system*. A file system is the format in which data is stored—a honey-comb of cells if you will, where each little piece of data gets placed.

Computers being computers, data storage is a little more complicated than that. Data for a single file, for example, does not get stored in data blocks that sit right next to each other. The data may be stored in data blocks 456, 457, and 458, and then block 6,134, then block 7,111, and so on. (This description is an oversimplification, but you get the idea.) It's the job of the file system to track where every part of a file resides. When you send a command to work with a file, the file system knows all the separate blocks where the file is stored.

Because of all this file tracking and retrieving, computer engineers came up with the idea of keeping the file systems small, even on large hard drives. In this way, the idea of partitions came into play. Basi-cally, the partition is a virtual barrier that tells the file system: "You used to be able to write to blocks 1 to 25,000 all over the disk, but now you're allowed to write only to blocks 1 to 17,500. A second file system will write to blocks 17,501 to 25,000, so hands off!" Thus, you have partitions, and each partition can use a different file system. As an analogy, honeycombs created by honeybees are different from those created by wasps—similar structure but different outcomes.

Windows XP uses two types of file systems: FAT32 and NTFS. FAT32 is a file system used by Windows 9x versions (along with plain old FAT). Windows XP (like Windows 2000) runs on FAT32 mostly for the sake of backward compatibility. It can run well enough on a FAT32 partition, but XP will really shine on an NTFS partition.

NTFS supports a number of features that NT-based operating systems such as Windows XP can capitalize on. For instance, NTFS uses transaction logs to help recover from disk failures. NTFS files are not easily accessible from other operating systems, which gives an NTFS-formatted drive a little added protection right from the get-go.

NTFS is also the only file system that will allow you to use Active Directory features. It is also the file system that will actually enforce network file access restrictions. If you have set up access protection on files and folders on a FAT32 partition, the restrictions will simply not matter. Thus, it is important to move your partitions over to NTFS.

TIP: *Don't convert your partitions over to NTFS if you're sharing your system with another operating system such as Windows 95 or 98. If you do so, you will not be able to share files between partitions.*

When you installed Windows XP, you were given a choice to convert your hard drives to NTFS at that time. If you chose not to do so, you can still make the change after XP installation. Moving a partition over to NTFS is simple but time-consuming. The best time to implement the change is at the end of the day, when you can leave the conversion running while you are away from the computer. To run the conversion to NTFS, you need to use the Convert application on the command line, as shown in these steps:

1. Click Start|Run to open the Run window.

2. Type "cmd" in the Open field and press Enter. The Command Line window will open (see Figure 19.1).

3. To convert the D:\ drive to NTFS, type "convert d: /fs:ntfs" and press Enter. You will be asked to force a drive dismount because Windows is currently using the drive.

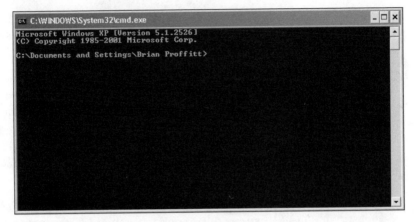

Figure 19.1   The Windows XP command line.

4. Type "n" and press Enter. You will be asked to initiate the conversion upon the next restart.

5. Type "y" and press Enter. The Convert application will stop.

6. Click the close icon to close the Command Line window.

7. Restart the computer at your earliest convenience if the converted drive is in use. Upon restart, the drive will be checked and converted, and Windows XP will restart normally.

TIP: *You don't have to restart the computer right away. You can set the conversion for the computer at any time and then just forget about it.*

Related solution:	Found on page:
Upgrading to Windows XP Professional	29

Exploring Local Security Settings

If you want to protect your system from unauthorized use, you will need to be familiar with the primary security tool within Windows XP: the Local Security Settings application. Local Security Settings is actually not a separate application at all. Rather, it is a component (called a snap-in) of the Microsoft Management Console (MMC). The MMC has various snap-ins, each designed to manage separate areas of XP administration—from users to devices to network security. The

MMC also has the distinct advantage of being completely customizable. Think of it as a big toolbox that you can toss all your favorite tools in before your next job.

Local Security Settings is one such toolbox—preloaded by Microsoft to provide you with all the really good tools to manage security on your local PC. You can find it, along with other MMC snap-ins, in the Administrative Tools section of the Control Panel by following these steps:

1. Click Start|Control Panel to open the Control Panel window.

2. Click the Performance And Maintenance link to open the Performance And Maintenance window.

3. Click the Administrative Tools link to open the Administrative Tools window (see Figure 19.2).

4. Double-click the Local Security Policy icon to open the Local Security Settings window (see Figure 19.3).

When the Local Security Settings window is open, you can make some pretty helpful changes to your security.

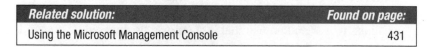

Related solution:	Found on page:
Using the Microsoft Management Console	431

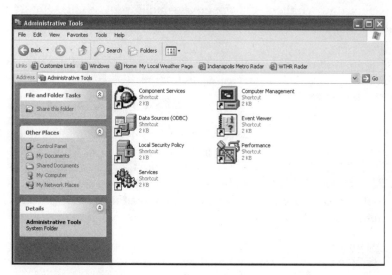

Figure 19.2   The Administrative Tools window.

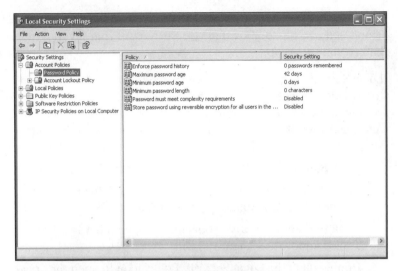

Figure 19.3   The Local Security Settings application.

Changing Password Settings

In Windows XP, users are encouraged to set strong passwords for
their user accounts. Strong passwords are not easily deduced by someone trying to get into your system. This means not using common-
language words and names that can quickly be guessed or cracked.
Strong passwords should instead have numbers and symbols inter-
spersed within them. Use uppercase and lowercase characters, too.
This will foil all but the most hardened password cracker.

TIP: *Having trouble figuring out a good password? Try using the first letters of a favorite line
of your favorite song. For instance, if you like The Police, you could use Rydhtpotrl (which is
from a stanza of "Roxanne").*

Eventually, it is true, a password cracker will be able to figure out any
password. It merely takes a matter of time to try out all the possible
combinations of characters. But, even with the average eight-charac-
ter password, it would take a cracker application months to figure
out the password if it were strong. By this time, the savvy user will
have changed his or her password at least once.

Windows XP allows users to have up to a whopping 127 characters in
a single password. If we all used that many characters, no one would
ever crack a password again. But, such a length is far too unwieldy
for even the most paranoid users. And, if you are connected to a network with machines running older versions of Windows, you will be
able to use only 14-character passwords to connect to those systems.

Ironically, even though Windows XP contains all this great password technology, the default configuration for users is to *not need a password*! This situation, even on a standalone home machine, is absolutely unsafe, so you should change it as soon as possible after you start running Windows XP.

The Local Security Settings will enable you to force users to use a password and at the same time will set a minimum password length, thus making your users a bit more clever in creating their passwords. The next procedure shows how to set password policy:

1. In Local Security Settings, click the expansion icon for the Account Policies setting group to see its contents.

2. Click the Password Policy setting group to see its contents.

3. Double-click the Minimum Password Length setting to open the Minimum Password Length Properties dialog box (see Figure 19.4).

4. Enter a value for the length of the password. When the value is not zero, passwords will automatically be required for all user accounts on the system.

5. Click Apply to apply the setting.

6. Click OK to close the Minimum Password Length Properties dialog box.

Another handy policy is to require users to change their settings at regular intervals. This regular change will keep passwords from becoming stagnant and easily cracked. Follow these steps to require this change:

1. In Local Security Settings, click the expansion icon for the Account Policies setting group to see its contents.

Figure 19.4   Force users to have a password.

2. Click the Password Policy setting group to see its contents.

3. Double-click the Maximum Password Age setting to open the Maximum Password Age Properties dialog box (see Figure 19.5).

4. Enter a value for the number of days for the password to expire. Typically, a month is a good duration.

5. Click Apply to apply the setting.

6. Click OK to close the Maximum Password Age Properties dialog box.

If you are in a more secure environment, you may not want users just switching back and forth between two passwords every month. You can make the users use different passwords when they make their change by creating a password history. The password history will remember the last few passwords they have used and force them to create something different.

Using Local Security Settings, you can set the number of passwords the history will contain by following these steps:

1. In Local Security Settings, click the expansion icon for the Account Policies setting group to see its contents.

2. Click the Password Policy setting group to see its contents.

3. Double-click the Enforce Password History setting to open the Enforce Password History Properties dialog box (see Figure 19.6).

4. Enter a value for the number of passwords remembered. Three or four is a fair value to use.

5. Click Apply to apply the setting.

6. Click OK to close the Enforce Password History Properties dialog box.

Figure 19.5   Get users to rotate their passwords.

Figure 19.6   Now, users will have to get creative.

Finally, you can make the users put more than just alphabetic characters within their passwords by enforcing strong passwords as follows:

1. In Local Security Settings, click the expansion icon for the Account Policies setting group to see its contents.

2. Click the Password Policy setting group to see its contents.

3. Double-click the Password Must Meet Complexity Requirements setting. The Password Must Meet Complexity Requirements Properties dialog box will open.

4. Click the Enabled radio button to select it.

5. Click Apply to apply the setting.

6. Click OK to close the Password Must Meet Complexity Requirements Properties dialog box.

Implementing Ctrl+Alt+Delete Logon

Trojan horses and similar viruses often try to gain access to users' PCs by tricking them into giving away their passwords. One trick that used to be effective was placing a logon screen near the start of the operating system and letting the users cheerfully provide their usernames and passwords.

To ensure a true Windows logon screen, Microsoft added the Ctrl+Alt+Delete function to the login process. Pressing Ctrl+Alt+Delete just before the logon screen guarantees that the next screen you see will be the right logon screen.

To activate Ctrl+Alt+Delete logons, use the Local Security Settings in the following manner:

1. In Local Security Settings, click the expansion icon for the Local Policies setting group to see its contents.

2. Click the Security Options setting group to see its contents.

3. Double-click the Interactive Logon: Do Not Require CTRL+ALT+DEL setting. The Interactive Logon: Do Not Require CTRL+ALT+DEL Properties dialog box will open (see Figure 19.7).

4. Click the Disabled radio button to select it.

5. Click Apply to apply the setting.

6. Click OK to close the Interactive Logon: Do Not Require CTRL+ALT+DEL Properties dialog box.

Controlling Network Access

If you are concerned about someone logging in from the network using your account information, you can quickly use Local Security Settings to limit the user's rights when he or she logs on to your computer. This setting does have the effect of limiting your access if you are the one logging on from a network connection, so you will have to weigh convenience over security.

To make this setting change, follow this procedure:

1. In Local Security Settings, click the expansion icon for the Local Policies setting group to see its contents.

2. Click the Security Options setting group to see its contents.

3. Double-click the Network Access: Sharing And Security Model For Local Accounts setting. The Network Access: Sharing And Security Model For Local Accounts Properties dialog box will open.

4. Click the drop-down list control to display the options.

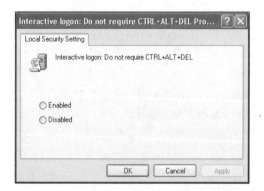

Figure 19.7   Setting up Ctrl+Alt+Delete logons.

5. Click the Guest Only option to select it.

6. Click Apply to apply the setting.

7. Click OK to close the Network Access: Sharing And Security Model For Local Accounts Properties dialog box.

You can also block out certain users altogether by following these steps:

1. In Local Security Settings, click the expansion icon for the Local Policies setting group to see its contents.

2. Click the User Rights Assignment setting group to see its contents.

3. Double-click the Access This Computer From The Network setting. The Access This Computer From The Network Properties dialog box will open (see Figure 19.8).

4. Click the name of a user or user group to select it.

5. Click Remove. The user or user group is removed and will be denied access to your computer.

6. Click Apply to apply the setting.

7. Click OK to close the Access This Computer From The Network Properties dialog box.

Figure 19.8   Decide who can log on and who can't.

Locking Out Unsigned Drivers

The use of unauthorized device drivers is an issue you will have to judge for yourself when the time comes. This is due to the fact that not every hardware vendor participates in the Windows Logo program and therefore may not have a digital certificate to authorize the driver.

Under the default settings, Windows XP will warn you if it detects an unsigned driver and let you make this choice. If your organization strictly uses Windows Logo-only products, you may want to use this opportunity to block those drivers. You may not stop a virus, but you could prevent someone from attaching an unauthorized piece of equipment on your network. To lock out unsigned drivers, follow these steps:

1. In Local Security Settings, click the expansion icon for the Local Policies setting group to see its contents.

2. Click the Security Options setting group to see its contents.

3. Double-click the Device: Unsigned Driver Installation setting. The Device: Unsigned Driver Installation Properties dialog box will open.

4. Click the drop-down list control to display the options.

5. Click the Do Not Allow Installation option to select it.

6. Click Apply to apply the setting.

7. Click OK to close the Device: Unsigned Driver Installation Properties dialog box.

Forcing Logouts at Certain Times

It's the dead of night, and one lone light from a monitor screen is shining in the forest of cubicles out in the office. Is some eager employee trying to get her work done? Or, is someone uninvited trying to get into the network?

To combat the problem of crackers trying to log on to the system at all hours of the night (when it presumably isn't monitored), many corporations establish network logon hours. During these times, any authorized user can get onto the network. After this period, only a select few can gain access to the network.

For those users who have to work late, logon hour policies will usually let them stay on the network, provided they were logged on before the end of logon hours. If you are more security conscious than this, you can have your computer kick off any user logged on to the network after logon hours are over. Just use this procedure to implement this policy:

1. In Local Security Settings, click the expansion icon for the Local Policies setting group to see its contents.

2. Click the Security Options setting group to see its contents.

3. Double-click the Network Security: Force Logoff When Logon Hours Expire setting. The Network Security: Force Logoff When Logon Hours Expire Properties dialog box will open.

4. Click the Enabled radio button to select it.

5. Click Apply to apply the setting.

6. Click OK to close the Network Security: Force Logoff When Logon Hours Expire Properties dialog box.

Handling Smart Cards

Smart cards, which are becoming prolific in European corporations, have not quite taken off in the United States—yet. Their simplicity of function and powerful security won't keep their widespread adoption from happening for much longer, though. But, like the best password system ever, smart cards can do little good if the computer is still on after the users remove them when they leave their desks. A better security policy is to make the system log off or lock up if the cards are removed, as shown in these steps:

1. In Local Security Settings, click the expansion icon for the Local Policies setting group to see its contents.

2. Click the Security Options setting group to see its contents.

3. Double-click the Interactive Login: Smart Card Removal Behavior setting. The Interactive Login: Smart Card Removal Behavior Properties dialog box will open.

4. Click the drop-down list control to display the list of options.

5. Click the Lock Workstation option to select it.

6. Click Apply to apply the setting.

7. Click OK to close the Interactive Login: Smart Card Removal Behavior Properties dialog box.

Monitoring Security Logs

All the best security procedures on the planet will not do much good if you don't see who's out there trying to get onto your PC. For the most part, many people go through their computer experience blithely unconcerned about who might be trying to access their computer.

After all, their security measures are in place. What's there to worry about?

Given the ingenuity of the average cracker, plenty. For every road-block you have set up on your computer, a cracker may have five ways of working around it. But, those methods take time. Cracker attacks may extend for days on your system without your realizing it, as the cracker slowly picks away at your defenses.

Along the way, the cracker will surely leave a trail behind, tripping little settings incorrectly. These mistakes will show up in your security log, Windows XP's way of tracking all the unauthorized users trying to get into your system

To view the security log, you will need another MMC snap-in, Computer Management. This snap-in will let you see the security log and find out whether something is amiss on your system. To use it, follow these steps:

1. Click Start|Control Panel to open the Control Panel window.

2. Click the Performance And Maintenance link to open the Performance And Maintenance window.

3. Click the Administrative Tools link to open the Administrative Tools window.

4. Double-click the Computer Management icon to open the Computer Management window (see Figure 19.9).

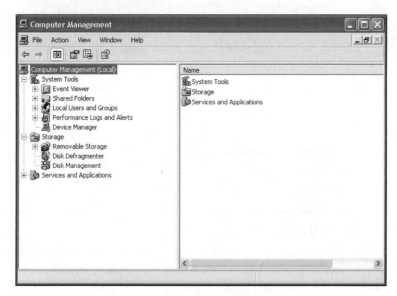

Figure 19.9   The Computer Management application.

5. Click the Event Viewer expansion icon to see the contents of the group.

6. Click Security to display the contents of the security log.

Sometimes, really sophisticated crackers will turn off the security logging feature so their efforts really go unnoticed. You can arrange this little surprise for the crackers in Local Security Settings:

1. In Local Security Settings, click the expansion icon for the Local Policies setting group to see its contents.

2. Click the Security Options setting group to see its contents.

3. Double-click the Audit: Shut Down System Immediately If Unable To Log Security Audits setting. The Audit: Shut Down System Immediately If Unable To Log Security Audits Properties dialog box will open.

4. Click the Enabled radio button to select it.

5. Click Apply to apply the setting.

6. Click OK to close the Audit: Shut Down System Immediately If Unable To Log Security Audits Properties dialog box.

As the name of this setting implies, if someone tries to disrupt the security log process, the system will immediately shut itself down, rendering it useless to a cracker.

Using the Encrypting File System

If you have formatted your hard drives with NTFS, you can use the Encrypting File System (EFS) to encrypt data on those drives. When the files are encrypted by EFS, only the user who originally performed the encryption can access those files. This encryption is very solid, too. No special user permissions can bypass this encryption. Even if someone were to steal the computer and install a new operating system on the machine (which would effectively wipe out most security settings), the files would still be encrypted and inaccessible.

Encrypting a file or folder is simple indeed. With NTFS, the encryption is completely integrated with the file managers in Windows XP. You will not know the files are encrypted because they will behave in exactly the same way.

19. Secure Windows XP

TIP: *Files and folders cannot be encrypted and compressed at the same time. You must perform one process or the other.*

To encrypt a file, follow this procedure:

1. Click Start|My Computer to open the My Computer window.

2. Navigate to the file or folder you want to encrypt.

3. Right-click the file or folder. The context menu will appear.

4. Click Properties to open the object's Properties dialog box.

5. Click Advanced to open the Advanced Attributes dialog box (see Figure 19.10).

6. Click the Encrypt Contents To Secure Data checkbox to select it.

7. Click OK to close the Advanced Attributes dialog box.

8. Click Apply to open the Confirm Attribute Changes dialog box (see Figure 19.11).

Figure 19.10   Setting advanced attributes.

Figure 19.11   Confirm your changes.

9. Click the Apply Changes To This Folder, Subfolders And Files radio button to select it.

10. Click OK. The Confirm Attribute Changes dialog box will close, and the Applying Attributes dialog box will open to mark the progress of the encryption.

11. Click OK to close the object's Properties dialog box.

NOTE: *Encrypted files and folders are listed in green type within Windows Explorer.*

Related solutions:	Found on page:
Sharing Files with Other Users	174
Compressing Data	426

Chapter 20

Administer Windows XP

In Brief

People being people, we tend to anthropomorphize the objects around us. Computers are no exception. For some reason, because computers are the keepers of much of our knowledge, we think of them as being knowledgeable.

A favorite author of mine, Diane Carey, once wrote a line of dialog for her character that went something like this:

"You know why no one puts legs on a computer? Because they would walk off a cliff if you told them to."

This line has stuck with me for quite some time because it cleverly illustrates something we have all suspected for quite some time: Computers are as dumb as a box of rocks. In fact, if you examine the components of a computer literally, it *is* a box of metallic and organic material forged by the hands of Humans. Which makes it a box of rocks and dirt.

This description is not meant to be insulting (though you should feel free to use it as an invective the next time your computer crashes); it is simply a more literal version of the truth. Computers have no sense at all about their place in the universe, nor can they think for themselves. They are complete *tabula rasas*, awaiting the instructions from a person to know what to do next.

Windows XP and all the other operating systems in the world are meant to be interfaces for us to deliver those instructions to the computer. We need these interfaces because very few of us can type the machine language the computer really needs to hear. Even software programmers can't: Applications are coded in natural language format and then translated into something the computer can understand.

Left to their own devices, computers would not function. They need human beings to provide energy and a benign environment in which to operate. But, even if those things were provided indefinitely, computers would eventually grind to a mental halt. Some little trip of logic, some minor error on a disk drive would spell curtains for the device. Computers, it seems, cannot manage themselves very well. They need us to care for them completely and regularly.

Windows XP has incorporated many tools to perform maintenance and upkeep on the computers on which it is installed—tools you will learn about in this chapter.

Helping Computers Help Themselves

Administration on a computer is composed of two parts: proactive and reactive. Reactive administration is what we all dread: Something has gone wrong on the computer, and now we have to fix it. This task is frustrating because often the problem will not immediately show itself, and we have to waste time trying to nail it down.

Being reactive in any crisis is simply not the best place to be because you start out behind the problem and have to work hard to catch up with it. Better to be proactive, where you're ahead of the game and not using a lot of time and energy.

The motto of the Boy and Girl Scouts is "Be prepared." That's a motto all computer users should have plastered right next to their computer monitors—right next to a copy of Murphy's Law. Your computer *will* break, something that will be discussed in Chapter 21. But, you can do many things as a proactive administrator to prevent these breakdowns as much as possible.

If you were to create a list of the leading causes of computer problems, it would look something like this:

- Hardware failure
- Software conflict
- Power failures
- User error

This list is a bit hard to pin down as far as order. Depending on whom you ask, the causes on this list can trade positions. What is important to note about all these causes is that all of them can be prevented by someone who is on his or her toes.

The damage caused by power failures can be circumvented by the installation of a good uninterrupted power supply (UPS). User errors can be reduced by proper training. Software conflicts can be minimized by the establishment of good configuration management practices and test machines.

And hardware failures? They can be prevented as well, especially when you consider that most computer hardware problems involve one of the most important parts of the computer: the hard drive. Since their invention in the 1950s, when they were 20 inches in diameter and stored a few megabytes, hard drives, or hard disks, have been the central storage component for memory on computers. Hard disks work by imprinting magnetic flux patterns on a magnetic medium in the shape of a small platter. The magnetic recording material is layered onto a high-precision aluminum or glass disk and then polished.

Data is read from the hard disk using a mechanical head arm that can move to any part of the disk almost instantly. The data from a single file, which is held in sectors and tracks on the disk, does not have to be stored all in one place. The file system can track where all the different parts of the data are located on the hard disk.

This capability to split related data into different pieces is critical to the speed of a hard drive. If the drive had to keep all that data together and store it exactly where it found the data in the first place, memory storage and retrieval operations would slow to a crawl. So, to keep itself happy, the hard disk stores files all over itself, letting the file system bear the brunt of keeping track of the data. But, this practice trades initial efficiency for long-term life.

By storing data willy-nilly on the hard disk, the drive creates a situation in which the head arm has to fly around the disk to pick up all the component bytes that make up a file. The more moving parts are used, the faster they will ultimately break down. (This situation also causes more inefficiency later, something to be examined in the "Defragmenting a Disk" section later in this chapter.)

The hard disk is one of the most important components of the computer, but it is also the one with the most moving parts. The key to keeping it healthy is to keep those parts from moving as much as is practical.

Hard drives are also problematic because of their finite nature. No matter how big a hard drive is, sooner or later, you are going to fill it up. With proper administration, you can prolong the life of the hard drive with better storage management. Compression and cleanup tools found in Windows XP are essential to this task.

Good administration of your computer involves more than disk and storage management. User policies, operating system configuration, and services are all a part of proper administration practices. The best tool to handle these functions is the Microsoft Management Console (MMC), a completely configurable application that lets you pick and choose the tools you need to manage your system better.

Like good security, the trick to good administration is staying on top of the situation with proactive tasks. With preventative maintenance, your system will enjoy a long and healthy life.

20. Administer Windows XP

Immediate Solutions

Managing with Computer Management

Users of Windows 9x operating systems may be surprised by the number of administrative tools contained within Windows XP. The inclusion of these tools is directly due to the Windows NT ancestry of Windows XP.

Windows NT's creators wisely concluded that a well-managed computer is a stable computer, so they threw every administrative tool they could think of into Windows NT. The trouble is, this solution may have backfired for the end user, who suddenly was buried in a host of tools with little guidance on how to use them. Training and certification took care of much of this problem, but Microsoft has also made some efforts in consolidating these tools into one manageable application. This, then, is the origin of the MMC.

The MMC can use whatever snap-in tools you decide to add to the console, as you will see in the "Using the Microsoft Management Console" section later in this chapter. To save some time, Microsoft has already provided users with premade MMC consoles that look and feel like individual applications. One of the most useful of these MMC-based applications is the Computer Management console. With this console, you can quickly and effectively manage your hard drive.

To open the Computer Management console, follow this procedure:

1. Click Start|Control Panel to open the Control Panel window.
2. Click the Performance And Maintenance link to open the Performance And Maintenance window.
3. Click the Administrative Tools link to open the Administrative Tools window.
4. Double-click the Computer Management icon to open the Computer Management window (see Figure 20.1).

Defragmenting a Disk

Fragmentation, as you have already read, is the effect created on a hard disk when data is stored in a noncontiguous way. Over time, this fragmentation forces the file system to work harder to keep the data organized and eventually will slow down the system as applications and data files alike take longer to be read.

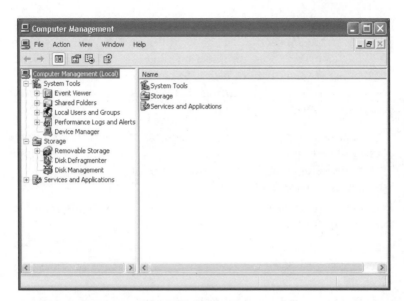

Figure 20.1   The Computer Management console.

The FAT32 and NTFS file systems have a weak spot concerning fragmentation. Other file systems, such as ext2, actively avoid fragmentation. The difference is the way ext2 stores files. The ext2 file system is designed to keep a list of all empty data blocks on the hard disk. When some blocks are needed to write a file, ext2 examines this list and finds contiguous free blocks to write the data to. FAT32 and NTFS, on the other hand, write the file in the first free blocks they find, until the entire file is stored. Clearly, the file system can be improved in this area. Until then, users must make do with what they have.

Experts disagree as to how much of a negative effect fragmentation actually has on hard drive performance, but it's a sure bet that if you can reduce the amount of fragmentation, your system will run faster. Is it significantly faster? The answer depends on how fragmented the disk is. Most experts think that if the disk is more than 10 percent fragmented, performance will begin to degrade quite a bit. If the level of fragmentation is more than 20 percent, you clearly need to defragment the drive as soon as you can.

Some third-party vendors have "sweetened the pot," as it were, and introduced a new feature to their defragmenting applications: optimization. Disk optimization is simple in principle: The defragmenter scans the drive and locates oft-used application executable files. When the defragmenting process is running, it not only defragments the executable files, but it also places them on one physical section of the disk with other applications that are well-used.

This concept is ingenious, because if all the application files are in
their own special section on the hard drive, there will be very few
free blocks in this application section and, therefore, very few writes
to that part of the drive to further fragment these files. The application files are not being written themselves, further reducing the
chances for them to be fragmented.

This optimization feature is also incorporated into the Microsoft
defragmentation tool. Disk Defragmenter is one of the tools found
within the Computer Management console, and following this procedure will enable you to run it:

1. In Computer Management, click the expansion icon for the
   Storage settings group to display its contents.

2. Click Disk Defragmenter to open the Disk Defragmenter page
   (see Figure 20.2).

TIP: *You also can start the Disk Defragmenter by clicking Start|All Programs|Accessories|
System Tools|Disk Defragmenter.*

---

3. Click a hard drive to select it.

4. Click the Analyze button to begin analyzing the contents of the
   drive. When this process is complete, the Disk Defragmenter dialog box will appear, notifying you of the results (see Figure 20.3).

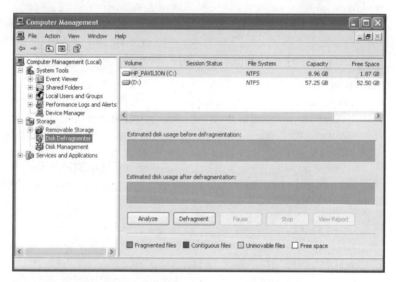

Figure 20.2   The Disk Defragmenter.

Figure 20.3   Always perform an analysis before defragmenting the drive.

NOTE: Drives are always analyzed before defragmentation to prevent the accidental shift of data onto an unidentified bad disk sector.

5. Click the View Report button. The Disk Defragmenter dialog box will close, and the Analysis Report dialog box will open (see Figure 20.4).

6. Examine the report. If you agree with its findings, click Defragment. The Analysis Report dialog box will close, and the defragmentation process will begin. When the process is complete, the Disk Defragmenter dialog box will open.

7. Click Close to accept the notification. The Disk Defragmenter dialog box will close.

TIP: If you have more than one hard disk, try to keep all your data files on one drive and your application and system files on the other. By keeping files that are written on a separate drive (or partition), you reduce the chances of your important system files getting fragmented.

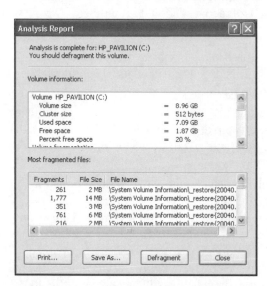

Figure 20.4   Viewing the analysis report.

Converting to Dynamic Disks

Every operating system uses partitions to help organize the data stored on hard drives. In all Windows and DOS machines, all physical hard drives are completely filled with one partition each, unless you indicate otherwise. These partitions are denoted by a drive letter (C:, D:, and so on).

You can divide these physical partitions into what is known as a logical partition. Logical partitions look and behave like separate physical drives on your computer system. Each logical partition gets its own drive letter and directory system, separate from the other partitions.

In Windows XP, such partitions, physical or logical, are referred to as basic disks. They are what Windows 9x and Windows NT users have grown accustomed to using. In Windows 2000, a new type of disk volume, the dynamic disk, was introduced, bringing with it some incredible new features.

A dynamic disk is a physical hard drive that foregoes the use of physical and logical partitions. Instead, it contains only dynamic volumes that you create in the Disk Management console. Dynamic volumes do not use any drive letter notation and can even be extended on the computer without restarting the system.

The five kinds of dynamic volumes are simple, spanned, striped, mirrored, and RAID-5. The latter three types—striped, mirrored and RAID-5—are known as fault-tolerant volumes. This means they are designed for excellent data recovery should something go wrong with the hardware.

To get all these cool features, though, you have to upgrade your drives from basic to dynamic. This procedure is relatively painless, but you should be aware of some limitations:

- You cannot use dynamic disks on a portable computer. Nor can you use them on removable drives, detachable disks, or disks that share a SCSI bus. If you have any of these configurations, you're out of luck.

- You cannot access dynamic volumes with any operating system other than Windows 2000 and Windows XP Professional, no matter what file system you're using for the volume. This means that MS-DOS, Windows 9x, Windows ME, Windows NT, and Windows XP Home Edition are right out. You can, however, get to any folder that is shared from the network, just as before. Because of this access limitation, though, you will have great difficulty booting multiple operating systems on any system with dynamic drives. It is strongly recommended that you don't even try.

You should also note that although the change to dynamic disk is reversible, reverting from a dynamic disk back to a basic disk is not an easy matter because the disk must be completely empty before you convert it back to basic.

TIP: *You should close all programs before starting a conversion to dynamic disks.*

If you understand these limitations and you still want to use dynamic disk features, you can use the Computer Management console to make the conversion, as shown in the following steps:

WARNING! **Back up all data before converting a drive to dynamic status.**

1. In Computer Management, click the expansion icon for the Storage settings group to display its contents.

2. Click Disk Management to open the Disk Management page (see Figure 20.5).

3. Right-click the drive icon of a basic drive. The context menu will appear.

4. Click Convert To Dynamic Disk to open the Convert To Dynamic Disk dialog box (see Figure 20.6).

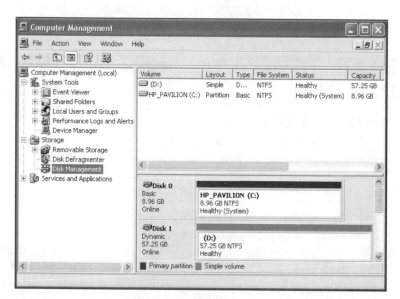

Figure 20.5   The Disk Management screen.

Figure 20.6   Be very sure you are converting the right disk, especially if you
use multiple operating systems.

5. Confirm the choice of disk to convert and click OK. The
Convert To Dynamic Disk dialog box will close, and the Disks
To Convert dialog box will open.

6. Confirm the listed drive is the one you want to convert and
click Convert. The Disks To Convert dialog box will close, and
the Disk Management dialog box will open.

7. Read the warning regarding not being able to open another
operating system on this new volume and click Yes to continue.
The Disk Management dialog box will close, and the Convert
Disk To Dynamic dialog box will open.

8. Read the warning regarding the file system being unmounted
on this new volume and click Yes to continue. The Convert Disk
To Dynamic dialog box will close, and the drive will be converted to a dynamic drive with a simple volume.

Related solution:	Found on page:
Backing Up Your Data	19

Optimizing Your System

By default, Windows XP is built to run applications with utmost efficiency. If this seems like a no-brainer, think again. Windows XP, like
its Windows NT ancestors, can run services in the background as well,
including IIS, Microsoft's Web server platform.

This is not to say that Windows XP is another version of Windows
2000 Server. No, that accolade is going to be reserved for the Server
edition of Windows XP due out in 2002. But, XP Professional does
have the tools to run some basic services on the platform. If you
plan to use your Windows XP machine in this manner rather than a

workstation, you can configure the performance of the processor and memory storage to accommodate these actions, thus optimizing the system to run services.

Use these steps to optimize the system:

1. In Computer Management, right-click the Computer Management (Local) listing. The context menu will appear.

2. Click Properties to open the Computer Management (Local) Properties dialog box.

3. Click the Advanced tab to open the Advanced page (see Figure 20.7).

4. Click the Settings button in the Performance section to open the Performance Options dialog box (see Figure 20.8).

5. Click the Background Services radio button in the Processor Scheduling section to select it. This will give more priority to applications running in the background on your XP computer, such as mail and Web server applications.

6. Click the System Cache radio button in the Memory Usage section to select it. This will enhance the system's access of its own system cache for any servers that might be running.

7. Click OK to close the Performance Options dialog box.

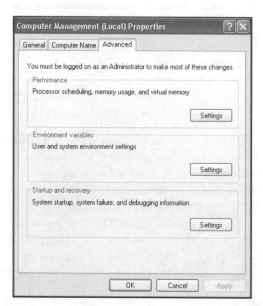

Figure 20.7 Advanced settings for your computer.

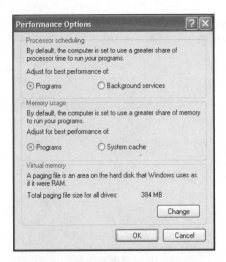

Figure 20.8   Optimize your system based on its job.

8. Click Apply to apply the settings.

9. Click OK to close the Computer Management (Local) Properties dialog box.

Checking for Drive Errors

The medium for a hard drive works almost exactly like that of a cassette recording tape. Information signals are imprinted on the hard drive using tiny fluctuations of magnetic force on tiny little parts of the disk called sectors. A sector is the smallest physical unit of data a hard drive has.

Every once in a while (usually at the factory), a sector of a hard drive gets damaged in some way. This is cleverly called a bad sector. Bad sectors are troublesome because they cannot be used for storage. You never want to write data to a bad sector because it takes special utilities to get at that data, and sometimes you cannot get to it even then. The best thing to do is to check your disk for bad sectors and other errors so that your file system is aware of the exact physical location of these faults on your hard drive. Then, the file system will automatically adjust itself to work around the bad sector.

Checking for bad sectors is also a good idea because you will want to keep an eye on the general health of your disk. If you suddenly start seeing a rise in the number of bad sectors, you may have a mechanical fault in your hard drive. Move critical data off the drive immediately and get the drive replaced as soon as you can.

To begin the disk-checking procedure, follow these steps:

1. Click Start|My Computer to open the My Computer window.
2. Right-click a drive icon. The context menu will appear.
3. Click Properties to open the drive's Properties dialog box.
4. Click the Tools tab to open the Tools page (see Figure 20.9).
5. Click the Check Now button to open the Check Disk dialog box (see Figure 20.10).
6. Click the Automatically Fix File System Errors checkbox to select it.

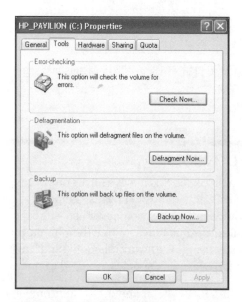

Figure 20.9   Tools to tweak your hard drive.

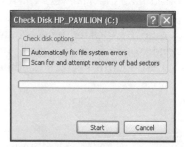

Figure 20.10   Check disk settings.

423

7. Click the Scan For And Attempt Recovery Of Bad Sectors checkbox to select it.

8. Click Start to open the Checking Disk dialog box (see Figure 20.11).

9. Click Yes to start the disk check the next time you restart Windows. The Checking Disk and Check Disk dialog boxes will close.

10. Click OK to close the drive's Properties dialog box.

The disk check will be performed the next time you restart Windows, at your convenience.

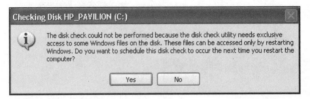

Figure 20.11   Because you started Check Disk in Windows, this message will always appear.

Cleaning Up Hard Drives

When you use a computer, a bit of detritus always forms on your hard drive from normal operations. Cached Internet pages, temporary files that were not deleted, old application files you never use—a real collection of digital junk. In this case, machines imitate their human creators very well because human beings are always shedding and leaving body oil all over everything. We are, as a species, pretty darn messy.

We are also (on average) fanatically clean about our environments. We sweep, we dust, and we wash. And, because we interact with computers, we have turned our cleaning frenzy on them as well. The tool Windows XP has for this, er, dirty job is appropriately named Disk Cleanup. Disk Cleanup tackles all those extra files left lying around on your hard drive that you don't need. You have full control over which files get swept out, so there's little fear of losing something important.

To run Disk Cleanup, follow these steps:

1. Click Start|All Programs|Accessories|System Tools|Disk Cleanup to open the Select Drive dialog box (see Figure 20.12).

Figure 20.12   Choose the drive to clean.

NOTE: *The Select Drive dialog box will not appear if you have only one hard drive on your computer. If this is the case for your computer, proceed to Step 4.*

2. Click the drop-down list control for the Drives field to display the list of drives.

3. Click a drive to clean to select it.

4. Click OK. The Select Drive dialog box will close, and the Disk Cleanup dialog box will open to track the progress of its analysis. When the analysis stage is complete, the Disk Cleanup dialog box will change to a list of items to delete (see Figure 20.13).

5. Click the checkboxes for the items you want to clean up to select them.

6. To view a detailed list of what you are cleaning, click the View [Objects] button, where [Objects] is the type of item you are

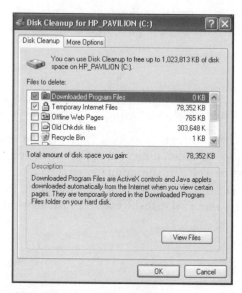

Figure 20.13   Pick the items to pitch from your computer.

examining. Windows Explorer will open and display the items in a folder.

7. Click the close icon to close the Windows Explorer window.

8. Click OK to open another Disk Cleanup dialog box.

9. Click Yes to confirm the action. Both Disk Cleanup dialog boxes will close, and the original Disk Cleanup dialog box will appear, marking the status of the cleaning operation.

When the Disk Cleanup dialog box closes, the operation is complete.

Compressing Data

You may not have realized it, but computers are full of redundancies—at least within the data.

A few years back, programmers noticed that within the raw data of any given file were patterns of data that were repeated over and over. This is a normal occurrence for all files, but the thought of then-precious storage space being used for storing a file full of redundant data really irked some of these programmers. So, some of them put their heads together and figured out a way to compress data files and still maintain their integrity.

The idea behind compression is easy to understand. Say you have a file filled with data that, when read by a human, would look like this:

```
arfrturssoejkflsuelf
selfsdlalrtursvaafdp
hfrtursffcsidrturste
skjflselfnrturswnfds
```

Now, let's say someone wrote a program to look for repeating patterns in data like this and the program noticed a high occurrence of the character strings **rturs** and **elf**. The program would then replace these patterns with a marker that would serve as shorthand for this data. After these strings were replaced with the marker, the data would look like this:

```
arfYsoejkflsuZ
sZsdlalYvaafdp
hfYffcsidYte
skjflsZnYwnfds
```

What was once an 80-character set of data is now just 54 characters, a reduction of nearly 33 percent. Of course, the reduction will be a bit less because at the end of the file will be a small table explaining which patterns were replaced by which markers. But, you get the idea.

In Windows XP, you can compress individual files and folders, or you can compress an entire hard drive at once. Compression is great if you have a tight fit on a drive, but it is not recommended you use it forever. You can't encrypt compressed files (keeping track of encryption ciphers and compression markers would likely make your computer processor go on strike), and there is a performance hit when you compress data because your system has to take the time to rebuild the data whenever you use the compressed file.

Compression, therefore, should be used as a stopgap until you can acquire more storage. With memory prices so low these days, there's no reason not to purchase more.

To compress an individual file or folder, follow these steps:

1. Click Start|My Computer to open the My Computer window.
2. Navigate to the file or folder you want to encrypt.
3. Right-click the file or folder. The context menu will appear.
4. Click Properties to open the object's Properties dialog box.
5. Click Advanced to open the Advanced Attributes dialog box.
6. Click the Compress Contents To Save Disk Space checkbox to select it.
7. Click OK to close the Advanced Attributes dialog box.
8. Click Apply to open the Confirm Attribute Changes dialog box.
9. Click the Apply Changes To This Folder, Subfolders, And Files radio button to select it.
10. Click OK. The Confirm Attribute Changes dialog box will close, and the Applying Attributes dialog box will open to mark the progress of the compression.
11. Click OK to close the object's Properties dialog box.

NOTE: *Compressed files and folders are listed in blue type within Windows Explorer.*

You can also compress the entire contents of a drive. This process is easy but time-consuming. You might want to start these steps before the end of the day or right before lunch:

1. Click Start|My Computer to open the My Computer window.

2. Right-click the drive you want to compress. The context menu will appear.

3. Click Properties to open the drive's Properties dialog box (see Figure 20.14).

4. Click the Compress Drive To Save Disk Space checkbox to select it.

5. Click Apply to open the Confirm Attribute Changes dialog box.

6. Click the Apply Changes To This [Drive], Subfolders, And Files radio button to select it.

7. Click OK. The Confirm Attribute Changes dialog box will close, and the Applying Attributes dialog box will open to mark the progress of the compression.

8. Click OK to close the drive's Properties dialog box.

Related solution:	*Found on page:*
Using the Encrypting File System	405

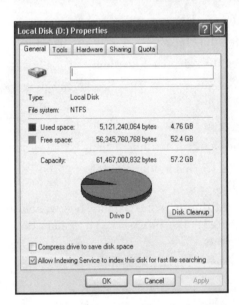

Figure 20.14   The properties of a hard drive.

Scheduling a Task

So, you know all the things you need to do for good system administration. Now, you're thinking to yourself that if only you had an extra 24 hours in the day, you could get all that work done.

Knowing full well that some of these administration tasks take awhile to run, you can schedule them to be run after hours, when no one needs to use your system. With Windows XP's Scheduled Tasks application, setting up this schedule is very simple.

Scheduled Tasks is also useful for users who leave their systems running all night in standby or hibernation mode. You can use Scheduled Tasks to automatically start your favorite applications just as you come into your office, giving you that extra time to get to the coffee room.

To create a new task, use this procedure:

1. Click Start|All Programs|Accessories|System Tools|Scheduled Task. The Windows Explorer window will open to the Scheduled Task folder (see Figure 20.15).

2. Double-click the Add Scheduled Task icon to open the Scheduled Task Wizard.

3. Click Next to move to the Program page (see Figure 20.16).

4. Click the application you want to start to select it.

5. Click Next to move to the Name And Duration page (see Figure 20.17).

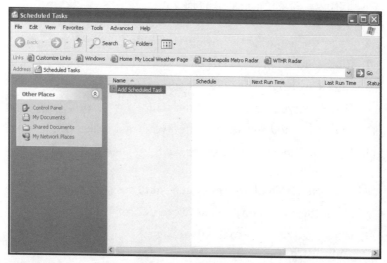

Figure 20.15   The Scheduled Tasks folder.

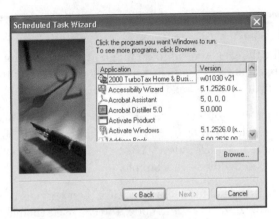

Figure 20.16   Select a program to start.

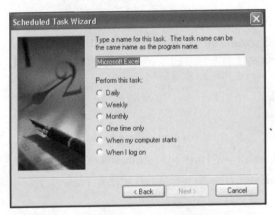

Figure 20.17   Pick a name for the task.

6. Enter the name for the task in the name field.

7. Click a duration radio button to select it.

8. Click Next to move to the Schedule page (see Figure 20.18).

9. Use the spinner control to enter a time for the program to start.

10. Click the frequency radio button you want to select it.

11. Click the calendar control for the Start Date field and select a start date.

12. Click Next to move to the Name And Password page.

13. Enter the username and password information, if necessary.

14. Click Next to move to the final page.

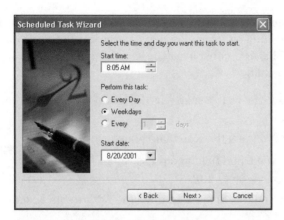

Figure 20.18   Schedule a task down to the minute.

15. Confirm the settings and click Finish. The Scheduled Task Wizard will close, and the new task will be listed on the Scheduled Tasks folder.

After you create a task, you can modify it at any time. Follow these steps to change the frequency of occurrence for a task:

1. In the Scheduled Tasks folder, right-click the task you want to modify. The context menu will appear.

2. Click Properties to open the task's Properties dialog box.

3. Click Schedule to open the Schedule page.

4. Edit the schedule as needed.

5. Click Apply to apply the settings.

6. Click OK to close the task's Properties dialog box.

Deleting a scheduled task is no problem when you use these steps:

1. In the Scheduled Tasks folder, right-click the task to delete. The context menu will appear.

2. Click Delete to delete the task.

Using the Microsoft Management Console

Throughout Chapter 19 and this chapter, you have used various consoles of the Microsoft Management Console (MMC) application. The MMC uses a "snap-in" metaphor that gives this application a great deal of flexibility.

Each snap-in is essentially a little mini-application that can be snapped into an empty MMC unit to form a unique combination of tools that fits you perfectly. This new console can be saved and retrieved at any time, so it's always handy.

Making a new console is, well, a snap—as the following steps demonstrate:

1. Click Start|Run to open the Run dialog box.

2. Type "mmc" in the Open field and press Enter. A blank MMC window will open (see Figure 20.19).

3. Click File|Add/Remove Snap-In to open the Add/Remove Snap-In dialog box.

4. Click Add to open the Add Standalone Snap-In dialog box (see Figure 20.20).

5. Select a snap-in to add to select it. Table 20.1 lists the available snap-ins.

6. Click Add. The snap-in will appear in the Add/Remove Snap-In dialog box.

NOTE: *For certain snap-ins, you might need to take additional actions, such as determining which computer this snap-in is destined to control.*

---

7. Repeat the preceding steps until all the desired snap-ins are in the console.

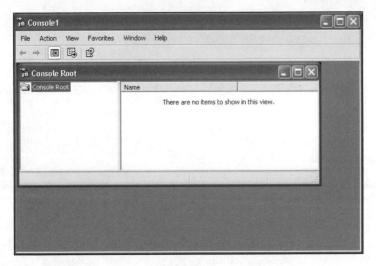

Figure 20.19   The template for an MMC window.

Figure 20.20 You can add as many snap-ins as you like.

Table 20.1 MMC standalone snap-ins.

ActiveX Control	Certificates
Component Services	Computer Management
Device Manager	Disk Defragmenter
Disk Management	Event Viewer
Folder	Group Policy
Indexing Service	IP Security Monitor
IP Security Policy Management	Link to Web Address
Local Users and Groups	Performance Logs and Alerts
Removable Storage Management	Resultant Set of Policy
Security Configuration and Analysis	Security Templates
Services	Shared Folders
WMI Control	

8. Click Close to close the Add Standalone Snap-In dialog box.

9. Click OK. The Add/Remove Snap-In dialog box will close, and the snap-ins will appear in the console.

10. Right-click the Console Root folder. The context menu will appear.

11. Click Rename and rename the console root folder to something more descriptive for your toolset.

12. Click File|Save As to open the Save As window.

13. Save the file under a new name and click Save to close the Save As window.

14. After using the tools, click File|Exit to close the new console window.

Chapter 21

Troubleshoot Windows XP

In Brief

Windows XP is being heralded as the most stable consumer-oriented operating system to ever be released.

That statement is from the Microsoft Marketing department. Looking closer at the operating system in action, I can tell you that for the most part it *does* seem very stable—but it's not perfect. I say this from experience at this point. I will let you in on a little secret as to why. Have you ever wondered why the troubleshooting chapter is always one of the last chapters in one of these computer books? It's not because the author is trying to hide the flaws in the topic he's writing about; it's because he needed all the time writing the rest of the book to figure out where and how the topic application or operating system will break!

When application failures have occurred (three while I wrote this book: one for Word XP and two for Windows Explorer), the system has always recovered nicely. This is saying something, too, because if Windows Explorer crashed in Windows 98, it was a sure bet the system would continue to behave abnormally until I restarted the machine.

As far as full-fledged system failures, I had only one and it was on a beta version of the product, which means it doesn't really count. I have run the full test on the system, too, letting my family work with the XP machine with all their different applications. And, if they can't bring up the dreaded Blue Screen of Death, no one can.

But, let's not kid ourselves, shall we? The fact is, sooner or later, something is going to go awry with your interaction with the computer. Either you are not going to remember how to do something, some application is going to choke and die on a file, or Windows XP itself will suddenly just break and you won't know why.

In this chapter, you'll learn how to respond to those unfortunate times and get back to your work in no time flat.

Yes, It Will Break

Experts disagree as to what is the leading cause of computer failure. Some consistently blame the user, citing poor understanding of how the computer works, leading to user errors that, in turn, lead to system problems. Other experts maintain that computer applications and operating systems have become so complex that they have become an open invitation for code incompatibilities to rear their ugly heads and cause system problems.

And, so the argument rages, each side trading barbs and technical papers until it has gotten to the point where you should never invite members of both camps to the same social function. If you do, they'll just sit sullenly around the room, glaring at each other and calling each other names until there's an explosion of canapés, and the whole party is engulfed in a food fight.

Well, perhaps it's not quite that bad. But, the two sides to this argument both make compelling statements that lead you to wonder which side might be right. Being the fence-straddling moderate that I am, I tend to think both sides are correct.

In my days as an IT staffer, I have seen users make some real whopper mistakes. Things that I could never imagine someone trying to do with a computer. This does not make the users stupid, not by any means. Using computers does not come instinctively. The idea of a metal box storing information is not a natural process, and it hasn't been very long (culturally speaking) since we figured out how to build the wheel. To expect people to just "pick this up" is a bit silly.

Computer developers recognize this problem and are working harder than ever to simplify their programs' interfaces. At the same time, the need to sell software is driving them to build more and more features into the software, in the hopes that someone will buy it. These conflicting methods are leading to some interesting new forms of software conflict—one of the big reasons an application will roll over and crash.

Software conflict is a direct result of living in a free-market system. Competitors work to build a better piece of software and often don't take into account what some other piece of code that might be installed on someone's machine might do. Windows has standards to prevent something like this from happening, but no one has anticipated every possible conflict yet. So, even if a program is fully Windows-compliant, it may still conflict with another application on your computer because the standard-setters never anticipated that kind of error.

The situation is getting better, though. Applications will still crash once in a while, but not as often. And, Windows XP has improved on the protected mode so richly enjoyed by NT and 2000 users. Protected mode means that when an application crashes, it does not touch the operating system of any other application. Thus, it can be shut down, and the rest of the session can continue like nothing happened.

Windows 9x users were supposed to enjoy this same sort of protection mode as well, but somehow the concept was never properly implemented on any of the Windows 9x platforms. A crash on a Windows 9x machine was like a crash on the Long Island Expressway—everyone stops to look and causes more crashes.

Until operating systems become truly self-diagnostic and self-repairing, we will always find faults and glitches in their operation. Anything built by human beings will have flaws. It's the nature of the beast. Windows XP is no exception.

What Windows XP does have is some useful tools to help you cut through the occasional blooper and error on your computer. It even has a new application, Remote Assistance, which will let others help you if you haven't quite got the knack of something. Microsoft recognizes that you'll have mishaps when you're using Windows XP. With its system recovery and diagnostic tools, you should be able to minimize the effects of these mishaps.

Immediate Solutions

Taking Over with Remote Assistance

You hear a knock at the cubicle entrance behind you. You turn to see one of your coworkers standing there, looking sheepish and forlorn.

"I can't seem to hook up to that big printer over near Sales. I know you showed me once, but could you run it past me again?" he asks.

Sighing, you get up from your chair and follow him into his cubicle to show him how to accomplish the task one more time.

All of us have been in either of these situations at one time or another. It's a part of working in the corporate environment. Somebody in the office always seems to know a little more about some aspect of the computer than you, and everyone always seems to go to that person for advice. That person is the office guru; it is his or her privilege and curse to be the keeper of knowledge about computers.

Office gurus have an interesting existence. They are lauded by the colleagues they help and reviled by the IT staff who think the gurus are poaching on their domain. Regardless of the respect gurus get, no one seems bothered by the fact that the guru can hardly get any of his or her own work done by being helpful.

Windows XP has a new tool that may alleviate some of this hassle for the gurus and their disciples: Remote Assistance. Remote Assistance enables users to ask other users for help online and let the guru take over their desktop to *show* them exactly what steps need to be taken. The task is completed, the user has learned something new, and the guru can get right back to work.

This use of Remote Assistance seems exactly like the situation described at the start of this section but because it is all happening online, the speed of the events is much faster. No walking to the guru's cubicle, no walking back and forth for the guru. Time is saved and stress levels are reduced. Also, because the initial request for help is online as well, the guru does not have to endure the sad puppy eyes if he or she really is very busy and has to say no.

Remote Assistance is extremely useful in the home environment as well. How many times have you run into a problem at home and had to wait until the next time you saw a guru friend to ask for help?

Remote Assistance is part of the Help And Support Center application, Windows XP's revamped online help tool. It needs either the Messenger service or a Messaging Application Programming Interface (MAPI)-enabled email client (such as Outlook and Outlook Express) to function. The procedure for using Windows Messenger is shown in the following steps:

NOTE: *Both machines must be running Windows XP for Remote Assistance to work.*

1. Click Start|Help And Support to open the Help And Support Center window (see Figure 21.1).

2. Click the Invite A Friend To Connect To Your Computer With Remote Assistance link to open the Remote Assistance page (see Figure 21.2).

3. Click the Invite Someone To Help You link to open the Invitation page (see Figure 21.3).

4. In the Use Windows Messenger section, click a contact to select it.

5. Click the Invite This Person link. The Remote Assistance Web Page dialog box will appear, indicating the status of the invitation.

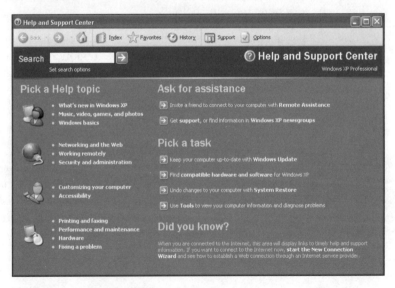

Figure 21.1   The Help And Support Center.

6. If the invitation is accepted, the Windows Messenger application will open a conversation window on both machines. The guru's machine will also open a Remote Desktop window and will be able to guide your mouse pointer through the steps while showing you how to perform the task.

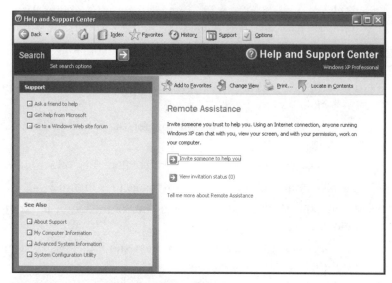

Figure 21.2   Starting Remote Assistance.

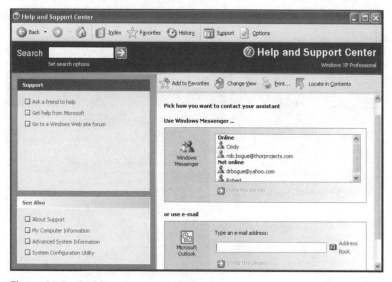

Figure 21.3   Inviting someone to help.

If the user you ask for help is not online with his or her Messenger client, you can use an email message to ask for help, as shown in these steps:

1. Click Start|Help And Support to open the Help And Support Center window.

2. Click the Invite A Friend To Connect To Your Computer With Remote Assistance link to open the Remote Assistance window.

3. Click the Invite Someone To Help You link to open the Invitation page.

4. In the Or Use E-Mail section, enter an email address in the Type An E-Mail Address field.

5. Click the Invite This Person link to open the E-Mail An Invitation page (see Figure 21.4).

6. Enter a personal request in the Message field. Be polite.

7. Click Continue to open the Security page (see Figure 21.5).

8. Enter a time for a valid invitation in the Set Invitation To Expire field.

9. Type a password for the helper to use in the Type Password and Confirm Password fields.

10. Click Send Invitation to send the email message.

11. Call or otherwise contact the helper and inform him or her of the password to use. It will not be sent in the original invitation note.

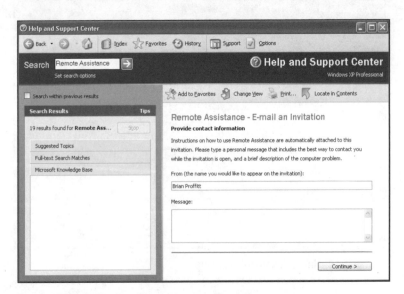

Figure 21.4   Write a polite note requesting help.

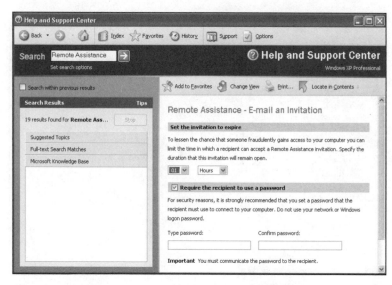

Figure 21.5   Protect yourself from unauthorized "help."

12. If the invitation is accepted, the Windows Messenger application will open a conversation window on both machines. The guru's machine will also open a Remote Desktop window so that your guru can guide your mouse pointer through the steps while showing you how to perform the task.

If you are a system administrator, you can proactively offer your services through Remote Assistance without waiting for a user to ask for help. This function is a little hard to find in the Help And Support Center, so you should add it to your Help And Support favorites list after you call it up on your screen, as shown in the following steps:

NOTE: *You must be logged on with an administrative account before performing this next procedure.*

---

1. Click Start|Help And Support to open the Help And Support Center window.

2. Type "Offer Remote Assistance" in the Search field and press Enter. The results of the search will be displayed.

3. Click the Offer Remote Assistance link to open the Offer Remote Assistance page (see Figure 21.6).

4. Enter the network name or IP address for the computer in the Type Or Paste The Computer Name Or IP Address field.

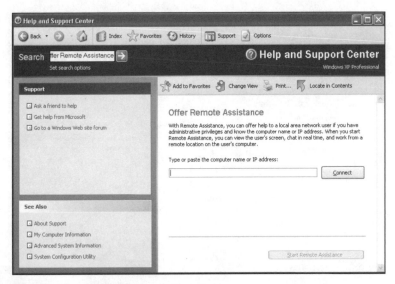

Figure 21.6   Offer help as an administrator.

5. Click Connect to establish the connection to the remote computer.

6. Click Start Remote Assistance to begin the Remote Assistance session.

To save the Offer Remote Assistance page in your Help And Support Favorites list, click the Add To Favorites button.

Related solutions:	*Found on page:*
Using Windows Messenger	292
Running Remote Desktop on the Remote Machine	331

Repairing Program Incompatibility

"Daddy."

The sheer bliss of darkness is replaced by utter confusion. Through the gloom, I do not remember my own name.

"Daddy!" the voice hisses more urgently. I know that voice from somewhere. I roll over in the bed and open my eyes to see my four-year-old standing there in the morning light. Behind her, I see my alarm clock shining 5:48 in green glowing numbers. In a language that approximates English, I mutter for my youngest to please go back to bed.

"Daddy!" she screeches as I close my eyes. I jerk to a sitting position by parental reflex.

"What? What is it, honey?"

"The computer is broken! I can't play my game!"

"Oh, sweetie, it's 5:30 in the morning. Let Daddy sleep." But, as I focus on her with bleary eyes, I realize that is the end of my Saturday morning sleep-in.

My four-year-old, who has the unnatural ability to wake up wide-eyed and bushy-tailed at any hour with the word *Ungodly* in front of it, has awakened me with an urgent crisis. Though she knows how to start the computer and run her educational game (which autoruns when she sticks the CD into the drive), something has gone wrong. In her opinion, the computer is broken.

I stagger into the other room and look at the screen. No error messages. I click the application icon and the program starts—only to halt with an error message that reminds me that the game must be played in 256-color display mode. This makes sense because it is an older game that belonged to her older sister at one time.

Thankfully, I breathe a sigh of relief. I can fix this problem quickly and stagger back to bed before I wake up too much.

I bring up the display properties and click the Settings tab—only to find that Windows XP no longer has a 256-color setting. What the heck is this? I just installed the new operating system on the kids' computer the day before to ideally decrease the number of crashes. Now, I am faced with a possible problem. The application will not run in more than 256 colors, and XP seems unwilling to use this mode.

Wide awake by now, I search high and low through the display drivers, looking for a solution. Finally, I find it. Older programs running on Windows XP can get some help to run on the new platform using the Program Compatibility Wizard. In no time at all, I run the wizard and solve the problem.

I start the game and turn to my daughter to tell her the good news—only to find she isn't there. She has gone downstairs to play with her toys and is no longer interested in playing on the computer.

Broken, I stumble into the shower to start my day.

To save you time so that nothing like this ever happens to you, here are the steps to run the Program Compatibility Wizard yourself:

1. Click Start|All Programs|Accessories|Program Compatibility Wizard to open the Program Compatibility Wizard page (see Figure 21.7).

2. Click Next to move to the Program Location page.

3. Click the I Want To Choose From A List Of Programs radio button to select it.

4. Click Next. The Program Compatibility Wizard will scan for a list of applications installed on your computer and display them on the Program page (see Figure 21.8).

5. Click an application you want to test to select it.

6. Click Next to move to the Compatibility Mode page (see Figure 21.9).

7. Click a compatibility mode radio button to select it.

8. Click Next to move to the Display Settings page.

9. Click a display setting radio button to select it.

10. Click Next to move to the Test page.

11. Review the settings and click Next. The program will be tested on the new compatibility mode. After you view the test, the Results page will appear.

12. Click the Yes Results radio button to select it.

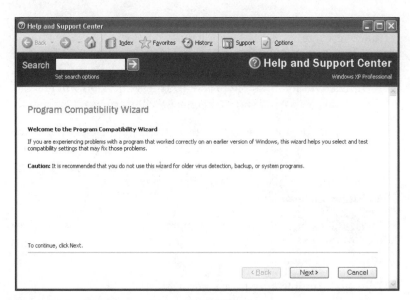

Figure 21.7   The Program Compatibility Wizard.

13. Click Next to move to the Send Results To Microsoft page.

14. Click the desired radio button to select it.

15. Click Next to move to the Completing The Program Compatibility Wizard page.

16. Click Finish to close the Help And Support Center window.

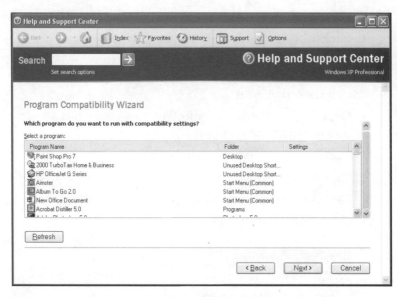

Figure 21.8   Pick an application to configure and test.

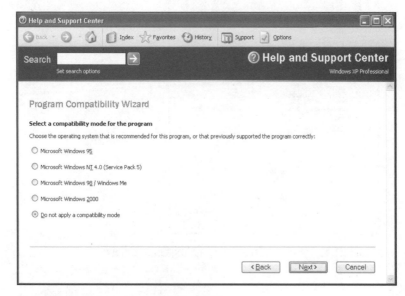

Figure 21.9   Select a compatibility mode.

If the Program Compatibility Wizard is something you don't need to step through, you can change the compatibility properties of an application more directly, as you can see in the following procedure:

1. Click Start|My Computer to open the My Computer window.

2. Navigate to the program file you want to change and right-click the executable file. The context menu will appear.

3. Click Properties to open the file's Properties dialog box.

4. Click the Compatibility tab to open the Compatibility page (see Figure 21.10).

5. Click the Run This Program In Compatibility Mode For checkbox to select it.

6. Click the drop-down list control for the Compatibility Mode field to display the options.

7. Click the appropriate option to select it.

8. Click the appropriate Display Settings checkboxes to select them.

9. Click Apply to apply the settings.

10. Click OK to close the file's Properties dialog box.

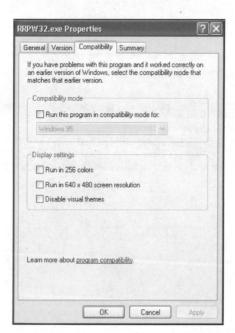

Figure 21.10   All the compatibility settings in one place.

Exploring System Information

When something goes really wrong on your computer, you will need the assistance of support technicians to get it repaired. Although no one wishes for this kind of event to happen, you must be ready for it.

Should this kind of event happen, the technicians will want to know what's on your computer so they can see whether any obvious conflicts are going on between hardware or software components. Instead of plowing though all the different settings dialog boxes virtually scattered all over the operating system, they will use the System Information application instead. System Information gathers up all the important settings and values about your system in one neatly organized package.

You can use System Information, too, if only to learn more about the inner workings of your machine. To start System Information, click Start|All Programs|Accessories|System Tools|System Information to open the System Information window (see Figure 21.11).

The System Information application is primarily a passive information tool, used to display the various settings on a computer. Navigate through the different categories to view all the information for yourself.

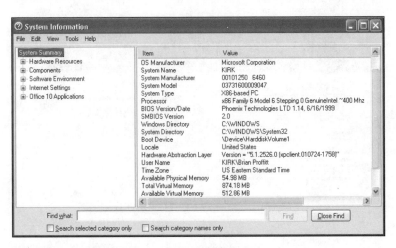

Figure 21.11   Check out your PC's vital statistics.

Falling Back with System Restore

If you have made a recent change to your computer that has brought your system to its electronic knees, it would be nice to turn back the clock and restore your system to the way it was before the change. Unless you have a time machine lying about, the best tool for this job in Windows XP is the System Restore application.

Whenever a change occurs on your Windows XP system, such as new hardware or software installations, the operating system will briefly pause and take a snapshot of the computer exactly as it is at that moment before continuing to implement the change. This snapshot is known as a restore point, which is a picture of all the settings and file locations on your computer at the moment the restore point is formed. When you elect to restore your computer, it will go back to the setting stored in one of these restore points.

Windows XP should automatically form a restore point any time a major system change is made, but to be absolutely sure, you should make a restore point before making any such change. To do so, follow these steps:

1. Click Start|All Programs|Accessories|System Tools|System Restore. The System Restore window will open to the Welcome To System Restore page (see Figure 21.12).

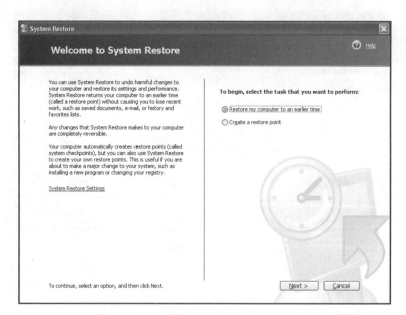

Figure 21.12 The System Restore application.

2. Click the Create A Restore Point radio button to select it.

3. Click Next to move to the Create A Restore Point page.

4. Enter a plain-language description in the Restore Point Description field.

5. Click Create to open the Restore Point Created page.

6. Click Home to open the Welcome To System Restore page.

After you make your system changes, all should be well. If something is still wrong with your computer after you make the system change, try uninstalling the software or hardware. If the problems continue, you can get the PC back to an earlier state by using System Restore, as shown in the following steps:

TIP: *You should close all applications before starting this procedure.*

1. Click Start|All Programs|Accessories|System Tools|System Restore. The System Restore window will open to the Welcome To System Restore page.

2. Click the Restore My Computer To An Earlier Time radio button to select it.

3. Click Next to move to the Select A Restore Point page (see Figure 21.13).

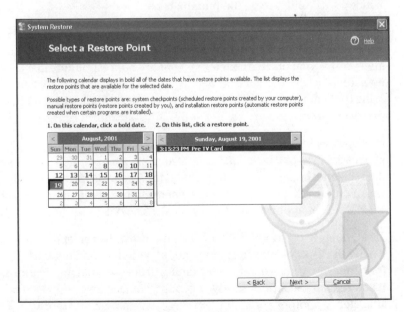

Figure 21.13   Choose how far to turn back the clock.

4. If no restore point appears on today's date, click a date on the calendar control.

NOTE: *Bold dates contain restore points.*

---

5. Click the restore point in the restore point list.

6. Click Next to move to the Confirm Restore Point Selection page.

7. Review the settings and instructions and click Next. System Restore will restore the settings and restart the computer. The Restoration Complete page will appear.

8. Click OK to continue with the system restart.

Using the Task Manager

Experience tells us that if something is going to freeze in a computer, it will most likely be one of the applications.

Applications lock up for various reasons. Perhaps your application could not handle a piece of data, which gave it the virtual version of indigestion. Or, maybe it tried to perform an illegal system call and Windows XP told it to go jump in the lake.

Whatever the reason for the problem, it is important to close down applications that are frozen (known as "not responding" in the Microsoft vernacular). Applications that are not responding just take up screen space and need to be closed. But, it is also important to bring them down as gently as possible so that they and the data files they were working with will not suffer any damage.

In Windows 9x, the best way to try to shut down an unresponsive application was to use the Ctrl+Alt+Delete key combination and close the recalcitrant application in that manner. The same principle holds with Windows XP, except that now users get to use the more robust Task Manager application to accomplish this goal.

Task Manager can do more than just shut down frozen applications. It actively displays live information about computer and network performance, as well as data on all running processes and applications. If you're using an administrative account, you can also connect Task Manager to another computer and see what's happening there.

To access Task Manager, you can use the Ctrl+Alt+Delete key combination or use these quick steps:

1. Right-click an empty area of the taskbar. The context menu will appear.

2. Click Task Manager to open the Windows Task Manager window (see Figure 21.14).

If an application is shown as Not Responding in the Status column on the Applications page, you can gracefully shut it down like this:

1. Click the unresponsive application to select it.

2. Click End Task to close the application.

Figure 21.14   The Windows Task Manager.

Recovering with Safe Mode

Some days, you just can't get a break. You've tried System Restore, the Task Manager—everything you can think of to fix the problem before you. Nothing seems to work. Before giving up, you can pull out the big guns to start repairing what's wrong. The first major method to try is to use Safe Mode.

Safe Mode is an operating mode that is found within all versions of Windows. Safe Mode will run Windows XP for you in a very basic form. Only the drivers and processes that are absolutely necessary for running the skeleton version of XP will run. Running this bare-bones version gives you a chance to perform diagnostic and repair actions in a cleaner environment.

If you have been consistently meeting process difficulties in the Normal Mode of Windows XP, try running Safe Mode to see whether you can repair the problem. To run XP in Safe Mode, follow this procedure:

1. Click Start|Turn Off Computer to open the Turn Off Computer window.

2. Click Restart to restart the system.

3. Early in the rebooting process, press the F8 key to open the startup menu.

4. Move the cursor to select one of the three Safe Mode options: Safe Mode, Safe Mode With Networking, and Safe Mode With Command Prompt.

5. Press Enter. The startup will continue to the Welcome screen, which will display logons only for the Administrator and administrative group accounts.

6. Click the account icon you want to use. The system will log on to that account, and the Safe Mode desktop will appear (see Figure 21.15).

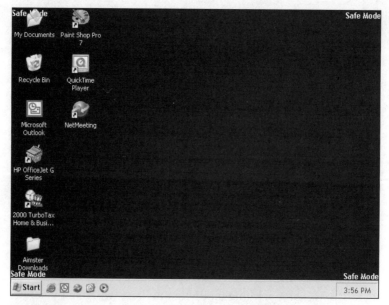

Figure 21.15   Safe Mode in Windows XP.

Using the Recovery Console

If all else fails, including Safe Mode, you can try one last procedure: using the Recovery Console.

The Recovery Console is a command-line interface that is a last-resort option meant only to be used by advanced users to work with services, format drives, and perform other high-level administrative services. The Recovery Console is not something you should use lightly, but it may be the tool that will save your bacon when all else fails.

The Recovery Console is not installed in Windows XP by default. Nor is it something that you can install using the Add/Remove Windows component tool in the Control Panel. To install this application, you will need to follow this procedure:

1. Insert the Windows XP Professional CD-ROM in the CD drive. The Windows XP Welcome screen will open.

2. Click Exit to close the Windows XP Welcome screen.

3. Click Start|Run to open the Run dialog box.

4. Type "d:\i386\winnt32.exe /cmdcons", where "d" is the drive letter of the CD-ROM drive, and press Enter. The Windows Setup dialog box will appear.

5. Confirm the installation of the Recovery Console by clicking Yes. The Windows Setup Wizard will install the Recovery Console and display a completed message.

6. Click OK to close the setup dialog box.

To run the Recovery Console, use these procedures:

1. In system startup, the Options menu will be displayed. Select Microsoft Windows Recovery Console and press Enter to start the Recovery Console.

2. Type the number for the Windows installation for which you want to apply the Recovery Console. The Administrator password prompt will appear.

3. Type the Administrator password to open the command line.

The Recovery Console uses a select group of commands to perform its functions. Table 21.1 lists those commands, derived from the Recovery Console's own help function.

Table 21.1   Recovery Console commands.

Command	Function
attrib	Changes the attributes of a file or directory
batch	Executes the commands specified in the text file
bootcfg	Configures and recovers the boot file (boot.ini)
cd	Displays the name of the current directory or changes the current directory
chkdsk	Checks a disk and displays a status report
cls	Clears the screen
copy	Copies a single file to another location
del	Deletes one or more files
dir	Displays a list of files and subdirectories in a directory
disable	Disables a system service or a device driver
diskpart	Manages partitions on your hard drives
enable	Starts or enables a system service or a device driver
exit	Exits the Recovery Console and restarts your computer
expand	Extracts a file from a compressed file
fixboot	Writes a new partition boot sector onto the specified partition
fixmbr	Repairs the master boot record of the specified disk
format	Formats a disk
help	Displays a list of the commands you can use
listsvc	Lists the services and drivers available on the computer
logon	Logs on to a Windows installation
map	Displays the drive letter mappings
md	Creates a directory
more	Displays a text file
net use	Connects a network share to a drive letter
ren	Renames a single file
rd	Deletes a directory
set	Displays and sets environment variables
systemroot	Sets the current directory to the systemroot directory of the system you are currently logged on to
type	Displays a text file

Index

B

Back button, 253–254
Background, 57
Backup data, 19–22
Backup files for upgrade, 26
Backup utility, 19–22
Backup Wizard, 19, 22
Bad sectors, 422–424
Basic disks, 418
    upgrading to dynamic, 418
Basic input/output system. *See* BIOS.
Batch files
    and answer files, 42
    for unattended installation, 40, 43
Batteries
    laptop, 347
    setting alarms, 356
    spare, 350
BearShare, 208
Berners-Lee, Tim, 250
BIOS
    incompatibility of, 16
    upgrading, 16–17
Blocking users, 401
Bridging nodes, 221
Briefcase synchronization, 362–363
Broadband connections, 183
    advantages, 179
    costs, 180
    and online upgrading, 369
    PPPoE, 189, 190
    setup, 186 (fig.)
    and shared Internet accounts, 197
Browsers, 49, 250
Browser Wars, 246–249
Browsing, 251
    with IE6, 250–254
Buffer underrun, 301
Burning CDs, 300, 301, 318
    problems, 301

C

Cable modems, 183, 197
Calling card function, 194–195
Calls (placing), 294
Call-waiting, 194

Camera, 220, 293
Carey, Diane, 410
Category View, 129
CB radios, 274
CDDA, 308
CDR, 300
CD Read-Only. *See* CDR.
CD ReWritable. *See* CDRW.
CD-ROM drives, 8
CDRW, described, 300
CDs, 300
    audio, 301
    burning, 300, 301, 318
    playing music, 306–308
    recording, 318
CD writer drive, 318
Cellular telephones, 274
Chat
    sending messages, 287, 294
    using, 286
Check Disk, 423, 424
Citrix, 325
Classic View, 129, 130 (fig.)
Classic Windows, 85
    desktop, 64–65
    Start menu, 100
Clean installation, 27, 162
    with Sysprep, 27
    of Windows XP, 24–25
ClearType, 348
    activating, 363–364
    anti-aliasing scheme, 349
Close button, 50
Code Red virus, 388
Color
    applying to desktop, 58
    and printer connectivity, 146
    problems, 445
    Remote Desktop, 333
Communicator 5, 248
Compact Disk Digital Audio. *See* CDDA.
Compatibility
    backward, 93
    changing properties, 448–449
    of drivers, 126
    mode, 446
    of software, 92
    tool, 7 (note)

N

O

Windows ME, 229
Windows Media, 8, 300, 308
Windows Messenger, 367
   audio and video transmissions,
      295 (tip)
   configuring, 291
   drawbacks, 278
   features, 277
   for initiating NetMeeting, 280
   placing calls, 294
   Remote Assistance, 440–441
   sending files, 295
   sending messages, 294
   using, 292–294
Windows 98
   Active Desktop, 84
   restoring backup files, 22
   upgrade, 94, 230
Windows NT, 3, 4, 330, 414
Windows platforms, 2–4, 24, 109–110
Windows Registry, 25
Windows Setup Wizard, 455
Windows 2000, 4, 94
   hardware requirements, 230
   problems, 228–229
   Remote Desktop, 329
   upgrade to Windows XP, 230
Windows Uninstaller, 123
Windows Update, 128, 376–372
Windows Update Web Site, 368, 373
Windows XP, 4
   activating, 33–34
   compatibility, 94
   deployment, 27
   and dual-processor systems, 5
   files/file system, 71, 73, 74, 81
   Home/Professional versions
      compared, 5–6
   interface, 46
   and NTFS, 393
   optimizing, 420
   passwords, 396
   Plus, 300 (note)
   primary hardware inventory for, 11
   remote access, 327
   upgrading, 230, 368
Windows XP Professional
   CD-ROM, 327

Yahoo, 270
Yankee Group, 206
Winmodems, 126
Winprinters, 126
WinZip, 89
Wireless networks, 210
   adding, 219
   configuring, 218–219
Wireless Zero Configuration
   Service, 218
Wizard disk, 224 (tip)
Workarounds, 209
Workplace computer
   connectivity, 188
World Wide Web. *See* Web; WWW.
World Wide Web Consortium.
   See W3C.
Worms, 388
W3C, 246–247
**www.microsoft.com/hcl/
   default.asp**, 15
**www.microsoft.com/windowsxp/
   guide/comparison.asp**, 6 (note)
WWW pages, 251

X

Xerox 8010 Star computer, 46
Xerox Palo Alto Research Center.
   See PARC.
XML, 366, 367

Y

Yahoo, 270
Yankee Group, 206

Z

Zip files, 89
Zombies, 390
Zone security, 258–261

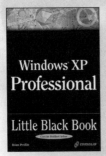